THE BUTCHER OF POLAND

Also by Garry O'Connor:

THE BUTCHER OF POLAND

HITLER'S LAWYER HANS FRANK

GARRY O'CONNOR

Cover illustration: Hans Frank, circa 1940. (brandstaetter / TopFoto)

First published 2013
This paperback edition published 2024

The History Press
97 St George's Place, Cheltenham,
Gloucestershire, GL50 3QB
www.thehistorypress.co.uk

British Library Cataloguing in Publication Data.
A catalogue record for this book is available from the British Library.

ISBN 978 1 80399 590 8

Typesetting and origination by The History Press
Printed and bound in Great Britain by TJ Books Limited, Padstow, Cornwall.

MIX
Paper from
responsible sources
FSC® C013056

Trees for LYfe

Contents

Acknowledgements

Many have provided insights and ideas which have been helpful in the writing of *The Butcher of Poland*, or, as it was called before the final, uncompromising title, *The Ultimate Doctor Faust*, *The Penitent of Nuremberg*, and *Poland is Nowhere*, but especially I must thank Ian Hogg and Nigel Bryant for theirs. Thanks are due to Bill Traherne-Jones who read the book in draft, to Annette Fuhrmeister who also helped with the German, Julian Friedmann, Julia Reuter and Michael Holroyd, all who read the book in various drafts. I thank Claus Hant for meeting me and talking at length, and for the depth and fascination provided by the lengthy and revelatory notes to his novel *Young Hitler*.

Had I not stumbled upon Niklas Frank's *In The Shadow of the Reich*, I wouldn't have become involved with the subject, and I can't emphasise enough what an extraordinary and inspirational memoir this is. I thank him very much for his contact with me over writing my book in its early stages, and the corrections and insights he gave me. Two other works I must mention which are crucial to understanding the Nazi mentality and German historical guilt are Bernhard Schlink's *The Reader* and Gunter Grass's *Peeling the Onion*. I would also like to thank all those at The History Press who have aided the production, especially my editor Shaun Barrington, who, as with the two previous books of mine The History Press have published in 2013, has been tirelessly enthusiastic and helpful.

To tell you the truth, they think whatever you want them to think. If they know you are still pro-Nazi, they say, 'Isn't it a shame the way our conquerors are taking revenge on our leaders! – Just wait!' If they know you are disgusted with Nazism, the misery and destruction it brought to Germany, they say, 'It serves those dirty pigs right! Death is too good for them!' You see, *Herr Doktor*, I am afraid that twelve years of Hitlerism has destroyed the moral fibre of our people.

German lawyer at the Nuremberg Trials, 1945 in conversation with US Army psychiatrist, Dr Gustave Gilbert

I am absolutely convinced that Adolf Hitler was just a name representing the total worldwide collapse of ethics in the twentieth century. It began in 1914 with the First World War, when everyone killed everyone and there were no longer any moral standards. Revenge was the order of the day, every excuse justified.

Whitney Harris, leader of US prosecution team at the Nuremberg trials

Occupied Poland, 1939–1944

— Poland, 1939   — — Frontiers, 1939

Incorporated into the Reich

General Government

Soviet occupied until June 1941

○ Extermination camps

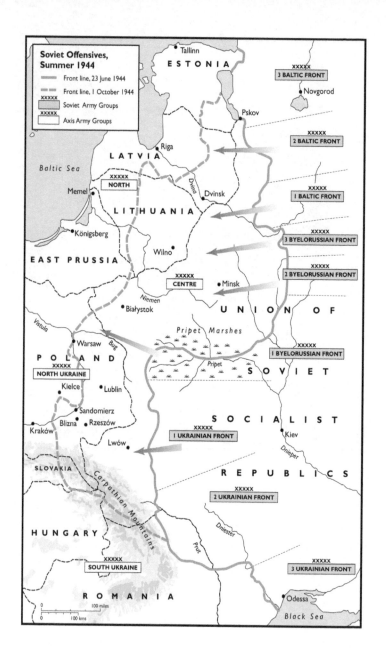

Soviet Offensives, Summer 1944

Front line, 23 June 1944
Front line, 1 October 1944
Soviet Army Groups
Axis Army Groups

Tallinn

E S T O N I A

xxxxx
3 BALTIC FRONT

Novgorod

Pskov

xxxxx
2 BALTIC FRONT

Riga

L A T V I A

xxxxx
NORTH

Baltic Sea

Memel

Dvina

Dvinsk

xxxxx
1 BALTIC FRONT

L I T H U A N I A

Königsberg

Wilno

xxxxx
3 BYELORUSSIAN FRONT

EAST PRUSSIA

xxxxx
2 BYELORUSSIAN FRONT

xxxxx
CENTRE

Minsk

Niemen

Białystok

U N I O N   O F

Pripet Marshes

Vistula

Warsaw

Bug

xxxxx
1 BYELORUSSIAN FRONT

P O L A N D

Pripet

xxxxx
NORTH UKRAINE

Kielce

Lublin

S O V I E T

Sandomierz

Blizna

Rzeszów

Kraków

Lwów

S O C I A L I S T

xxxxx
1 UKRAINIAN FRONT

Kiev

Dnieper

SLOVAKIA

Carpathian Mountains

R E P U B L I C S

xxxxx
2 UKRAINIAN FRONT

H U N G A R Y

Dniester

Prut

xxxxx
SOUTH UKRAINE

xxxxx
3 UKRAINIAN FRONT

R O M A N I A

Odessa

0   100 miles
0   100 kms

Black Sea

Introduction

This is a cautionary tale that can never be told too often. Hans Frank's colourful and sensational life has up to now only once been revealed in its vivid and dramatic colours – by his son, Niklas, in his book *In the Shadow of the Reich* (*Der Vater*, Munich, 1987; English version Alfred A. Knopf, New York, 1991), with a different emphasis from what follows. Niklas Frank's coruscating and shocking account, bravely honest and compelling in judgement, and entirely unforgiving, is an autobiographical stream of outrage, related in the first person by the son who was brought up in his father's shadow and had to deal with what his father had done, and his reputation. This cry of rage was followed by two further books, both as yet untranslated into English: *Meine Deutsche Mutter* (*My German Mother*, Munich, 2007) and *Bruder Norman! Mein Vater war ein Naziverbrecher, aber ich liebe ihn* (*Brother Norman: My father was a Nazi criminal, but I love him*, Munich, 2013). The trilogy, in 'discharging Niklas' heavy burden', has been described in the German press as 'taboo-breaking, tragic and painful'.

Otherwise, apart from a factually meticulous and exhaustive life in German by Dieter Schenk, untranslated into English, and a primarily academic account of his legal career by Dr Martyn Housden, an English historian, Frank's life has in the English-speaking world tended to be overlooked or overshadowed in the lurid and overpopulated gallery of Nazi criminals – swamped by the tens or hundreds of books written on his *confrères* in evil that even today continue to flood the market.

Frank's life has for me one particular fascination: I believe no one has remarked on it except for the subject himself. In an extraordinary and rather eerie way it reflects the universal story of Faust. It was of course Hitler who, as Mephistopheles, was behind this weak Faustian central figure, and pulled his strings, first in Bavaria, then in Poland. So it is Hitler as much as Frank who shares the ghastly limelight as 'The Butcher of Poland'.

It provides a new twist to, or development, of the Faust theme and legend, and it has many points of contact with *Sophie's Choice* and *Schindler's List*, although without the inspirational central figure of the latter. It would more than lend itself to be being filmed. The force of destiny, the good angel, the alleviating spirit which finally prevails in the face of unimaginable evil is Poland itself, and the Polish people. The story is unremittingly dark, yet hardly darker than *Doctor Faustus*, Marlowe's great play. The raging doubts and weakness of Frank's character, and the sacrifice of his soul to eternal damnation are seen to be constantly at play, and provide the dynamic of the drama.

I have come to this subject in a curious way. First, I have known three actor friends and subjects of biography who have had a connection with the Third Reich: two of these gave memorable film performances as Hitler. First, Alec Guinness enacted his crisis and torment in *Hitler: The Last Ten Days*, in 1973; the second, Derek Jacobi, was cast as the Führer in *Inside the Third Reich*, in 1982. Ian Hogg, the third, played Alois, Hitler's father, in *Hitler: The Rise of Evil*, a Canadian production. All three had in common the fact that they contributed to a knowledge of what made Hitler tick, what his inner life consisted of, and how it was ever possible that he became the destroyer and supreme tyrant of the last century.

There is a more intimate or personal touch which, from a family point of view, brought me slightly closer to the subject. Maggie Teyte, the operatic soprano who was my great aunt, when her career was in its heyday in the 1930s, took part in a triumphant London Philharmonic tour of Germany with Sir Thomas Beecham, who at the time was her lover.

Hitler, who wooed all celebrities, especially musical celebrities, who could be seduced to his mission, told Beecham, 'I should have liked so much to come to London to participate in the Coronation festivities (of George VI), but cannot risk putting the English to the inconvenience my visit might entail.'

Beecham's subtle reply apparently left Hitler looking bewildered: 'Not at all. There would be no inconvenience. In England we leave everyone to do as he likes.'

Maggie Teyte was also introduced to Hitler. She told me in the 1970s, 'he was an awful little man and he smelt.' She refused to sing for him. This reminded me of a story about C.J. Jung, whom the Führer tried to summon to analyse him: Jung refused to leave Switzerland to meet him and take part in his charade. Yet others, like the Mitford sisters, queued up to meet him and found him charming.

Hitler played a great part in the life of Hans Frank, spiritually and emotionally a greater part than anyone else. It stimulated Teyte's imagination for, later, when she came to prepare a concert version of Gounod's *Faust*, she said, 'Hitler really started it all. I could just see him – reaching out, twisting, destroying. He was the real Mephistopheles. I always thought he should be the centre of the opera – not that milksop Marguérite or that weakling Faust.' So for her, as for Frank, the Satanic or Mephistophelian figure in Germany was always Hitler.

It will hardly come as a surprise, then, that the main thematic influence on what follows is Thomas Mann's great flawed masterpiece, *Doctor Faustus*, which I have read and drawn on in the

Penguin Classics translation by H.T. Lowe-Porter. Mann sees the origin and roots of Nazism in the formation of character, personality and actions of its leader, as deeply embedded in German cultural history. To give one example, the following statement of the novel's narrator, Serenus Zeitblom, is an indication of the main concern of Mann's fictional investigation:

> In a nation like ours, I set forth, the psychological is always the primary and actual motivation; the political action is of the second order of importance: reflex, expression, instrument. What the breakthrough to world power, to which fate summons us, means at bottom, is the breakthrough to the world – out of an isolation of which we are painfully conscious, and which no vigorous reticulation into world economy has been able to break down since the founding of the Reich. The bitter thing is that the practical manifestation is an outbreak of war, though its true interpretation is longing, a thirst for unification (*Doctor Faustus*, p. 297).

Thomas Mann might well have put his finger on the deep cultural roots of Nazism in *Doctor Faustus*. There is a further consideration, however, often neglected by those who write up the crimes of the Third Reich and their perpetrators and hold them wholly and solely responsible for what they did, which of course they were. This other factor, which it is wrong to overlook, is the dynastic importance of German families and German family life.

In Western culture the interrelation between gods or God, the spiritual aspect of life and the responsibility of man, especially in the working out and influence of the family on history as well as the personal fate of individuals, find repeated and profound expression in the deep-rooted family drama. These emerge in such seminal works as the Oresteia trilogy of Aeschylus,

Sophocles' Theban plays, which depict the life of Oedipus and his family, and then in the body of works by Shakespeare, Racine, Chekhov, Ibsen and, closer to our age, O'Neill, Miller and Tennessee Williams.

Likewise, in the drama of the Third Reich's birth and rise to power, the importance of the families who were its progenitors has largely been overlooked, forgotten or deliberately white-washed in the fear that so many of their components and features are common to the universal human family. For example, in the Canadian film, all the scenes depicting Hitler's family life and in particular his crucial and influential relationship with his cruel father, were cut prior to being broadcast.

In Heinrich Himmler's family, where three brothers, Gebhard, Ernst and Heinrich all joined the SS, the impeccable middle-class professional, teaching, religious, patriotic background of the family, stretching far back into the past, was a formative influence that was duplicated thousands if not millions of times in German families in 1900, the year both Heinrich Himmler and Hans Frank were born.

What is described in the following pages by its adherents and followers as a heroic epic, namely the two Hitler putsches – the earlier failure in 1923 and the ultimate seizure of power in 1933 – were great days for the mainly very young participants; to be compared, for example, to the formation of the Irish Free State, to the birth of Israel, or the emergence of an independent India after the turmoil of the Raj withdrawal, and the civil war in which hundreds of thousands died – and to the present-day events in the Middle East in which the same constituents seem all too prevalent. The fact they all led to very different ends is not the point I am trying to make here.

During the First World War German boys who were left at what was called 'the home front' saw war as 'a game in which, according to certain mysterious rules, the numbers of prisoners taken, miles advanced, fortifications seized and ships sunk, played almost the same role as goals in football, and points in boxing'. A game that provided a whole generation of boys far more profound excitement and emotional satisfaction than anything peace could offer.

Here was one of the strongest roots from which the vision of Nazism grew. In fact, this underlying vision of Nazism experienced war, not by what happened and was experienced by soldiers of the front, but more crucially for the future, in the battle games of German schoolboys playing at home and school. It was, then, that generation born like Frank in 1900 and after, who became keen and ambitious in their early twenties, fuelled with the romantic heroism of boyhood and with the emotional and sexual drive of early manhood (and an unexpressed sexual and power drive seeking expression and fulfilment), which became the engine in the powerhouse of National Socialism.

But it was not only the younger generation. Fathers, mothers, grandfathers and grandmothers were all behind it, too. For instance, in June 1936, when Heinrich Himmler was made head of the German police in the Reich ministry of the interior, his parents and brothers, all of whom had received the highest possible educational grades and qualifications as upholders of German society had, according to Katrin Himmler (the daughter of Heinrich's younger brother Ernst), no reservations about the all-powerful position of the SS and the police:

> In their letters [to Heinrich] his parents express their admiration for the 'magnificent black columns that are your creation', as his father wrote on the occasion of the SS parade on 9 November in memory of the fallen 'heroes' of the Beer Hall Putsch. Heinrich had secured seats for them for both the 1934 and 1935 ceremonies. Gebhard and Ernst used meetings with Heinrich to put the case for further promotion within the SS. And they too, thanks to their brother, had the opportunity now and then to meet those who wielded power in the Reich (Katrin Himmler, *The Himmler Brothers*, p. 163).

They were not the exception but the rule. The collective general crime of almost all Germans of that time was that they not only lacked the courage to speak, as Primo Levi asserted, but they lacked the desire to do so. They embraced Hitler's apparently invincible totalitarian regime.

Once established, 'The pressures it can exercise over the individual are frightful. Its weapons are substantially three: direct propaganda or propaganda camouflaged as upbringing, instruction and popular culture; the barriers erected again pluralism and information – and terror …' (Levi, *The Drowned and the Saved*, p. 35 *ff*).

The Canadian film *Hitler: The Rise of Evil*, shown in Britain on Channel 4, in which Ian Hogg played Alois, Hitler's father, was an attempt to bring a more balanced view of Hitler's origins. It showed Alois bullying and beating his son. One scene had Adolf setting fire to his father's beloved beehive out of revenge, and his subsequent brutal chastisement by Alois; during this, Klara, Adolf's mother, tries to intervene and in turn is hit. Another time, Alois humiliates Adolf in front of his work colleagues.

These scenes were either cut or reduced to a tiny glimpse as part of the producers' or distributors' urge not to portray Hitler as too human a figure, or, as he emerges in those early scenes, with his inability to make relationships and his obsession about sketching buildings, as a sufferer from autism. While never mentioned in the film, this is how the producers and actors thought of the young Adolf – as a withdrawn victim of paternal violence.

Before Derek Jacobi played Hitler, he had played Dietrich Hessling, a Teutonic louse, in the television series *Man of Straw*, adapted from the satirical novel written by Heinrich Mann, Thomas Mann's brother, which exposed to ridicule the pre-First World War German family. In Hessling's slavish worship of the Kaiser, Mann mocks the habit of obedience, the unbending adherence to rigid family values, which gave rise to Nazism.

When he came to play Hitler, Jacobi's take on the role was Hitler the actor, Hitler the performer, Hitler as written up in that multi-faceted portrait of him by Albert Speer, his Minister of Armaments. So here again was the revelation of a very different aspect of the dictator's mind and actions.

Derek told me of an incident when filming on location in Munich. They had roped off a central *platz* where he had to make a speech. All the young children around wanted his autograph. Then, for a key speech, they employed a crowd of local students as extras. They stood there as he spoke and were told to react and applaud at the end. 'I made the speech. I came to the end. They clapped. Silence. And then slowly they all raised their hands in the Nazi salute. I shuddered. It was so inbred. A reflex …'

The most expanded character study of the dictator was that of Alec Guinness in *Hitler: The Last Ten Days*. Guinness spent many months getting inside the evil character, so many that his behaviour upset his wife and friends – but he said this didn't depress him so much as obsess him.

He showed Hitler first and foremost as the artist *manqué*, which of course he was, who sacrificed his vocation to save and rebuild his country. Guinness' Hitler had a sense of humour, he was an anti-bourgeois misfit, and a puritan. So Guinness explored this inner life, and it is an irony that this puritan, anti-smoking tyrant was beaten by leaders who were all heavy smokers and not noted for temperance.

The film was banned in Israel for showing Hitler in too human a light, which is perhaps another irony. It was also heavily reduced on the cutting room floor in order not to provoke too much empathy for the man, and to conform to the reigning demonisation. It thus never made the impact the director and star hoped.

In the authoritative endnotes to his novel *Young Hitler*, the contemporary German writer Claus Hant provides convincing evidence that Alois was a petulant know-all and miser, a brutal, choleric type with few friends who often, when coming home drunk at night, would beat his wife or young son with a hippopotamus hide whip similar to the one Adolf carried setting out as a party leader. According to Hitler's sister Paula he got a beating every night. Only when his father died in 1903, when Adolf was 14, did relative peace come to the family.

Four years later his mother Klara was operated on for breast cancer. Contemporary witnesses, as cited by Hant, confirm that Adolf was particularly self-sacrificing in taking care of his mother:

> When she died later that same year, three days before Christmas, the young Hitler was overcome with profound anguish. The Jewish physician Doctor Bloch, who treated Hitler's mother until her death, recalled later in exile in America that 'he had never in his career seen anyone as filled with grief as Adolph Hitler'. Karl Krause, his butler, recalled in his memoir: 'he had a photo of his mother on his night-stand, it was on his writing desk, in the library, and in the study.'

Significantly, indicating his vulnerability over any exposure of what happened in his family past, as well as his own unresolved and repressed or suppressed feelings over it (as well as changing his family name from Schicklgruber to Hitler), Hitler eliminated all traces of his past. To erase the truth, not just the details of his parentage, he even went to the point of murder, and the demolition of town and building. He hardly spoke of his father beyond the briefest of mentions.

Joachim Fest, a biographer of the Führer, concluded that 'to veil and transfigure his true person was one of the main endeavours of his life. Few other figures in history have stylised themselves so forcibly and concealed their true selves with such seemingly pedantic consistency' (*Young Hitler*, p. 345, note 102).

Finally, I should mention that I have taken a liberty in two sections, where the sources are so many, the citations themselves hearsay, speculative dialogue or verbatim report, to use this dialogue, add to it, and knead the narrative into what is known as 'faction'. My precedent for this is the practice of Peter Ackroyd in his monumental *Charles Dickens*. Elsewhere Ackroyd has made the claim, with which I heartily concur, that 'Biography is convenient fiction'.

PART ONE

1

Saving Germany from Self-Accusation

'The Russians,' said Deutschlin sententiously, 'have profundity but no form. And in the West they have form but no profundity. Only we Germans have both.'

Thomas Mann, *Doctor Faustus*

President Woodrow Wilson, a good Presbyterian, put forward plans to reform the United States by taking business out of the hands of businessmen, and turning it over to the politicians. Now, in 1918, with the brief of changing the wider world after World War One, to make Europe a safer and saner place to live, he had selected a cohort of distinguished American scholars, men like himself, an ex-President of Princeton, who derived their ideas from books, to eradicate evil forever from the conduct of governments. He had the whole civilised world for his classroom. 'Open covenants of peace openly arrived at' stood at the heart of President Wilson's Fourteen Points to which the Germans had agreed as the basis for the Armistice on 11 November 1918.

At Versailles, in May the following year, the Germans found themselves not so much an active participant in peace negotiations, as passive recipients of what became known as the *diktat* of Versailles imposed on them. Wilson, dressed in black, lean in figure and face, eyes magnified by shiny lenses, presided. Président Clemenceau of France, aged 78, a diabetic with grey silk gloves hiding his eczema, made it clear revenge would be his agenda: 'The hour has struck for the weighty settlement of our accounts.' But while in the West it had lost, Germany had been winning the war in the East and still had an army of 9 million men under arms. Count von Brockdorff-Rantzau, Germany's negotiator to whom Clemenceau addressed these words, did not deign to rise from his seat to read a bitter reply. Wilson's response to this strengthened the perception of his growing anti-German animus: 'What abominable manners! ... It will set the whole world against them.' So much for peace.

The *Diktat*, signed finally on 28 June 1919 by the German Social Democrat Government yielding to overwhelming force, described by Robert Lancing, Wilson's Secretary of State, as Germany 'being forced to sign their own death warrant', provoked fury not only in Germany. Maynard Keynes, British Treasury representative at the Paris Peace Conference, resigned. He thought the economic reparations forced on Germany by the 'Damned Treaty' were a formula for economic disaster and future war. In a letter to a friend he called Wilson 'the greatest fraud on earth'; to Lloyd George, British Prime Minister, he wrote, 'I am slipping away from this scene of nightmare.'

Keynes returned to his alma mater, King's College, Cambridge. Here, he penned a blistering condemnation of the Conference, as much to re-enlist himself, it seemed, with his cultural peers in the Bloomsbury set – they disapproved of his *Realpolitik* engagement. His *The Economic Consequences of Peace* reverberated with coruscating force around the world. It was written to warn how the effects of imposing a 'Carthaginian peace' on Germany would contribute directly, as the French historian Etienne Mantoux said later, to the future war Keynes sought above all to avert.

For all his academic aestheticism, his attachment to the pacifist sensitivities of his Bloomsbury peers and sponsorship of the arts, especially the theatre, Keynes was an economist. He knew, as Thomas Mann said, 'the economic is simply the historical character of this time, and honour and dignity do not help the state one bit, if it does not of itself have a grasp of the economic situation and know how to direct it.'

Like the subject of this book, Keynes was a man of two worlds. Not so that master progenitor of twentieth-century evil who, in August 1914, aged 25, had fallen on his knees at the outbreak of war and thanked God. This was the moment he termed, in high-sounding phrases, of 'unity and integrity', the moment that National Socialism was begotten, when Germany was freed from a world of stagnation which could go on no longer, an appeal to duty and manhood, an opportunity for heroism. But above all, it was a means of achieving a life in which state and culture could become one. This book is about Hans Frank; but without some consideration of Hitler, we cannot know Frank, so I hope the reader will forgive what may seem like digressions both here and in what follows, but, it is hoped, will not prove to be so.

Adolf Schicklgruber, although born on 20 April 1889 in Braunau am Inn just over the Bavarian border in Austria, was bursting with the consciousness that his adopted land was to become the dominating world power. He was convinced the twentieth century would be Germany's century: that after Spain, France and England in previous eras, it was Germany's turn to lead the world. War would be the means, an understanding of power combined with a readiness for sacrifice.

Defeat and Hitler's wartime experiences drove home that earlier flash of subjective truth. His dangerous role in the war was that of a volunteer dispatch runner; he was an infantryman but was close to officers in command who were ready to use men as cannon fodder. He had already lived the life of a down-and-out in Vienna from 1908 to 1912 before he moved to Munich. On the very edge of society, scratching a living by whatever means he could, he had written or worked on plays and novels and even a musical drama in the style of Wagner. He painted pictures which he tried to sell and while the general misconception is that he gained his political insights from newspapers and magazines, in time he became more famed for burning books than reading them. The truth is that he was obsessed with books and read voraciously. His roommate in Munich, Rudolf Hausler, complained he read until three or four many mornings. Not only did he have a photographic memory, but the range of his reading was immense, from the *Divine Comedy*, Goethe's *Faust* and *William Tell*, to Carl May's Wild West stories for boys. Much later, Hans Frank recalled that Hitler claimed to have had works by Homer and Arthur Schopenhauer with him in the First World War trenches. Ernst Hanfstaengl, at one time close to the Führer before becoming an opponent, stated that 'Hitler was neither uneducated nor socially awkward ... My library came to experience his voracious appetite for books.'

At the front Hitler had found himself engaged in fighting 'man-to-man' and overcome the instinctual aversion to killing, confirming his social-Darwinian worldview that life was a continual savage battle. Combat was for him a great formative event. The community of comradeship, in the absence of homeland and family, grew to be overwhelming. The Bavarian or 'List' Regiment comprised 3,600 men when first deployed. Four years later, by the time of the armistice in November 1918, 3,754 of the troops that had served in the regiment had been killed. So few of his comrades survived that it is not surprising Hitler came in time to believe Providence was on his side. Wounded twice, he received six medals and decorations, including the exceptional Iron Cross 1st Class, usually only won by officers. But he was not officer material in the opinion of his military superiors, despite this bravery, and never rose above corporal. Complimented later on this promotion, Hitler admonished his superior Max Amann: 'I would ask you not to do that, I have more authority without stripes than with stripes.' It enabled him later to separate himself from the career officers who were seen as the architects of German defeat. It would become commonplace to state that at heart and soul, together with all his ex-servicemen followers, he never stopped being a soldier. Some psychologists have claimed the traumatic but positively experienced war motivated him subconsciously and that this created a 'repetition compulsion' that stayed with him.

After being blinded by gas at the front line at Werwick in October 1918, Hitler was taken to the Bavarian Field Hospital stationed near Brussels to be treated. Then, exceptionally, he was separated from his fellow wounded and sent 1,000km to a small hospital in Pasewalk, near the Polish border, which specialised in treating 'war neurotics'. The authorities were determined to separate these from other serving men lest they spread the infection of hysterical or psychotic behaviour to other men and affected morale.

No documentation exists of how or with what he was treated, though various testimonies were collected by the US Secret Service which confirmed that what Hitler called his 'blindness' caused by the gas poisoning had an unadmitted, psychopathological dimension. It was undoubtedly at Pasewalk that Hitler experienced a transformation – whatever the effect of the assumed mustard gas, both physical and psychological – from an unexceptional introverted 'armchair scholar' and practical joker, lax in attitude and with eccentric ideas, into a visionary with a burning mission. It was there, hearing of the unrest and armed uprising in Munich, that he became seized with certainty, in the form of supernatural, ecstatic visions, of a victorious Germany, in the course of which his eyesight was restored. Such delusion, reported the *Frankfurter Zeitung* on 27 January 1923, 'eliminates any complexity, and that alone makes a huge impression in the spineless times we live in. These people are certainly not lacking in activity, but rather in the sense and value of the goals by which their will is achieved – which is why they are so dangerous in their obsession to the nation as a whole.'

Before this transfiguration Hitler had believed himself to be a genius; now he 'knew it'. Before, he had believed divine Providence protected him; now he was utterly convinced. Likewise, his convictions became 'absolute truths'. It was this transformation, this unshakable certainty in his own power, which gave him unlimited authority and empowered him to represent his views with an unparalleled fanaticism.

Not surprisingly, then, he kept quiet about what had happened to him in Pasewalk, only given a mention in *Mein Kampf*, never refeering to it as 'paranormal' again for political reasons, nor that he had been diagnosed as a war neurotic. This became another secret for, as he often said, 'a secret known by two people is no longer a secret.'

He left Pasewalk Hospital on 11 November 1918. The news of the German Army's surrender brought on the sickening sense, as he later described it in *Mein Kampf*, of selling out, of a stab in the back that gave him both a personal and national sense of utter collapse. The total despair served only to bolster his visionary or hallucinatory summons to free Germany from bondage.

It was a conversion as powerful as any in religious history, a spiritual shock and re-orientation of such enormous proportions it transformed Hitler's whole personality. Unlike Nietzsche, he never believed God was dead. God was alive and well and infused him with power, took him away from his early failure and depression, and gave him a feeling he was the new Godhead. Hysterical blindness and autism may also have contributed to his certainty that Providence had chosen him to perform the mission of liberation. He was, from now on, to be guided 'with the certainty of a sleepwalker along the path laid out for me by Providence'. His sight, so he claimed, came back the next day.

It was the prohibition, the disbanding of the German Army, which spurred him into action in 1919. He had to recreate that moment in 1914 when Germany had been conscious of its military power; when she united in it, and exulted in it. Had not the Treaty of Versailles robbed Germany of its decisive character, denied the activities that were its very life-blood, Hitler would never have come to power. 'The exercises, the receiving and passing on of orders, became something which [Germans] had to procure for themselves at all costs,' wrote Elias Canetti, the Nobel Prize-winning author:

> The prohibition on universal military service was the *birth* of National Socialism ... The party came to the rescue of the army, and the party had no limits set to its recruitment from within the nation. Every single German – man, woman, or child, soldier or civilian – could become a National Socialist. He was probably even more anxious to become one if he had not been a soldier before, because, by doing so, he achieved participation in activities hitherto denied him.

So, for Hitler, the prohibition of the army by the *Diktat* of Versailles became the prohibition of the specific and sacrosanct practices he could not imagine life without. Every man's sacred duty became the re-establishment of this faith of his fathers. Hitler could whip up resentment and a desire for revenge against the world, could rally support for his vision, by repeating and repeating the slogan *Diktat* of Versailles with unwavering monotony. The paranoiac could probe the nation's wound and keep it bleeding, proclaiming the phrase at mass meetings with terrifying and coercive force.

So he joined up again as soon as he could, enrolling in the remnant German Army as a press officer and propagandist in what was now a politically motivated force. From now on, from that moment of rebirth or conversion, Hitler was to act with a kind of genius. He was able to make things happen exactly as he had foreseen and wanted them to happen. Here was a satanically inspired Mephistopheles who, in the future and among his legion of servile subordinates, would find many fanatic followers, and one young Faust in particular, close to his mind and will, ready to sell his soul for lavish reward.

2

In the Superior Range

Hans Michael Frank, Nazi Germany's top lawyer, was born eleven years after Hitler in Karlsrühe, Bavaria, on 23 May 1900. He was christened a Catholic and, as he said himself, adhered to the liberal doctrine of being 'an Old Catholic'. This meant he belonged to a breakaway body of the Munich Church which, led by the famous theologian Ignaz Döllinger, didn't adhere to the nineteenth century edict of papal infallibility, and was in some ways akin to the Anglican Protestant Church.

On the face of it, his childhood was not all that extraordinary. He had a younger sister, Elizabeth, and a brother, Karl junior, nine years older. Magdalena, his mother, was an independent-minded, sensual, irrepressible woman of old Bavarian stock, but neither particularly intelligent nor spirited. The daughter of a small food shop owner in Munich, she was obliged to work and did not attend any schools. She married the much older Karl Frank to find a better life, but was bored after some years.

Karl senior was an outwardly respectable middle-class lawyer originally from the Rhineland; according to his grandson Niklas, he was 'a very uninspired mediocre character and a bad lawyer because he was not very bright'. A photograph of him with Hans aged 12 shows a bald man in his fifties, wide and bushy browed, sporting a walrus moustache. He is formally dressed, and has his hand on Karl junior's thigh. Hans has dark hair parted on the left and is wearing a brass-buttoned sailor suit. In another photo we see a younger Hans in Bavarian top hat with boots and knotted scout tie, his doll-sized sister in headscarf and rural waistcoat and skirt, standing next to him. A solid, ordinary middle-class Bavarian boy, one might think – in appearance at least.

All was not as it seemed on the surface. Magdalena, increasingly bored, fled the marital home and set up house in Prague with her lover, a teacher, not really an intellectual but more a dealer in foodstuffs and coal. Elizabeth and Karl Junior joined her there. Judging by the accounts we have of Hans' early years, his mother was around him perhaps to the age of 10. He was a quiet lad, of an obstinate frame of mind. He preferred studying to frivolous games with other boys. Magdalena was especially proud that, on his first day at school, he took a newspaper with him and could already read it.

By the age of 10, Hans had moved in with his father running a law practice in Munich, and there he went to the famous Staatliche Maximiliansgymnasium attended by many eminent Germans, including the Nobel Prize-winning physicist Werner Heisenberg and future pope Joseph Ratzinger. Hans excelled at everything; he was an all-rounder, although apparently keen on outward form and display more than inward commitment. As one of his school friends described it, he accumulated information in order to show off.

He lived with his father in a second-floor flat in Munich's Barerstrasse, where they kept chickens which sometimes ran free. The desertion by his mother must have told heavily on him, judging by what he was to say later: 'The mark of the man is to be unconditionally the master. Weak men are worse than women, for when they are weak they are cripples.' Presumably he referred to his father, who had been unable to hold on to his mother in the family home. The absence of this feisty woman would seem to have made him a lonely, introverted boy, studious and quick to engage with and embrace a higher purpose in life, as well as devote himself to dedicated and intense study – with the caveat given above, that such learning was for display more than for intellectual nourishment.

He formed some homoerotic friendships at school, none of them lasting. He passed through fairly usual phases, first with a platonic attachment to an older art and music teacher known as Ernst Sp., a 'free spirit' who encouraged him to breed tropical fish, and started to give him 'thirsty glances' before the First World War separated them. At school one playground companion was Karl Sch., the same age, believed to be homosexual. They went hiking together in the countryside around Munich. 'He played an important role in my life,' said Hans; they wrote each other letters with amusing wording and thought they were clever.

The father's presence exacerbated the brooding resentment of the son, who each lunchtime would meet his father in the pub near his office in Schelling Strasse. We are unsure at this stage whether Karl senior had already been disbarred a first time for embezzlement, but we do know it happened later. There is a description of him as a freelance lawyer working from this public house on Schelling Strasse. For cash-in-hand he would write letters, advise and even take on cases on a very *ad hoc* basis. He seems to have had friends who helped him find briefs. In 1945, in his prison cell at Nuremberg, Hans spotted a newspaper report that Dr Jacoby, 'a Jewish lawyer in Munich, who was one of my father's best friends, had been exterminated at Auschwitz'. One thing is certain: Karl was a deceitful, crooked lawyer, whose conduct instilled or provoked in his son a strong need to profess rectitude and honour, although this tended rather to fluctuate. How relative this would become to circumstances and opportunity will in time grow clear.

It seemed Karl senior gave Hans, without the latter knowing it, early master-classes in corruption. The old man had, so his grandson Niklas wrote, 'a way of getting experienced women into the sack: somehow or other he would sweet-talk them into it with his clever chit-chat about being a lawyer, at the same time he was taking off his skivvies.' The Creszentia Breitschaft affair happened later, when Hans was on the threshold of fame; but it was indicative of the whole process of the Frank *modus operandi*. As Niklas said, 'Anyone who got involved with the Frank family was caught like a fly in a Venus flytrap.'

The way 'Zenzi', as she was known in the family, fell victim to the swindling lawyer is a grotesque farce that could have been written by Bertolt Brecht, another Bavarian, born in Augsburg two years before Hans. An unscrupulous 'procuress', Fran Elise Lutze, used to steer unmarried or widowed women of some means between 40 and 50 towards the dapper legal rogue. Zenzi owned a railway-station restaurant in Lentkirchen, and she fell for Frank senior. They began an affair, and Frank set financial terms on marriage: meantime, as the liaison went on Frank took money from Zenzi with the promise he would marry her if she paid for his divorce from Magdalena, Hans' mother. Not only had she to pay 1,200RM, but also a regular 50RM a month. And this was not all he extorted from her. By this time, having joined in the deception too, Hans got his father's mistress to loan him 500 marks to help him move house. Even though he was by now a Reichstag deputy, Hans also asked for more:

My dear Frau Breitschaft, I ask you for a great favour. Constituents of mine in Silesia have suffered enormously in consequence of the ban on the publication of two newspapers, the *Schlesischer Beobachter* and the *Schlesische Tageszeitung*. I, too, have suffered serious personal loss. Would you help out just one more time? You know, of course, that you are my only creditor, and also that all banks are closed to us. Grant me a final one-year loan of 1,200 reichsmarks. I shall then pay it all back in regular monthly instalments. You would be doing us a huge service. The battle is difficult, but Germany must be free! Can you send the money – 1,200 reichsmarks –

directly to my address at the Reichstag, Berlin? This will be the last time.

Father and son milked the poor woman for all they could. Karl senior found another mistress, a Fräulein Donauer. Ultimately, after he and his son conspired together to steer themselves through the *dreck* (mud), Zenzi, reduced to physical and verbal threats and then bankruptcy and joblessness, won a token law case against them.

This was but one of the family skeletons serving to harden Hans' relatively young heart. There were more. Yet alongside this dark, early material of personal corruption, the idealist, infused with the same biological mysticism of Germany's future leader, had long been sketching paths of his own future glory.

Just before his eighteenth birthday, Hans began to keep a diary in which his sense of race, of nationhood, loomed ominously large. On 6 April 1918 he wrote:

Today I mustered in as a recruit [in the army], one of the generation born in 1900. Having been declared fit for active service in the infantry, I was assigned to the imperial regiment. Today, for the first time in my life, I learned from personal experience how crude the executive mind of the Prussian military system really is, that compulsive outgrowth of pedantic discipline in the spirit of Frederick the Great. We Bavarians, members of a genuine Germanic race, have been armed with a powerful sense of free will; only with the greatest reluctance and under duress do we tolerate this Prussian military dominance. It is this fact above all that constantly renews for us the symbol of the great, unbridgeable dividing line made by the mighty Main River, which separates

South Germany from the North. To our way of thinking, the Prussian is a greater enemy than the Frenchman.

His regiment was the 1st Bavarian *König* Infantry, stationed at Marsfeldt Barracks, and he was about to experience war for the first time. But Hans already seemed to lead a charmed life. Germany laid down its arms and he started classes again at the Maximiliansgymnasium. Perhaps it was the *schuld* (guilt, but the German word has a double meaning, *viz* debt) of his personal family circumstances, as much as the Kaiser's defeat, that inclined him to idealism and purity – and to hold forth in airy *rodomontade*:

> People of Germany, return to your roots, as long as there is still time. Preserve your ideals. With all your might, pull yourselves up out of this swamp of speculation and materialism that threatens to seduce and engulf you. Return to Nature, return to your own soil. Only there will the healing process you so badly need come to fruition.

He was not quite eighteen. Into this frothy outpouring a note of bitterness has already crept. He wrote of 'A nauseating and unfortunately typical scene in a café. A Frenchman – surrounded by flirtatious German females entertaining him with their foolish giggling. Is that not a derision of our people, our nation? Unconscionable!'

In fact, a combustible contrast to idealism – the cumulative repression of feelings of hatred (towards his father, possibly also towards the mother he loved but who had not found a way to stay with his father), towards the victors of the war, and envy – were already building up in Hans. *Ressentiment*, resentment, a concept defined by Friedrich Nietzsche, had been the obsession of Max Scheler, the Munich-born philosopher, who had, even before the Great War, defined it as a universal, negative condition of man, both in its personal and historical contexts. In the Bavarian capital city, *ressentiment* was set to become a dominating feature.

His undoubted sharpness of mind notwithstanding – he had an IQ of 130 or more, 'in the very superior range of intellectual abilities' – manifest at the age of 18, Hans showed these feelings of nothingness, the release from which was soon to dominate several powerful, disaffected political movements. While Scheler believed in the unique significance of human emotions, especially love, and the importance of heroic or saintly models for the development of the moral life, Frank, like a small but significant minority of Germans, was increasingly caught up in a widespread moral and ethical vacuum and seeking other mentors. He found himself questioning the existence of God and decided that the Almighty, who most decidedly had shown himself not to be on the side of the Germans, had some important questions to answer: 'How futile is the question, whether there is a God, since after all there is a soul, which leads us, a flame from the everlasting fire. But can anyone answer the question, where is this God?'

In the context of Germany in late 1918 to early 1919, this questioning young German wanted and was looking for a heroic model; instead of God, he found Napoleon:

> Once again the story of Napoleon's life, which I am reading now for the third time, touches me profoundly. Whence comes this compelling urge in me to pattern my life after this man's? It must be truly glorious to rise in dizzying flight to such heavenly heights, no matter how great the fall that must follow … The desire to experience these heights burns like a fire within me. But my path shall go, not like that of Napoleon, over the bodies of those cursing and seeking to destroy him, but instead past the milestones on the way to the liberation of humanity. A united and free World Reich will then be the ultimate creation of the Germans.

On 19 December 1918 he writes (temporarily reinstating the Almighty): 'Lord God, send us now the man who will bring us order ... I wish for our nation men who can once again restore it to universally acknowledged prominence, while keeping it firmly anchored within. We must succeed in this!'

He was by no means pessimistic: on 2 January 1919 he writes, 'With shining eyes I look to the future.' Then he backpedals – maybe, he thinks after all, he is up to it: 'Our nation today is incapable of leading a state able to flourish. Shall I be the one to lead the revolt of the slaves?'

Hans was not an exception in the Germany of his day. In many ways he was the intelligent German norm. Heinrich Himmler's background was even more normal and not subject to the vicissitudes of Frank's family life. He and his two brothers, all talented scholars, had the most sheltered but at the same time stimulating early years. Their parents took care to ensure their sons, who had the best gymnasium educations on offer in Munich, 'were suitably prepared for their future professional and social positions, and this demanded not only an all-round education in the humanities, which was chiefly their father's responsibility, but also the secondary virtues that were so highly valued in those days'.

Heinrich was a meticulous recorder of all details of life, a fervid family correspondent, and attentive to all aspects of social respectability. As his grand-niece records:

The ties between Heinrich and his family, which remained stable and unbroken, are misrepresented both in historical and biographical research as well as in the family folklore – perhaps because they all wanted to keep their distance from such a criminal character as Heinrich Himmler, to see him as a 'one-off', as someone abnormal that they and their normal environment had nothing to do with.

But Heinrich had no overpowering belief in himself, for all his skill in organisation; he was denied robust good health, and never thought of himself as a supreme leader: he sought a Messiah.

Not so Hans Frank, who entertained much more grandiose ideas. Was he destined to become the German Napoleon? Was he to be the one to lead – or was it to be another?

3

Gretchen

A woman is loved by a proper man in three ways. As a dear child that one has to scold and perhaps punish in its irrationality, that one protects and cares for because it is delicate and weak and because one loves it so much. Then as a wife and as a faithful understanding comrade who fights her way through life at one's side, ever loyal and without hampering the man's spirit and putting him in shackles. And as a wife whose feet one kisses and who, through her feminine softness and childlike, pure sanctity, gives one the strength not to weaken in the hardest struggles, and grants one at ideal moments of the soul the most divine bliss.

Heinrich Himmler

There was for Hans Frank, even in the Napoleonic mind-set he favoured, a redeeming angel. He had met, and fallen in love – to the intense, romantic degree of which he was capable – with a fellow student. But she wasn't a Josephine. The chrysalis Doctor Faustus had found his Gretchen: Lilli Gau, if that was her name. Later we learn her married name, which was Wertel. We imagine her, tall, slender, blonde-haired, with blue-black eyes, a lovely line of lips, a soft maidenly bosom. In fact, later descriptions confirm she was tall and beautiful. Cupid's dart struck into the heart of 18-year-old Hans.

She was from the start forbidden fruit. She lived with her family in a secluded villa in a choice residential area, the English Garden. Her father, a rich Munich banker, on hearing of this young man's love for his daughter, forbade Lilli to go out with him. He was a poor lawyer's son, his father expelled for malpractice from the Munich Law Society, reduced to touting for legal custom in the Schelling Strasse tavern: and even worse, like country bumpkins, the father and son kept chickens in their flat. Hans felt his insecurity and humiliation keenly.

'What did you do?' he interrogated himself. 'Did you think also for, or against yourself?' He uses the formal second person plural *sie*, which is odd. 'I need, I believe, somebody, who will bring to me a fresh, healthy, and clean young love. L. is the perfect wife for me.'

This is especially revealing of his burning sense of rejection. The cold formality, the hygienic precondition, the overweening egotism; this statement displays how Hans was hardly Goethe's Young Werther, or Byron's Childe Harold, losing himself in youthful identification with his beloved. The sanitised love object is an odd departure from the Teutonic, romantic mystic soul Hans believed himself to be, which retains something appealing about it.

Now Hans was handsome, powerfully built, with smouldering dark eyes, a resolute, firm chin, sensual mouth, fine head of hair; altogether a highly presentable young man with a keen intelligence. Yet, confronted with the potentiality of loving a tall, compatible young woman he saw as his equal, do we hear virtue, courage, self-sacrifice, high-mindedness – and above all objective love – expressed in his soul-searching? He backed off. He withdrew. He nursed his self-pity and sense of rejection. He fought for, and found, a different self-love to sustain him through the shame and guilt of his broken family and his disreputable father's life. But, like that of his future mirror image, the Führer – who apparently had no early sweetheart, but had suffered extreme brutality from his father as a child and then

rejection as a budding artist – it wasn't at all a genuine self-love
in the way it was defined by the philosopher Scheler. Scheler had
defined the distinction between a genuine self-love and what
he calls 'a peculiar sham form of love, founded on self-hatred
and self-flight':

> In his *Pensées*, Blaise Pascal has drawn the classic picture of
> a type of man who is entangled in many worldly activities
> (games, sports, hunting, also 'business' or increasing work for
> the 'community'), and all this because he cannot look at him-
> self and continually tries to escape from the vacuum, from his
> feeling of nothingness.

This was often, too, as Scheler shows, the prototype for the politician's self-love, or that of the narcissist actor or performer.

Frank's diary at this crucial time is full of this vacuum, this
sense of nothingness. It is therefore perhaps not so strange that
he did not pursue Lilli vigorously and wholeheartedly, but
indulged instead in a mooncalf love, hanging about in the street
near his sweetheart's villa, indulging himself with fantasies of
her unattainable beauty – none of these, it must be said, particularly physical or erotic. No doubt, too, he dreams of the
financial advantages for the impecunious Frank family in marriage to Lilli.

He moans endlessly, 'Oh why am I so alone?' He upbraids
God a second time. He wanders through the English Garden of
Munich and, occupied with thoughts of Lilli, sits himself down
on a wooden bench in front of her house. He searches the surrounding streets. He sees a light within. Asks himself if she is
there. On 3 March 1919 he blames his creator 'for his wretched
state', writing about himself in the third person.

This posturing is perhaps superficial. The harder qualities
inside the 18-year-old are those of the resentful, turbulent spirit
of the times. He has, we remember, already been a German soldier, albeit briefly. Clever, adaptable, with a calculating mind,

one thing obsesses him more than Lilli, and this is his desire for security. In this vacuum of spirit, what does this much vaunted soul – *meine Seele* – feed on, where does it gain its nourishment? On the one hand, it joins with the infinite, it connects with the universe through philosophy, through music, through concert-going, through listening to one form of music in particular: German music. Music, not love for Lilli, is the vital force, the connecting tissue. On the other hand, there is the quest for order. For Frank, epitome of an ambitious young German male of his time, cultural order and political order are the same thing, or if not the same, then closely related.

The problem for even highly intelligent Germans as we see only too well through Frank's outpourings in his diary was that at every level of their society they were unable to think objectively about the nation, and therefore morally. We hear this comment from numerous American and English writers. Every discussion anyone held with a German began with the assumption that Germany was misunderstood and wronged, 'even to the extent of a piteous martyrdom', as the exiled American socialist activist George D. Herron claims in Upton Sinclair's *Between Two Worlds*.

This nurtures the overriding idea that whatever achieves the aim, the thing in view, namely national pride and honour, becomes the supreme good, and to attain these, the end justifies the means. Ranks had to be closed and the nation had to act as one being. Germans held the view that it was Germany's national pride that had to be preserved at all costs, rather than the revelation of truth, or the discovery of her own responsibility in the war that had just passed. Germany had to be saved from the humiliation of a confession.

In 1919 a left-wing journalist, Felix Feuenbach, published Bavarian files from 1914 that suggested Germany had some responsibility for the outbreak of war. He was summarily condemned to eleven years in jail for treason by a 'People's Court' in Munich convened to deal with murderers and looters in

1918. Above all, Germans, in their nationalist and psychic being, thought collectively, so each saw him or herself as an agent or citizen of the State, and considered whatever accomplished the State's end both philosophically and scientifically justifiable.

Only twelve days after roaming round the English Garden dreaming of Lilli, Frank explodes with metaphysical righteousness:

> Is Western humanity to be extinguished? ... Our future is the future of the World, and the German nation is the saviour of mankind. Now be steadfast, all you who are German on God's wide earth. We are enslaved, we are reviled. From the suffering that awaits you, people of Germany, subtract that portion for which you are to blame – the rest will more than suffice for our retaliation at the everlasting court of universal justice ...

It is the most naked appeal to awakening the power within the nation – and the start of the divorce of power from morality. He continues: 'One thought fills me with ardour today: the statesman must be a priest among the people ... "Be sufficient unto yourself in true and virile humility, and strive for perfection. Behold, well-being must needs then be yours."' Religion, and culture generally, are political. Frank, unsurprisingly, is unimpressed by contemporary art:

> Mark you well, the art of today is like all the other vacuous posturings, empty and affected, puffed up. There is nothing in it of the truth of life, which one cannot create, which one can only feel and *live*! I read Rosegger's *The God Seeker* and am shattered. Religion, so deeply thought through. Humanity, so deeply sensed in all its memory. I am filled with bitter premonitions about our immediate future. How far – in his modest and mature depth of feeling – how far Rosegger stands above the literary insanity of our times, aesthetically and expressionistically depraved as they are.

Rosegger was an Austrian poet, who in *The God Seeker* (1883) conflates the nationalist and religious impulse. Then Frank goes off on a different tack concerning his feminine side, or *anima*, which might give rise to sexual speculation:

> Two different natures are within me. The one appears to me in the form of a sovereign queen, who, cool and secure in her power and might, causes me to gaze down upon my certain victory; yes, who compels and urges me forward, who makes me quiver aloud at the thought voiced within: You, do you see, yes, you of all the millions are the one who will accomplish the great task!

Then there is Frank's other nature:

> And opposed to that, my second nature, the one who makes me so self-conscious before my fellow man, who keeps pushing me along, saying: 'Look, bow down before this one, the one who knows more, can do more, understands more.' Hand in hand with this goes doubt: oh, this dreadful doubt of mine! The battles that arise from this confrontation! Really and truly, I shall either ascend to the heights – or go mad. Perhaps both?

These emotions expressed so woodenly and repetitively, yet with ferocious animus, come to the fore as Hans wanders about the Munich streets dreaming of Lilli Gau.

~~~

Enter Kurt Eisner, real name Salamon Kosmanowskis, a middle-class Jewish theatre critic from Munich's bohemian Schwabing district who brought mayhem to Munich in November 1918. This prompted Frank's first act of political commitment, of taking action on his principles.

Released from Cell 70 in Stadelheim gaol after a sentence for organising strikes to end the war, Eisner looked and played the role of fiery revolutionary and bohemian. Short of stature, he sported a heavy grey beard, a black cloak, and a huge broad-brimmed black felt hat in the style of Lenin. Small, wire-rimmed spectacles completed the image. He sneered at political convention. Eisner was no Marxist. When immediate social breakdown and anarchy threatened the Social Democratic Party's control of Munich in November 1918, Eisner organised a brass band and banners, summoned a crowd and exhorted it to occupy the army barracks and seize the Bavarian State Parliament.

He met no resistance from the diminished defence force allowed by the Treaty of Versailles, and was endorsed both by the revolutionary workers' and the soldiers' councils. Then, calling himself an Independent Social Democrat, and supported by the Majority and Independent Social Democrats, he proclaimed the Bavarian kingdom a republic, the 'People's State'.

As food supplies dwindled because the Bavarian peasantry withheld their support, Eisner's 'government' quickly foundered, while the Allied powers requisitioned the trains. In the ensuing paralysis, there was a severe, radical right-wing backlash. All sides condemned Eisner as a pacifist agitator, a Jew, a journalist, a bohemian and, worst of all, a Berliner. He had, even more nefariously and treacherously, published the secret and incriminating documents collected by Felix Feuenbach, who was his secretary.

On 21 February 1919, Count Anton von Arco-Valley, an aristocrat exactly Hans' age and a fellow student, shot Eisner twice at point-blank range in the street, killing him instantly. Arco-Valley was wounded by return fire from Eisner's guards, but, curiously enough, saved from lynching by Feuenbach, who was then dispatched to the Stadelheim jail from which Eisner had been set free. An Eisner admirer strolled into the Bavarian Parliament and shot Erhard Auer, majority Social Democrat Leader, and Eisner's harshest critic, who survived. Subsequently, a document was found in Eisner's pockets which tendered his resignation.

Huge demonstrations followed Eisner's funeral, and Munich sank deeper into unregulated mob rule, with scenes reminiscent of Thomas Carlyle's description of the French Revolution in July 1789. There was a legitimate Bavarian Government, formed of Majority Social Democrats led by Johannes Hoffmann; but it could not command authority. The Workers' and Soldiers' councils distributed arms and a Soviet-style putsch was in the offing. Writers such as the playwright Ernst Toller – 'coffee house anarchists' – proclaimed Munich University open to all applicants except those who studied history!

History was, as often in regime upheaval, considered hostile. Capitalism, it was claimed, would soon fall owing to the issue of free money. Armed clashes between the 'Red Army' and Social Democrats became frequent. Then more militant Communists squashed the airy-fairy idealists to proclaim a Bolshevik Bavaria. They contacted Lenin in Moscow. 'Have you nationalized the banks yet?' inquired Lenin politely (and sensibly). They did so, and took hostages from the aristocracy and middle class. The 'Goddess Reason' reigned in Munich's Catholic churches; priests, early liberation theologians, joined the insurrectionary forces, who were soon training a 'Red Army' of 20,000; many were boarded in churches and monasteries where weapons were stored. Bavaria was about to spearhead the Bolshevisation of Europe. As Gebhard Himmler wrote, 'Munich, from which the weak Hoffmann government had fled to Bamberg, had to be liberated from outside.'

All this sounds, and was, very dramatic. But on the global scale it was a sideshow. It counted for little in the colossal charnel-pit of Europe in early 1919, filled with the mangled flesh of countless millions. Desolation reigned everywhere. Vultures circled overhead. Upton Sinclair painted the European overview:

> Turks were slaughtering Armenian peasants. Civil war raging in Russia, the whites now being driven in rout to all points of the compass. In Siberia, a freight train loaded with Reds was

wandering aimlessly upon an eight-thousand mile track, the locked-in prisoners perishing of disease and starvation. The Polish armies, invading Russia, were still dreaming of a world empire. The White Finns were killing tens of thousands of Red Finns. The Rumanians were killing Red Hungarians. There were insurrections and mass strikes in Germany, a plague of labour revolts in France and Britain, millions unemployed in every great nation, famine everywhere in Europe, flu in the western half and typhus in the eastern.

And, in the middle of all this, the screams of dying populations, the wails of starving children, the moans of the hopeless, the insurrections of the frustrated, and in the chaos of Bavaria's capital city, wandered young Hans Frank. His fairy-tale world suddenly had become very dark and threatening, crammed with ogres of all political shades. On 14 April he writes: 'I put away my weapons (two knives, one revolver) in a hiding place; anyone who fails to give them up will be shot.'

He is full of energy and hope. He would soon be joining the forces to liberate Munich from mayhem and chaos:

Oh what energy is locked up within me. I sense my will, filled with restless urgings. I glow with the need to be the pilot of this ship! A great new Germany will arise from these ruins, a Reich that will signify a world of civilized culture and whose founder will be crowned with the diadem of a liberated humanity. I am replete with joy when I realize I can work without let-up sixteen hours at a stretch. That is a capacity I shall soon have need of. Humanity, awake! Let yourself finally be aroused! Cast aside the mundane rubbish that encumbers you. Why do you dwell in the depths when you have seen the heights? It has now become impossible for me to forgive the enemy. There is but one goal remaining: Germany, the heart and the brain of the world! I no longer mourn. Henceforth I observe what transpires here with the eye of vengeance. Vengeance will raise us high above our tormentors. I believe in the German spirit. It will pluck us from the misery into which the barbaric, mindless rabble would plunge us. By God, this mob will easily be brought under control. Only through dictatorship – but not that of the proletariat! – will Germany be saved.

Hans had his weapons (the knives and revolver) to aid him in realising this dream. He is only fifteen days away from that fateful day, 1 May 1919, when he takes the step which is to transform his life. It sows the seed which germinates as his life's sacred mission.

On that day, while the 'Red Army' had been ordered to lay down its arms, an army of 33,000, well equipped and disciplined, took to the field against poorly armed workers. Himmler took part in the march of Munich as a member of the Schaaf Detachment of the Landshut *Freikorps*, which became involved in heavy street fighting when they used methods that resembled Nazi storm troops.

4

The Mission

Later than Himmler, but also on the first day of May 1919, Hans joined the *Freikorps*, or Free Corps, the civilian volunteer force dedicated to 'order'. Munich was well on the way to becoming not, as a writer later dubbed Poland, 'God's Playground', but the devil's. Revolutionary or reactionary sects of every colour and dimension fought for dominance; every social and political grouping seethed with hatred, resentment, fear, and the lust for revenge. Public order, a state or condition everyone hungered for but no leader could deliver, had vanished. And of course, since the *Diktat* of Versailles, there was no German Army, only a small *Reichswehr* or regular army permitted for defence based in Berlin. There were thousands of disbanded military men loose everywhere. Locked in a general strike, Munich was at a standstill. Factories were closed, public services shut down, looting and theft were commonplace.

The newly enlisted men in the *Freikorps*, under the command of Franz Ritter von Epp, a Bavarian colonel, were the Majority Social Democrats' answer. Hastily recruited, they moved to take control of the city, backed by regular military units not yet disbanded, and an armoured train. The Communists, hastily ditched by the workers' and soldiers' councils, retaliated by seizing hostages, notably members of the Thule Society, an anti-Semitic, pan-German secret society which more or less excluded women, and which had adopted the Aryan swastika symbol as its emblem or logo.

Defeated Germany was rich compost for the fast growth of occultism of every shape and form, ready to nourish conspiracy theories, especially inclining to those which blamed the Jews for the evils attending the defeat of the Fatherland. Notable right-wing émigré White officers from Russia brought the notorious anti-Semitic forgery *The Protocols of the Learned Elders of Zion* into Munich in their baggage. They found a ready audience among *Freikorps* personnel. Another leader of the Thule movement was the theorist or self-styled philosopher of future Nazism, Alfred Rosenberg, who later ruled German-occupied areas of Soviet Russia. The toxic, hubristic mixture of mysticism with *völkisch* ideology and actual political power was soon swallowed down in large draughts by future Nazi leaders: as well as Hitler, Himmler and Rudolf Hess, in time the deputy Führer, were mystics or occultists of one kind or another; Hess was also a believer in astrology and a devotee of Rudolf Steiner. Hitler was especially taken with the racist 'Ariosophic' philosophy of Dietrich Eckart, describing him as his 'polar star'. Eckart called himself an expert in magic, studied the mystic Angelus Silesius and occupied himself with Hinduism, as did Rosenberg. The future collaboration of Germany and Japan in the Second World War was crucially influenced by Professor Karl Haushofer, an authority on Asiatic mysticism linked to Eastern secret societies. According to Hans Clunt, Himmler 'engaged passionately in esotericism and based his organisation of the SS leadership on the model of occult societies'. He planned to breed a racially pure elite of Aryan *Übermenschen* at his Ordensburgen School and familiarise them with occult teachings. Himmler also founded the *Ahnenerbe e.V.*, a research society which financed the exploration of secret esoteric wisdom not just in Germany, but also in occupied France, Tibet and India.

Eisner's assassin, Arco-Valley, now in jail, had affiliations with the Thule Society. Its leader at that time, a sham Baron von

Sebottendorf, a convicted forger, preached racial hatred. The Reds shot ten of their aristocratic hostages, including the Prince of Thurn and Taxis and the young Countess von Westarp, a start to the homicide that now erupted on the unlikeliest of pretexts – such as an uncomplimentary remark about a revolutionary poster. So the *Freikorps* invested Munich by force, and in the acts of revenge that followed, drunken units on the rampage beat up and slaughtered left-wing anarchists and communists by the hundred, including blameless members of a Catholic crafts society, accused in error of being revolutionaries. These were like blueprints of later Nazi terror. One Red Army leader, Gustav Landauer, was brutalised, his face smashed to a pulp, before he was shot, his corpse left to rot in Standelheim Prison courtyard.

As far as we know, Hans took little part in the blood-letting. Finding order of a kind had returned, he resumed his studies in law at Munich University. His revolver and knives had been supplanted by another deadly weapon. He had seen how much he needed to sharpen and perfect what would furnish the best armoury of all – for his self-advancement as much as for his self-defence: German Law and the legal system. Hans had formulated, by 9 December 1918, his wish to serve the German people, adding that he awaited the call. He didn't have long to wait.

While Frank spent much time reading and writing essays and poems, actively contributing to student magazines and playing chess, at which he excelled, he kept up his attachment to the *Freikorps*, a significant part of which joined up to support the 'White', counter-revolutionary government of Bavaria.

This new force, given the part fear of left-wing political ideology increasingly played in Munich life, was endorsed by Gustav Ritter von Kahr, the Bavarian Prime Minister. The *Freikorps* increased its numbers and became a bloodthirsty, anti-Republican paramilitary force. Frank's comment even before his 18th birthday, quoted earlier, on the distinct difference between Bavarians and Prussians in the view of the extreme far right, shows how Bavaria (and he himself) were ahead of the game as far as National Socialism was concerned. All through his life he would assert his credentials going back to this early commitment. Even so, determined as he was to master every aspect of German jurisprudence, Frank, in that early emotional insecurity, hungered after marriage and domestic order.

Meantime, in the Pan-German Thule Society, which Hans had also joined as an early member, racial mysticism was about to join in unholy matrimony with the German workers' and soldiers' grassroots need for work and political order.

This is how the marriage was contracted. Hitler, 29 years old, with his two Iron Crosses for bravery (the second time for capturing fifteen English soldiers single-handed), had left Pasewalk and committed himself to political activism. For him the Amnesty was a sell-out, a stab in the back for Germany, engineered by cowardly military leaders colluding with a weak Republican regime which had replaced the rule of the Kaiser. 'The more I tried to achieve clarity on the monstrous event in this hour,' he wrote, 'the more the shame and indignation and disgrace hammered my brow. What was the pain in my eyes compared to this misery?'

The depth of Hitler's suffering, which propelled him into politics in his adopted hometown of Munich, was immeasurable. He had hated Vienna, where he had been stung by rejection as a struggling, untalented artist, lived below the poverty line in soup kitchens and workers' hostels, hawking his tepid canvasses for small sums of money. Studying intensely the machinations of the three main political parties, which battled for hegemony in the multicultural and multi-racial morass of the Austro-Hungarian Empire, he was repelled: 'The conglomeration ... of Czechs, Poles, Hungarians, Ruthenians, Serbs, and Croats, and everywhere the eternal mushroom of humanity – Jews and more Jews. To me the city seemed the embodiment of racial desecration.'

He promised he would cleanse Munich of similar contamination. He told Josef Hell, editor of *Der Gerade Weg*:

> As soon as I have the power to do it I shall, for example, have erected in the Marienplatz in Munich gallows and more gallows, as many as can be fitted in without stopping the traffic. Then the Jews will be hanged, one after another, and they will stay hanging, until they stink. They will hang as long as the principles of hygiene permit. As soon as they have been taken down, the next ones will be strung up, and this will continue until the last Jew in Munich is destroyed.

In Vienna Hitler had discovered his true genius, a political acuity formed from study and judgement of the strengths and weaknesses of the three main political parties, the Social Democrats, the Christian Socialists, and the Pan-German Nationalists. Above all, he perceived with masterly clarity the success of the Social Democrats with their manipulation of the crowd through propaganda, 'the gigantic human dragon', and the value it attached to what he called 'spiritual and physical terror' – unleashing a 'veritable barrage of lies and slanders against whatever adversary seems most dangerous, until the nerves of the attacked person break down ... This is a tactic based on precise calculation of all human weaknesses, and its results will lead to success with almost mathematical certainty.'

Hitler also further developed, before arriving in Munich in late November 1918, an equal understanding of how actual physical terror towards the individual and masses could achieve political aims: 'While in the ranks of their supporters the victory achieved seems a triumph of the justice of their own cause, the defeated adversary in most cases despairs of the success of any further resistance.'

Hitler's astuteness impelled him back to Munich in November 1918, even though his previous experience of his adopted German city had been miserable and useless. Years on

from his first stay in the Bavarian capital, he had the same impo-
tent feelings of the much younger Frank, and expressed them in
almost the same words. Contemplating the anarchy, he wrote:
'For days I wondered what could be done, but at the very end of
every meditation was the sober realization that I, nameless as I
was, did not possess the least basis for any useful action.' Following the events of late 1918 and early 1919, and using the frame
of reference of pre-war Vienna, he saw his chance to become an
influence on the right among the disaffected monarchists, whose
Wittelsbach King Ludwig III had abdicated. His battalion, he
found, had joined the left-wing Soldiers' Council, so he resolved
to leave, but he spent the winter on guard duty in a prisoner-
of-war camp at Traunstein (the town where Joseph Ratzinger,
the future Pope Benedict XVI, would live from the age of 10 to
20). Back in Munich, in the spring, Hitler avoided arrest by what
he called left-wing scoundrels and began political activity as an
investigator, researching the causes of the brief 'Red' regime for
his infantry battalion.

Then, like some other future political leaders, he joined an
Army Press and News Bureau – in this case of a German Army
which had become, at least in Bavaria, politically motivated.
It now indoctrinated its men in conservative politics. Inter-
vening one day in a lecture with an anti-Semitic tirade against
the speaker, Hitler won the support of his superiors. He was
promoted to *Bündungsoffizier*, an instructor tasked to combat
dangerous ideas such as pacifism, socialism and democracy.

Up to this point Hitler, it might be claimed, was a product
or result of social conditions. But here his unique, demonic
genius came into play and flourished. There was nothing else,
except perhaps a frustrated artistic aspiration to create new cities
and monuments – no desire for sexual conquest or family love,
no burning need for money (he had lived thirty years without
it), no ostensible vice or desire for self-gratification to restore,
or, perhaps more accurately, create an identity for this broken
man, who had lost his soul with German defeat – nothing left

except that extraordinary power of speech. Life had stripped him of everything but the power to become a political agitator. Here, in Munich, he found the richest and most fertile soil to nourish that power.

The growth of his skills was swift. From years of listening, of attendance at rallies, he knew what people wanted to hear. He pressed into use techniques and tricks of every shade in the spectrum of popular demagoguery, from revolutionary atheist anarchism to high-flown, right-wing idealism and radical anti-Semitism, his 'ticket' in the early days. This was not only deeply embedded in him, probably for reasons beyond envy, it also enjoyed currency as a counter to the Red threat, identified with Jewish Marxist Leninism. Munich's Red Army had summarily executed the aristocratic patriots, who were now seen as martyrs.

In contrast to dull right-wingers delivering lectures, or the brutal, pompous or merely rambling majority of political speech-makers, Hitler's oration quickly won admirers. His confidence soared. He spoke simple, straightforward sentences. He drew on his own down-to-earth experiences. He spoke without verbs in powerful emotive slogans; as Jonathan Swift wrote in *A Voyage to Laputa*: 'The first project was to shorten discourse by cutting polysyllables into one and leaving out verbs and participles because in reality all things imaginable are but nouns.' Beginning by mastering the intoxicating tirade, Hitler went on to weave his magic spell over audiences: 'All at once I was offered an opportunity of speaking before larger audiences, and the thing that I had always presumed from pure feeling without knowing it was corroborated: I could speak.'

And it was during this new drama of projecting power, this drive to save and redeem Germany Hitler found in himself, that one day in June 1919 Hans Frank heard the call he had been yearning for.

5

Mephistopheles Unveiled

5 June 1919. It was, Frank recorded in his diary – although his son Niklas disputes this, claiming it is a fraudulent entry made later in 1942 – the day he first met the Führer at the University. This was 'at a lecture by [Gottfried] Feder to the "Cultural Attachés" of the Munich garrison, to which I had been sent as representative of my squadron'.

Gottfried Feder was the right-wing star of the month: a crank, an engineer who had become obsessed with the idea (today having some appeal) that 'speculative' capital as opposed to 'creative' or 'productive' capital explained Germany's economic mess. He formed 'The Green Fighting League for the Breaking of Interest Slavery'. The impecunious Frank loved the idea. Hitler saw it as the eventual premise for the formation of a new party.

After Feder sat down, a Munich professor rose and attacked his arguments. The academic proposed Bavaria should break away from Prussia and combine with Austria to form a South German nation. Frank had some sympathy with this idea. But not for long. He hadn't served in the Imperial Army at the front. Hitler rose in fury to denounce the proposition.

It was Hitler's anger, his passion, his crescendos that made an overwhelming impression on Frank. There were no qualifications in what he said; everything was absolute, uncompromising,

irrevocable, undeviating, final. To Frank, listening to this coruscating force, Hitler spoke from the heart. Here was someone, he
felt, who could express his own deepest fears and desires with
self-confidence, aggression, even a sense of destiny, a belief in
the ultimate triumph of his party.

The audience responded with astonishment to the then
unknown Hitler. Who was this madman? Later, Hitler was
to fine-tune his oratorical armoury. He taught himself all the
tricks: how to begin a speech quietly, to capture his audience's
attention, then gradually build to a climax. The deep, rather
hoarse voice would rise in pitch, climbing to a screaming
finale, accompanied by carefully rehearsed dramatic gestures,
by which time his face glistened with sweat, his lank, dark
hair falling forward over his face as he worked his audience
into a frenzy of emotion. The speeches found a formula he
often repeated. He began with an account of his own poverty-
stricken early life, to which he drew an implicit parallel with
the downcast, downtrodden and desperate state of Germany
after the First World War. Then, his voice building, he would
describe his own political awakening and point to its coun-
terpart in Germany's future recovery and return to glory. His
knack, without using overtly religious language, was to appeal
to religious archetypes of suffering – humiliation, redemption
and resurrection. Ultimately though, it was not what he said
but how he said it that stirred up frenzy. 'The public sensed,'
writes Claus Hant, 'that Hitler was something extraordinary,
nothing like the leaders of other parties, who came across as
mere mortals, weak and unsure, while he seemed to follow his
path with unswerving certainty ... Not only Hitler believed
he was the Chosen One, with a divine mission, but the world
around him began to share his vision of himself.' In the circumstances of post-war and post-revolutionary Bavaria, he
found a ready response. The effect was, perhaps, akin to hypnosis. Frank, so he claimed, went to the front of the assembly
to meet Hitler and express his admiration.

At this or a similar meeting when Feder spoke, Hitler met and shared ideas with Anton Drexler, by trade a locksmith, later claimed to be the actual founder of National Socialism. Drexler shared with Hitler a similar height and build (5ft 8in or 1.73m) and an all-round unprepossessing or insignificant appearance, hardly a good advertisement for the Aryan ideal. Ill more often than not, bespectacled, with an undisciplined, second-rate mind that nevertheless asserted fierce independence of thought, he wrote poorly and spoke even worse. But he was a virulent anti-Marxist and as a Munich railroad worker he had combated the red menace. He struck up a rapport with a newspaper reporter, Karl Harrer, with whom he found less than 100 like-minded souls to start the German Workers' Party, its clear ideals of a Nationalist Workers' Party outlined in a booklet, *My Political Awakening*. Drexler thrust it into Hitler's hand. There was a host of similar high-sounding groups and parties all over Germany vying for attention and support, but none would grow like the *Deutsche Arbeiter Partei*, or DAP. It was anti-middle class, anti-bourgeois and anti-liberal. Hitler felt reluctance at first to join this shabby collection of young working-class idealists who met in ill-lit, rundown premises:

> That I was poor and without means seemed to me the most bearable part of it, but it was harder that I was numbered among the nameless, that I was one of the millions whom chance permits to live or summons out of existence without even their closest neighbours condescending to take any notice of it. In addition, there was the difficulty which inevitably arose from my lack of schooling.

Hitler's self-schooling in fact had been prodigious. Not only did he maintain, and later even enforce with murder, a determined silence about the mentors who had influenced him and helped him, he also neglected to mention the prodigious effort of the autodidact in his 'down and out days' in Vienna and Munich. As well as the power of persuasion, Hitler also had an extraordinary power of recall. Like many who have not had education forced on them, or absorbed learning in competition to win places or awards – only to forget it instantly – what he read remained filed in his memory:

One trait of Hitler that always amazed everyone – even those not in his thrall – was his stupendous memory, which was able to retain even insignificant information precisely and recorded everything he had ever laid eyes on.

Later, at Nuremberg, Göring would observe: 'He knew the armament, armour, speed and draught of almost all important battleships in the world.'

A particularly chilling aspect of his poor mouthing and cementing over of his past was what he owed to Jews in his early life. He had earlier been generous about Jewish qualities, praising their business sense, you could 'do business with them because they were the only ones prepared to take a risk'. He called them 'a clever people who stuck together better than the Germans'.

In Vienna his best friend at the hostel where he lived was a Jewish copper polisher named Neumann with whom Hitler once disappeared for a week. Another Jewish resident, Siegfried Loffner, took Hitler's side when he felt conned by another (non-Jewish) resident, and reported the incident to the police. Another friend was the one-eyed Jewish locksmith Simon Robinson, who supported Hitler from his disability allowance. A Moravian Jew, Rudolf Redlich, was another Jewish friend. His roommate August Kubizek, who wrote a memoir, *Adolf Hitler, mein Jugendfreund* (1955), took him to a Jewish musical evening given by an affluent Jewish family called the Jahodas, about which Hitler commented admiringly.

Hitler sent hand-painted postcards to Dr Block, the Jewish doctor from Linz who treated his mother, and later saved him and his wife from being rounded up and taken to a camp.

Although he had treated Hitler's mother, Block's medical degree was not recognised when he emigrated to the US and he died penniless in the Bronx in 1945.

Not surprisingly, then, many younger men, such as Frank and Himmler, were impressed by the reach and power of Hitler's intellect and memory. Frank wasted no time in joining the DAP, together with names that were to form part of the roll call of infamous Nazis, such as Munich District Commander Captain Ernst Röhm and Dietrich Eckart, the bohemian writer who had staged his own plays, like the Marquis de Sade, when confined in mental institutions.

Eckart was of particular importance. He had wit and vision. He defined the *dramatis personae* of the DAP leadership as if he were writing a play. 'We need,' he told the party meeting in the Brennessel Wine Cellar:

> … a leader who can stand the sound of a machine gun. The rabble need to get fear into their pants. We can't use an officer, because the people don't respond to them anymore. The best would be a worker who knows how to talk … He doesn't need much brains … He must be a bachelor, then we'll get the women.

Frank knew he possessed no such qualifications. But there was one who did. Hitler happily fell in with the much older Eckart, who became his mentor. Eckart had found his leader. With Drexler he drew up his manifesto, or programme, for the DAP that on 24 February 1920 in the Brennessel Cellar promulgated the harsh directives against Jews which, it can be argued, were logically and inevitably to lead to genocide: denial of office and citizenship, exclusion from the press and expulsion of all those who had entered the Reich.

The emblem of the crooked cross (*Hakenkreuz*) as the DAP emblem was also Drexler's brainchild. It was strange that it should have been a distortion of the Catholic Cross, as well as incorporating the crooked imagery when tilted anti-clockwise that the Nazis so often employed for Jewish facial features. The swastika, then, was a gargoyle, a horror emblem to confront and frighten the enemy, as well as the symbol of Aryan power and ultimate knowledge. The word '*swastika*' is Sanskrit, meaning 'it is good' or 'so be it', but it is hard to attribute to the symbol a wholly negative or positive meaning: it was, in its importance, ambiguous, but for sure it was at first a secret and then a very public identification.

Yet another Bavarian, Thomas Mann, who left Germany in 1933, depicts Nazism as primarily a cultural, artistic phenomenon in *Doctor Faustus*. When his Faust, Adrian Leverkühn, contracts syphilis from a prostitute, he is led by his diseased hubris into madness and self-destruction. As Mann described it in the novel, the history of Germany under Nazism showed a desire to 'escape from everything bourgeois, moderate, classical, sober, industrious and dependable into a world of drunken release, a life of Dionysian genius, beyond society, indeed superhuman – above all, subjectively, an experience and drunken intensification of the self, regardless of whether the world outside can go along with it'. Mann identifies Nazism closely with the world of German music. Looking at the beginnings in Munich University, in the beer cellars, the cabarets and cafes, the crumbling army barracks, with characters such as Eckart, Röhm, Drexler and Harrer, and Hitler's intoxication with Wagner, one appreciates the force of Mann's analysis: Leverkühn, like Wagner, combined the esoteric German spirit, its aestheticism, with a dangerous collective primitivism destructive of bourgeois culture.

Apparently, at the time of *Parsifal*, Wagner signed a letter adding to his name the title 'Member of the High Consistory', aligning himself with the Thule mysticism.

The passage from Mann's novel below concerns that link between the German artistic soul and the rise of Nazism, for the narrator fears his friend's combination of aestheticism and barbarism and how close they are to each other:

> The revival of ritual music from a profane epoch has its dangers. It served indeed the end of the Church, did it not? But before it had served less civilised ones, the ends of the medicine-man, magic ends. That was in times when all celestial affairs were in the hands of the priest-medicine-man, the priest-wizard. Can it be denied that this was a pre-cultural, a barbaric condition of cult-art; and it is not comprehensible that the later revival of the cult in art, which aims at atomisation to arrive at collectivism, seizes upon means that belong to a stage of civilization not only priestly but primitive?

Hitler saw himself as a creative genius on the scale of Wagner, the world his medium instead of music:

> For myself, I have the most intimate familiarity with Wagner's mental processes. At every stage in my life I come back to him. Only a new nobility can introduce the new civilization for us. If we strip *Parsifal* of every poetic element, we learn from it that selection and renewal are possible only amid the continuous tension of a lasting struggle. A world-wide process of segregation is going on before our eyes. Those who see in struggle the meaning of life, gradually mount the steps of a new nobility. Those who are in search of peace and order through dependence, sink, whatever their origin, to the inert masses. The masses, however, are doomed to decay and self-destruction. In our world-revolutionary turning point the masses are the sum total of the sinking civilization and its

dying representatives. We must allow them to die with their
kings, like Amfortas.

Amfortas was king of the Grail knights in Parsifal who is injured
by his own Holy Spear and the wound will not heal. Amfortas
has a holy vision which told him to wait for a 'pure fool,
enlightened by compassion' (*Durch Mitleid wissend, der reine Tor*)
who will finally heal him. Fascinatingly, Amfortas' wound was
also significant to Jung, who in his *Psychological Types Revisited*
argued that we are divided into a civilised, socially adapted
part and a barbaric part that holds the secret of our individuality. We suffer from this internal split as from a never healing
wound. The relevance of this to the beginnings of Nazism is
not difficult to discover.

Hitler had already tried his hand at a musical drama
during his early days in Vienna, its subject the gory legend of
King Nidur who raped his daughter and killed his sons, later
using their skulls as bowls. Wagner's chosen one ruled with god-
like power, defeated his evil enemies, with blood sealing the
word of the truly pure. Hitler told Frank in those early days, 'I'm
building my religion from Parsifal ... One can only serve God in
the guise of the hero.'

Wagner was convinced that if the Jew wanted to become a
person he had to 'stop being a Jew', and frequently expressed
his instinctive aversion, comparing Jews to vermin in his letters
and using other pejorative terms about their personalities and
natures, similar to Hitler's. The latter, according to A. Kubizek
in *Adolf Hitler, mein Jugendfreund*, 'adopted Wagner's personality,
instilled him so completely in himself as to become part of his
own being'.

Hitler's early entourage soon also included the grotesque figure of Julius Streicher, founder of *Der Stürmer* (the
'stormer'), an anti-Semitic Nuremberg paper that became
Hitler's favourite. Streicher delighted in pornographic images
of Jews. He had been dismissed from his schoolteacher post for

pederasty and he became a full-time Nazi propagandist. He
said of first hearing Hitler:

> I had never seen the man before. And there I sat, an unknown
> among unknowns. I saw this man shortly before midnight,
> after he had spoken for three hours, drenched in perspiration,
> radiant. My neighbour said he thought he saw a halo round
> his head, and I experienced something which transcended
> the commonplace.

Significantly for the history of the German Catholic Church,
the future Cardinal Eugenio Pacelli, the papal nuncio to Bavaria
and then Germany, was also smitten by Hitler in 1919. Pacelli,
who had arrived in Munich two years earlier, would become
Pope Pius XII. The still impoverished leader walked into his
office without an appointment, and so impressed Pacelli with
his fanatical anti-communism that Pacelli even went so far as
to bankroll him. Some have seen in that meeting evidence that
Hitler gained some kind of psychological or spiritual hold over
Pacelli, which was to supply Hitler with all the high cards in
their future dealings.

Hans Frank shared at once with the Nazi leaders this hubristic
vision of epic conflict, incorporating as it did aestheticism and
cult-magic, uniting the barbaric and the collective with high
ideals and mystical hierarchy. There were special conditions in
Bavaria that bred such figures, their legions of support, and their
very special witnesses and commentators. The vision needed its
intellectual fixers, its legal manipulators, to give it credibility in
the real world. Here Frank saw his chance and defined his role.

He would, given that venal and corrupt potentiality,
fulfil all his earthly desires and become Faustus to Hitler's
Mephistopheles. From the very start he loved this identification
of himself with the learned doctor of legend, the alchemist who
turned base metal into gold. Like Faustus he saw his rewards
shimmering in a dream of endless wealth and power – and, of

course, sex. In this he was the opposite of Heinrich Himmler, whose commitment to Nazism, at least at first, was a form of complete self-abnegation, of disbelief in, or rejection of, anything in himself which had not been endorsed by or come from the leader, or did not serve the cause.

There was another good reason Frank could never be as set apart as Hitler. He liked women too much. He hungered for a partner and this could only ever be achieved through legitimate marriage, something which his Führer, from his own broken family background, eschewed for himself, but valued highly to the degree that he expected moral probity in the behaviour of his faithful followers.

This was to lead to some strange situations in the future married life of Hans Frank.

Hitler pursued a sexually abstinent, celibate vision of his own role in a future Germany. Early in his life he had renounced girlfriends, although he responded to a certain type of femininity found in the unthreatening joviality and silliness of 'young things'. Generally, in the intense scrutiny given to his life and personal motivation, the conclusion was that he had a low sex drive. He surrounded himself, almost as a stylistic backdrop, with blond Aryan aides-de-camp. Yet he worked hard all his life to veil and transfigure his true person and especially to hide his questionable lineage. After his death, speculation remained intense about his sex life, but detailed research has revealed the secret that there was no secret.

In 1920 Frank was still only 20 years old and he had a variety of pursuits apart from girls. He played chess, went on walking tours and climbed mountains, explored geology, collected books on the history of his beloved Bavaria. His diaries are full of enthusiasm for his leisure pursuits and his love of music, for he was also an accomplished pianist. On 11 May 1920 the

DAP became the National Socialist German Workers' Party, or NSDAP (*Nationalsozialistische Deutsche Arbeitpartei*). On 29 July 1921 it picked Hitler as its first Party Chairman. The party now had its expanding political programme. It was the party's paramilitary wing, under the command of ex-Captain Röhm, which Hans soon joined. It was to be inevitable that he would be a witness to, if not directly participate in, the violent tactics of the SA.

There is little doubt that Frank, for all his worship of Beethoven and Mozart and the tender, wifely potential of his early girlfriends, was attracted to the pornography of violence. What part sex had played in his relationship with Lilli at that time is not known, but they did begin, or resume, a sexual relationship later.

Röhm attracted Frank also in a different, though related way. What Röhm offered was direct and physical aggression against the enemies of the National Socialist programme, and the creation and installation of terror in the minds of those who opposed it – those, that is, who were spared the beatings and murder, but even so were intimidated *en masse*.

Frank was a *Freikorps* veteran, and had, although he never confessed this, been present at, and perhaps taken part in, the violent confrontations earlier in the anarchy on Munich's streets. From these veterans a 'Hall Protection Group' – the linguistic smokescreen of euphemisms began early – renamed the 'Gymnastics and Sports Section', were at first bully-boys, already a familiar sight in Munich's streets, attacking anyone who looked like a Jew. A couple of severe brawls following Nazi interventions at meetings of the Bavarian League, a separatist organisation, in beer cellars led to the Nazis arming themselves more effectively and expanding their forces to maintain Bavaria as the centre of anti-Republican 'order'.

Hitler himself, at the centre of this fanatical brawling, was briefly jailed in Stadelheim Prison for a month in October 1921. The local police and the Bavarian President Ritter von

Kahr were broadly sympathetic to the counter-revolutionary, anti-Republican extremists and they turned a blind eye to the political violence, which culminated in the murder of Walter Rothenau, the Reich Foreign Minister, a highly intelligent Jewish Social Democrat, hated by the Junkers because he wanted the Germans to make sacrifices. This provoked a clampdown from Berlin on the extreme right everywhere in Germany.

There exist early photographs of Frank looking proud in his SA Storm Division uniform. This division amalgamated with Gerhardt's Gymnastics and Sports Section in October 1921 under Röhm's command. Hans would now be serving under a man who championed ruthless and daredevil tactics, had a penchant for mindless violence and sneered at intellectuals, the middle class, and those who valued compromise. Frank nevertheless was still devoting himself to his studies of litigation, legal justice and jurisprudence.

Röhm was a stocky, bull-necked, scar-faced veteran: the upper part of his nose had been shot away in 1914. His credo was 'The Germans have forgotten how to hate. Feminine complaining has taken the place of masculine hatred.' War and unrest appealed to him, 'since I am an immature and wicked person'. Like several early Nazi leaders, Röhm was homosexual; he made a virtue of carousing and brawling with his comrades, while he treated women with disdain.

6

Sexuality

Many present-day analysts and historians of the Third Reich are drawn into investigating or speculating on this topic: the degree to which homosexuality was an important – not to say, in the opinion of some, crucial – factor in the rise of Hitler and the Nazi Party. On this issue there are opinions for and against, with evidence to support both sides. It is of course a subject fraught with danger and pitfalls for any analyst or historian today.

In Bleigiessen, on New Year's Eve 1920, Hans met a second girl who became his sweetheart. So precipitously did he fall in love with 17-year-old Gertrude H., that again he immediately began to see her as his wife. Her mother was a war widow. Her parental home appealed to Hans' taste as it encouraged music and drama. Gertrude learned the piano and also composed music. Hans, an accomplished pianist, was wildly enthusiastic about her, praising her 'delightful charm'. They found each other's circle and company congenial and stimulating. 'I was a poor student, I was the absolute taker,' he moans, although they became engaged in April 1921, when Gertrude was 18. Their engagement lasted two-and-a-half years until, in the summer of 1924, they broke it off. Hans had to go to Kiel for his legal studies, and she to Italy. But they separated, according to Hans, on the 'best of understanding'. Frank is discreet about whether or not they had sex during their engagement. He is also discreet concerning a common supposition about him – that he was bisexual.

Homosexuals enjoyed a relatively high level of freedom in Germany in the 1920s, perhaps a level unrivalled anywhere at that time. There were an estimated 1.2 million German homosexual men in 1928 (6 per cent of men over the age of 20). Berlin was reputedly the most liberal city in Europe with regard to sexuality, with a plethora of homosexual clubs, Turkish bathhouses, bars and brothels. By the time of the death of the famous homosexual lawyer Karl Heinrich Ulrichs, as early as 1895, the constituency had influence. Friedrich Engels wrote to Karl Marx about Ulrichs: 'The pederasts start counting their numbers and discover they are a powerful group in our state. The only thing missing is an organization but it seems to exist already, except that it was hidden.' The Scientific Humanitarian Committee was established in 1897, which opened later in Berlin as the Institute for Sex Research. This collected tens of thousands of case histories of people ostensibly being offered treatments for sexual problems and 'dysfunction'; however, some believe it served mainly as an introductory agency for homosexuals, including its leader, Magnus Hirschfeld, to make contact with others.

The more aggressive, masculine part of the early 'gay rights' movement founded a magazine, *Der Eigene* ('The Special'). In 1902 its militant organisation, 'The Community of The Special', espoused the active revival of Greek pederastic and Spartan military values of male bonding which, it was claimed, assured the success of renowned homosexual leaders such as Alexander and Frederick the Great of Prussia. The CS leaders were especially anti-Jew and anti-Christian because of the Judeo-Christian ethical condemnation of homosexuality. Adolf Brand, the CS chief, rejected Christianity as 'barbarism', exhorting his members to 'fight beyond good and evil, not for the sake of the masses, since the happiness of "the weak" would result in a "strong mentality", but for the human being who proclaimed himself a god and was not to be subdued by human laws and ethics'. Brand here echoed Nietzsche, who had dubbed Christianity 'the lie of millennia'.

Again, the hub of all this ferment was Bavaria in Hans Frank's time. He, too, was identified as an early Nazi homosexual, or bisexual, although there is little evidence to show he had ever been active. Julius Streicher was an open homosexual. Rudolf Hess was known in homosexual circles as *Fräulein Anna*. Baldur von Schirach, reputedly bisexual, was the head of the Hitler Youth movement, which, like the earlier *Wandervogel* youth movement begun in 1896, was obliquely associated with homosexuality. Walther Funk, the banker and the Austrian Reinhard Heydrich, later the notorious SS executioner, were also homosexual.

But it was Ernst Röhm, who became a friend of the young Frank, who was the driving force of homosexual recruitment for the SA. Drawn to meetings in the *Bratwurstglockl*, Röhm's favourite homosexual beer cellar, new recruits flooded in.

So was Frank drawn to Röhm for reasons other than shared political beliefs? Frank seems to have drunk deep of the intoxicating homoerotic atmosphere that bonded early SA members, until they became 2.5 million strong, larger than the German Army. Historian Alfred Rouse describes the culture thus: 'There was a very masculine brand of homosexuality, they lived in a male world, without women, a world of camps and marching, rallies and sports. They had their own relations, and the Munich SA became notorious on account of them.' Gisela High School and other Munich educational establishments were favourite hunting grounds for the SA to pick up recruits for Röhm's orgies. Röhm also believed homosexuality would be the basis for a new society.

Frank later publicly professed himself to be a homophobe (like Hitler). But it is claimed by several commentators that Frank was bisexual. If there was truth in this, he achieved little notoriety for it in practice. There is but one instance, much later, in an official record:

May, 21, 1944. Frank orders the dispatch of a memorandum
to *Obergruppenführer* Höfle *re*: the clash with Höfle on account
of alleged improper treatment of an NSKK [the elite Nazi
corps of drivers] man for Frank's own personal purposes.

Niklas Frank, in his memoir of his father, infers that for his 'own
personal purposes' could only mean one thing, and graphically
elaborates on the idea. Frank's official diary records that the
whole NSKK company was withdrawn from the Government
General, suggesting a pretty serious incident had taken place.
His son calls this his father's 'new amorous target'. It would, says
Niklas, at least have been an indication of one human trait.

That Frank participated in and embraced the all-pervading
male narcissism and self-glorification that spread the central
ethos of Nazism into every area of German life is undoubtedly
true. Nazi culture was one of meticulous style and male chic,
and for men mainly. It was, now Hitler's war plans and lust
for world domination no longer had to be secret, shamelessly
Nietzschean. Frank's pursuit of his early sweethearts for marriage and family could have been, as it was for some others, a
façade of bourgeois respectability. Power, the frustration of not
having it – and the naked full enjoyment of it when achieved –
was possibly Frank's main aphrodisiac and sexual gratification.
If he was then to go on to indulge in whoring and sex outside
marriage, it was to show he was one of the *Gauleiters*.

As for Hitler himself, here too suggestions have been made,
in the early days, of homosexuality. In Vienna, instead of working, Hitler had chosen to live in a Vienna flophouse, a habitat
of many homosexual men, and he was listed in his pre-Bavarian
days in Viennese police records as a homosexual. Walther Langer
suggests Hitler had a coprophiliac perversion, and while he
had abnormal relationships with four women, three of whom
attempted suicide and two of whom succeeded, the particular
episode which perhaps revealed an earlier homosexual influence
was his order in 1938 of the murder of Reinhold Hanisch, a close

associate of his in Vienna, who would have known his sexual secrets. While it is unlikely, as suggested by some, that Hitler had been a rent boy in Vienna, Hanisch's murder would be consistent with Hitler's attempt to bury his past, a period in which Frank figured. That he should surround himself, especially at first, with homosexual men and make use of their undivided adoration and talents is indicative of an easy familiarity with a homosexual ethos.

The burying of records and destruction of Hirschfeld's Sex Research Institute on 6 May 1933, only days after Hess was appointed deputy leader of the Nazi Party, was a cover-up. Forty thousand confessions and biographical letters, as well as 35,000 photographs and 12,000 books, were burned in a public ceremony in Munich on 10 May. Two truckloads of carefully selected incriminating material were taken away. An indicator of how close Frank had by then become to the centre of Nazi power was the confiscation of the Institute's headquarters, which were renamed the seat of the Nazi Association of Jurists and Lawyers that Frank was appointed to lead. Of course while Hitler would later use their homosexual affiliations as a means to stigmatise and dispose of his enemies, this subculture in German society was crucial if it wasn't exactly dominant in his rise to power. Hitler saw the value of highly articulate, homosexual support. Ludwig L. Lens, assistant to Hirschfeld at the Institute, asks why Hitler's first act was to destroy medical records:

> The answer is simple … We knew so much. It would be against the medical principles to provide a list of the Nazi leaders and their perversions [but] … not ten per cent of the men who, in 1933, took the fate of Germany into their hands, were sexually normal … Many of these personages were known to us directly through consultations; we heard about others from their comrades in the party … and of others we saw the tragic results … Our knowledge of such intimate secrets regarding members of the Nazi Party and other

documentary material – we possessed about forty thousand confessions and biographical letters – was the cause of the complete and utter destruction of the Institute of Sexology.

In the summer of 1923 Frank met Hitler by chance in a corridor of the NSDAP offices. Frank was considering whether his citizen unit should join with the NSDAP. Hitler, wearing his Bavarian *Lederhosen*, in outgoing mood, asked, 'What, are you really still studying? Since 1919 you've been studying. You must have everyone worried in your house!' Hans told him he had just taken his exams. Hitler replied, 'Then you must excuse me, please. Lawyers are such unimaginable people. That you, in your young years, want to spend your life spent ploughing through paragraphs – horrible! But our party can make use of lawyers, more and more.' Frank said he was thinking it over. Hitler laughed.

The idea of co-operation between the NSDAP and a *Freikorps* citizen unit had engaged Hitler's attention. 'But there are no terms. Men come to me, not me to them,' Hitler told Frank. Once again Hitler's eyes captured Frank, they were 'already a piercing, deep blue', which transfixed him. (The word 'already' is intriguing.) Frank signed up to the NSDAP while remaining attached to the SA.

Nietzsche declared that a person's sexuality had repercussions on the very foundations of his or her spirituality. In his incontinent outbursts of confession in Nuremberg prior and during his trial, Frank revealed how deeply his 'soul' had been 'seduced' in the early years of his manhood. 'I quoted from Goethe's *Faust*, "*Zwei Seelen wohnen, ach! in meiner Brust*" [Two souls dwell, alas, in my breast!]' he told Dr Gustave Gilbert, the US Army psychologist. He finished the quotation, and went off on the theme of split-personality in one of his careering, introspective monologues:

'Yes, we do have evil in us – but do not forget that there is always a Mephistopheles who brings it out. He says, "Behold!

The world is wide and full of temptation – behold! I will show
you the world! – There is just a little triviality of handing over
your soul!"' … He became more and more expansive, drama-
tizing his speech with all the appropriate gestures, waving his
arms to behold the world, and rubbing his fingers like a miser
asking for the triviality of a soul in payment. 'And so it was. –
Hitler was the devil. He seduced us all that way.'

He harped on the theme of surrender, seeing himself as
paradymic:

'You know, the people [*Volk*] is really feminine. – In its
totality, it is female. One should not say *das Volk* [neuter], one
should say *die Volk* [feminine]. It is so emotional, so fickle,
so dependent, on mood and environment, so suggestible – it
idolizes virility so – that is it.'

'And so it is ready to obey?' interpolated Gilbert.

'That, yes – but not merely obedience – surrender [*Hingabe*]
– like a woman. You see? Isn't that amazing?' He burst into
explosive laughter as though tickled by projection into a lewd
joke. The identification was unmistakable. 'And that was the
secret of Hitler's power. He stood up and pounded his body
shape, he was the man! – and he shouted about his strength
and determination – and so the public just surrendered to him
with hysterical enthusiasm. One must not say that Hitler vio-
lated the German people – he seduced them! They followed
him with a mad jubilation, the like of which you have never
seen in your life! It is unfortunate that you did not experience
those feverish days, *Herr Doktor* – you would have a better
conception of what happened to us. – It was a madness – a
drunkenness.'

Here Frank would have been in full accord with Mann's *Doctor
Faustus*. Gilbert believed this showed 'spontaneously' Frank's
latent homosexuality.

7

Bürgerbräu Cellar

The next phase of Frank's identification with Hitler's rise, deepening his envy of the Führer, came with the *Bürgerbräukeller Putsch*, the 'Beer Hall Putsch' of 8 November 1923.

The Nazi revolution was living up to its reputation for high drama on a world stage, and this attempted coup hit the headlines. To have taken part earned you a lifelong credential in Nazi mythology. Those who had not, who joined the party only after the March 1933 elections, mostly officials who became the backbone of the party, were known as March Violets.

Bavarian beer halls were, and still are, the favoured venues for combining on a gargantuan scale the quaffing of beer and discussion of politics. In November 1923, Gustav Ritter von Kahr, recently appointed with dictatorial powers as the Bavarian State Commissar, addressed an assembly of 3,000 of the most important burgers of Munich. They had gathered at the Bürgerbräu cellar, it was believed, to proclaim Bavarian independence and the restoration of the Wittelsbach dynasty. Since that September, in campaigning for his own party, Hitler had held mass meetings over Bavaria, stirring the authorities into declaring a state of emergency. With von Kahr on the rostrum were Police Chief Rutter von Seisser, and General Otto von Lossow, head of the German defence force permitted by the *Diktat* of Versailles.

While Hitler's strategy of creating a vanguard elite party on a mass working men's base followed Lenin's model, the actual seizure of power in his eyes had to come from a paramilitary coup.

In autumn 1922, Benito Mussolini, with his army of 40,000 Blackshirts, had marched on Rome and taken over Italy. The German currency collapsed in 1923, with farcical runaway inflation (tips in restaurants were 400 million marks). The poorest lost everything, while the winners were the landowners and the industrialists. This fermented unrest and blame centred on the Versailles Treaty and Jewish speculation. These factors, and Mussolini's success, encouraged Hitler to believe his hour had come.

By now he had adopted a folksy, Bavarian persona. With High Court Judge Theodor von der Pfordten, an undercover supporter of the Nazis, and General Erich Ludendorff, a hero of the Great War, Hitler planned a provisional constitution for a national dictatorship shared between himself and Ludendorff. An uprising by Communists in Saxony added further stimulus to Hitler's march on the *Bürgerbräu Keller* with a detachment of steel-helmeted SA men under Röhm at 8.45 p.m. on the cold night of 8 November. While the SA set up a machine gun in the gallery, Hitler stormed into the *Keller* and up to the rostrum, pushed the pale and confused von Kahr aside, and shouted:

> The national revolution has broken out! The hall is filled with six hundred men. Nobody is allowed to leave. The Bavarian government and the government in Berlin are deposed. A new government will be formed at once. The barracks of the *Reichswehr*, and those of the police are occupied. Both have rallied to the swastika.

The three leaders were forced at gunpoint into a reception room outside the main hall where Hitler threatened them with a pistol which, he said, held four rounds. He would shoot if they did not support him. He promised them posts in his government, but they said nothing. This provoked him even further. In a state of high histrionics he pointed the gun to his temple, saying again he would shoot them and himself if they did not join him. They argued with him and still refused. Waiting no longer he abruptly left the room, bounded back into the hall itself, mounted the rostrum, addressed the hall and lied to the audience that the three leaders were on his side. He extemporised with such skill and power that he changed the crowd's hostile mood, 'turned them inside out as one turns a glove inside out, with a few sentences ... [with] something of hocus-pocus – magic.' At a stroke he had stitched up Kahr, Lossow and Seisser, weaving them into his plan, claiming they were struggling to reach a decision. Now, by demonstrating his support from the floor – 'May I say, you will stand behind them?' – he would hoodwink the three leaders into agreement.

By such chicanery Hitler had the assembly cheering and feeding from his hand. It was the Nazi debut of the masterful political lie, the prototype of hundreds if not thousands of political party speeches, where speakers whip up support to a point of frenzy little short of magic and hypnosis.

What we know of the attempted putsch from Frank, there on the spot, he renders in a lengthy, rather wooden account in *Facing the Gallows*. A little earlier the same evening as a member of his SA unit of 150 men under Gerhard Rossbach, Röhm's deputy, Frank found himself summoned to an extraordinary meeting in his local restaurant. This was at 7 p.m. 'We were invited by a flying officer named Göring at the behest of Hitler to join him in the Beer Hall demonstration.'

Arriving there, while the horse-trading and drama unfolded, Hans met Hitler, Göring and von Ludendorff in an entrance hall. 'You, come here!' Hitler ordered Frank. He told Frank and his detachment to head off in different directions 'to proclaim all over the city the new Reich government'.

Hans was driven with comrades in an eight-seater vehicle to the Hotel Vier Jahreszeiten (Four Seasons), where they met

French and English officers of the Allied Control Authority. They promised them, with the new government seizing power, 'protection at every imaginable step taken'. This place was of particular significance. With its royal associations and luxury, it was Munich's top hotel. The Thule Society had taken up rooms there to spread its message of brotherhood.

The heady excitement among the SA and Hitler's followers promised to evaporate when Hitler ill-advisedly left the Beer Hall to settle an armed skirmish between storm troopers and some regular troops in the army barracks. Ludendorff released the three detained leaders. They slipped away to organise a counter-attack.

The rest of the night passed in confusion and chaos. Hitler's subordinates failed to centralise and co-ordinate the putsch. Units of the *Reichswehr* garrison ambushed SA men leaving the hall with orders to capture its barracks. SA squads were dispatched to round up prominent Jews.

As he felt success had slipped away, the next morning Hitler was desperate. He sent an envoy to enlist the help of Crown Prince Rupprecht of Bavaria to approach von Kahr and work out an honourable settlement. Hitler's messenger was delayed. Frank, marching under arms and reunited with his 150 men of the 2 Rossbach Battalion, had meanwhile returned to the Beer Hall.

'To the fore came all that was high romantic, and as much that was unpolitical,' he reports. Each man in this little 'cavalry group' – as he describes them, almost as if they were members of a chivalric knighthood – was paid two billion marks (approximately two and a half US dollars). Later in the morning, as confidence drained away, Ludendorff cried '*Wir marschieren*' ('we march'), and together with Hitler they led a force of two to three thousand storm troopers armed with carbines and fixed bayonets towards the centre of Munich. Flag-bearers with banners and swastikas, and Ludendorff's house retinue, preceded the Nazi leadership. Hitler took pride of place in the centre, slouch hat in hand, collar turned up against the cold. Ludendorff wore a loose *Loden* coat and green felt hat. They did not have much of a destination to aim at, other than the Bavarian War Defence Ministry.

Frank says they were heading for the *Feldherrenhalle* and, on the way, they encountered a large crowd at the Marienplatz listening to an anti-Jewish tirade from Julius Streicher. To reach their objective the column passed through a narrow street blocked by a police detachment numbering only 100 men. Armed with carbines, they stood their ground. Hitler's bodyguard, Ulrich Olaf, a dab hand at employing his master's trickery, regaled them with the magic name of Ludendorff, who had commanded millions in the Great War, telling them to give way – 'His Excellency Ludendorff is coming.' But the police had no love for the German Army. Hitler shouted 'Surrender!' and then in the ensuing kerfuffle someone fired a revolver. No one knew who this was, but Hitler believed it was Streicher and vowed never to forsake him.

As the Nazis advanced towards the police, the police opened fire or returned fire. Hitler locked his left arm with the right arm of Erwin von Scheubner-Richter, who was shot dead and fell. He pulled Hitler down with him onto the pavement. In the exchange of shots virtually the whole Nazi vanguard flung itself to the ground. And then, according to a Dr Walter Schulz, Hitler was 'the first to get up and turn back', leaving his dead and wounded brethren lying in the *Residenzstrasse*. He was hustled into a waiting car and spirited away. He had been wounded, and was arrested two days later. Göring was seriously wounded in his thigh, and was given first aid by a Jewish banker in his branch, the effects of which launched his addiction to morphine. He escaped and fled to Sweden.

There was only one courageous exception to the cowardly flight. Erect and proud at the head of a ragged force which had now vanished, Ludendorff stood alone. He marched forward, passing between the raised Bavarian police muzzles, to the Odeonsplatz. The sight bordered on farce. He was arrested and subsequently

tried with Hitler and Röhm. Furious, feeling deserted by the
German Army, Ludendorff declared that he would never again
wear uniform (although he did so for his trial). But he now knew
Hitler to be a *Feigling* (a coward). When Ludendorff died in 1937,
Hitler attended the funeral but declined to speak in praise of the
war hero, who had refused to have further dealings with him.

With hindsight, Frank appears to have an elegiac, if not
deeply melancholic, view of their 'heroic' march. The *Stosstrupp*
SA Infantry School and *Oberlander*, comprising the rank and file,
seemed to him very sad – a defeated army which had not actually yet met its defeat. As the 'salvo' from the exchange of gun-
fire sounded, a man 'barked out at the top of his voice – "Hitler
has been hit! Ludendorff is even dead!" We were a lost, fated
army,' wrote Frank.

How near Frank was to the exchange of fire is not specified.
Not for the first time one suspects he may have been lying in this
self-serving memoir, placing himself at the centre of the action.
'Then suddenly all was quiet,' he goes on:

> Hitler dead. Germany dead. I ventured into the *Residenzstrasse*.
> There two ambulance men were carrying away a corpse.
> Horrified, I saw the face of Theo von der Pfordten, my dear,
> marvellous friend, the Judge of the Bavarian High Court,
> who also had been shot dead. And with that horrifying pain I
> went away with many a detour to my house.

The folded draft constitution was discovered in von der Pfordten's pocket.

Heinrich Himmler and his older brother Gebhard found it
deeply uplifting to have taken part, and in Heinrich's case it fulfilled a lifelong frustrated urge to be a soldier. Gebhard summed
up the withdrawal of the epic heroes:

> In the middle was our fallen comrade Faust, carried on
> a stretcher. We wanted to take him out to his parents. I

remember the smirks on the faces of many a worthy citizen, while the previous evening they had cheered us on. We expected there would be another brawl. How wrong we were! Not one harsh word. The workers stood in silence and took off their hats and caps as we marched past with the dead man; a few women went up to the stretcher and gently stroked the canvas sheet covering the dead body.

Ten years later, in 1933, in the commemorative photo of all those who took part, we see Frank also marching through the streets of Munich, strutting proudly, chest erect, if just behind the leaders. Their part in the affair had been much more important than his.

This failed attempt by Hitler and his NSDAP confederates, backed by a strong force of heavily armed storm troopers, became, in the way it was conceived, executed and then unravelled, the *lehrstück* for Hitler's future seizure of power.

Afterwards, like Göring, Frank left Germany to avoid arrest, travelling to Naples and Palermo in Italy, where he stayed until April 1924, learning Italian and continuing his law studies. Like many of his unit he had retained and carried loaded weapons.

Hitler, under arrest and on trial for treason, became a political celebrity. As he stood in the Munich dock on 26 February 1924 the world at large as well as the German press gave him the limelight he craved, and knew how to exploit. He dominated the courtroom, claiming full responsibility for the uprising: 'There is no such thing as high treason,' he trumpeted, 'against the traitors of 1918.' He proclaimed himself as having the most noble, selfless intentions, as the future 'destroyer of Marxism'. Dominating the proceedings of the court with an hour-long address, he turned the tables on the uneasy, guilty triumvirs of Bavarian legitimacy, implicating them in his crime.

Before a sympathetic judge he received a lenient, scandalous verdict and sentence of five years (this was for treason), and police efforts to have him deported back to his Austrian homeland were quashed. As often happened to right-wing offenders who committed 'high treason', he subsequently had his sentence cut, and served only nine months.

Nazi propagandist Dr Joseph Goebbels – a PhD from Heidelberg University – had studied arts and humanities at no less than six other leading German universities. He was a failed novelist, a failed playwright (he had written a play about Jesus), and a failed journalist. He would soon transform the farcical putsch into one of the great legends of Nazi history.

Hitler spent his nine months comfortably ensconced in Landsberg Fortress as a privileged prisoner with a room of his own, a cosseted 'Easterner' who dressed in Lederhosen, a Bavarian peasant jacket, and a green hunting hat with a feather. He received endless homage – 'admiring women and cringing politicians' – while his cell, overlooking the River Lech and overflowing with gifts, 'looked like a delicatessen store'. He was now a folk hero and one writer in the same year depicted him as 'the living embodiment of the nation's longing'. His appeal widened; no longer was he just the 'drummer', the herald, the prophet of the one to come, the long-awaited saviour as many Thules saw him, he was the redeemer himself.

He began tapping out *Mein Kampf* with two fingers on an ancient typewriter, but soon stopped as he preferred dictating it, and had just enough time to finish it before his release. It came to rank as one of the most horrifically influential ideological tracts in world history. During his jail sentence a new German in charge of the Reichsbank stabilised the currency by ceasing to print money and slashing government expenditure. During his last weeks in prison, as Hans Frank attests in his Nuremberg memoirs, now armed with his prophetic text, Hitler designed a 'people's car', a *Volkswagen*, manufactured to drive on specially designed roads, or *autobahns*. His first port of call, on release before Christmas 1924, was the house of Ernst Hanfstaengl where, suffering extreme Wagner withdrawal symptoms, he commanded, 'Play the *Liebestod*.' Next morning he purchased a Mercedes, and, as his valet Otto Dietrich asserted, overtook every other driver on the road. 'Poop, poop!' – he reminds one of Mr Toad in *The Wind in the Willows*. Fast, beautiful and expensive cars were the only luxury he allowed himself.

8

Marriage

Brigitte Maria Herbst came from Forst in Lausitz. The daughter of a banker, writing in a beautiful italic hand was her hobby. She was born in 1895, five years older than Frank. She qualified as a typist and stenographer. She had two lovers before she met Frank and was therefore very different from Hans' early sweethearts like Lilly Gau, Brigitte S. and Gertrude H., who were Frank's age or younger. The first lover we can identify only as Hans S., an engineering student at Munich's Technical High School. From Hamburg, and the son of a shipping magnate, he was a far better marriage prospect than Hans Frank.

Her other lover – and it would seem that both his and Hans S's primary interest in Brigitte, at first, was her sexual availability – was Baurat R., an easy-going artist type who proposed marriage. She refused, as his prospects were poor. But while Hans S. was her 'first lover' according to her, Baurat R. was her 'secret cushion', a more intimate monicker. Apparently, Brigitte would gladly have married Hans S., her shipping heir, but he would have nothing to do with it. According to Niklas Frank, her and Frank's fifth child, born in 1939:

He was Mother's lover, but out of consideration for his Hanseatic interests, he neither would nor could marry her.

Instead, he used and abused her according to the practice of
his class. It was usually at Lake Starnberg, where he owned a
house; sometimes Tuesday evenings, occasionally Thursdays;
mostly, however, on weekends.

Judging from photographs, and discounting the uncomplimentary descriptions by Niklas, Brigitte was not a bad-looking
woman. But she was not exactly a great beauty either: we
see her as a brunette in a first photograph with a long, loose
necklace and bare shoulders, and a faraway, mystical expression in her eyes, which also suggests a knowing femininity. 'I'm
putting on this look just for the camera.' Perhaps she is merely
saying, 'Come and get me, and I'll turn out different from what
you expect.'

Later photographs show a stern, matronly figure, displaying
a Christian cross on a necklace, and close plastered, centrally
parted hair – a typical middle-class *Hausfräu* and mother of five
small children, two girls and three boys. Even later, there is a different image. Wrapped in furs, under imposing headwear, surrounded by the heavy furniture of Krakow's Wawel Castle, she
is now the 'Queen of Poland', as she derisively became known.
She stares with smug, dowager confidence at the photographer.

Brigitte met Frank on 27 May 1924, shortly after his return
from Italy. She had been working as a secretary to the *Landtag*,
the Bavarian State Parliament, and at the Institute of Technology. She also typed doctoral theses for postgraduates.

Hans was working on his legal dissertation 'on the public
person' and brought it into her office for her to make a fair copy.
Sunburnt, 5ft 10in (1.77m) tall, a strong figure, flourishing and
well-fed from his Italian trip, he looked quite a handsome prospect. She must have been decisive in her assessment of his future
potential, and was 'instantly smitten' by his looks, his charm, and

impressive legal mind. She typed the thesis by which he gained his Doctorate of Jurisprudence in 1924.

Niklas makes it clear that it was Brigitte, now almost 30, who had her sights on the future, and that her choice of Frank was pushed forward by Frank's Aunt Margot, who worked in the same office as Brigitte. She suggested Brigitte type his thesis and then acted as go-between. Niklas addresses his father throughout his book as if he is writing a personal letter to him, or cross-examining him in court, calling him to account:

> Your fate was sealed. Mother took your manuscript, engaged you in conversation, did her little Circe act on you – and *poof*! Soon you were invited for a little *souper à trois*, the third being a painter (Baurat R.) in Schwabing Mother knew. He, of course, had been bribed to let her have his studio for the night [this was also in Schwabing]. And what happened after that, you know better than I do. You arrived with flowers. Mother put on her coy look, said that unfortunately the artist friend would not be joining you after all. (I used to know his name, but Aunt Margot is dead, Mother is dead, and I just can't remember.) After a cold supper and some fiery Italian wine, she gave you no other choice but to mount her. In matters pertaining to lovemaking, she was an experienced woman, orgasm or not. You were proud as a foolish peacock afterwards, and by the very next day it was clear that Mother was not letting you go. Again, you had no other choice: you had to propose.

Brigitte had succeeded, according to her son, barely eight months after she had set herself that goal. She was 29, and Frank 'a lawyer without hopes or prospects'.

It was later, in a black mood, that Frank was to call this a 'momentary erotic intoxication'. It seemed that during that time, and after the eight months of courtship – they became engaged in October 1924 – Hans was generally in low spirits. In addition to this, his father Karl's life of embezzlement had caught up with him. During their engagement, Karl was disbarred on many counts involving considerable sums going back as far as 1903. Brigitte appeared fairly sanguine about her prospective father-in-law's disgrace. Nothing could stop her – and she was approaching 30.

The couple married on 2 April in Munich in a Catholic ceremony. Hans, according to his own assessment, was hardly a believer. Strangely enough, even for those bizarre Weimar years of sexual laissez-faire, they took Hans S. along with them to Venice for the honeymoon, which the shipping magnate's son paid for. Frank confessed, when awaiting trial in Nuremberg: 'My sorrows began as soon as we went on our honeymoon, the three of us! With Hans S., Brigitte's friend.' The marriage, he believed, had been some kind of aberrant whim of the moment. 'Your lovey-dovey snapshots of Venice have an added irony,' is Niklas' sour observation, 'because I know who is behind the camera.' Even in those photos Brigitte has 'that loose fat flesh of certain thirty-year-old women who can't control their weight. From Venice on,' Niklas tells his father, 'that meat was your flesh course.'

While Frank married very young, he now had his nose firmly to the legal grindstone. Although for the moment he was without money, 'without profession, without pleasurable deployment', in the forests of the German night, his National Socialist ideals burned with feverish brightness. One can only believe that, like the majority of the 35 million dutiful women in Germany, Brigitte supported his ideals 100 per cent. And now he had a wage-earning anchor in Brigitte, who began to take up her wifely duties as a model Aryan spouse, giving birth quickly to two children, a daughter, Sigrid, born in March 1927, and Norman, born in 1928.

Hans worked intensely to rescue his father's legal fortunes and took over the practice, letting his father work in it again illegally, while maintaining he was employed in a non-legal capacity as book-keeper. In 1926 Hans passed his Bavarian State legal examination and was in a position to take on lucrative briefs.

There was by now an increasingly well-funded political party
ready to employ him in lawsuits. And he seemed to have access
right to the very top. Bearing in mind the disparaging things he
said about Brigitte, Hitler was the truer, if non-physical, object
of his adoration.

By the time Frank married, that earlier possibility of Germany's reunion and reconciliation with Western Europe had ebbed
away. The German spirit had returned to its fascination with
the destructive East that produced Attila the Hun. In a masterly
analysis of the new German atmosphere, D.H. Lawrence wrote
in the *New Statesman* on 13 October 1924:

> ... at night you feel strange things stirring in the darkness
> ... There is a sense of danger ... a queer, *bristling* feeling of
> uncanny danger ... hope in peace-and-production is broken.
> The old flow, the old adherence is ruptured. And a still older
> flow has set in. Back, back to the savage polarity of Tartary, and
> away from the polarity of civilized Christian Europe. This, it
> seems to me, has already happened. And it is a happening of far
> more import than any *actual* event.
>
> It is the father of the next phase of events.

Without modernisation, without all the technical and legal factors which were to become harnessed as interlocking cogs in this
huge new machine of evil, Hitler's goal of world domination
and the application of genocidal policies would not have pro-
gressed beyond wild fantasies. Frank, an intermediary of evil,
was to find an important role in that next phase of events, as
Hitler moved nearer to his seizure of total power.

Late in 1925, Frank was still mired in self-pity, only months
after his wedding. He took up his diary, which he had abandoned on 18 March 1921:

> Before me, a picture of Caesar's bust. Above me on the wall,
> Bismarck and Frederick the Great. Between them, a picture

of a woman. Spirits that are so near, and yet I cannot reach them. [Who was this woman? Lilli Gau? Gertrude H.? His new wife? Surely this last was one he could reach and touch.]

To think that I have had the boldness to write this down in this book, in all my poverty, in the chilly, empty space surrounding me. To think that in all my unspeakable worthlessness I still have dared to ally myself with a movement that supposedly has brought me to the heights, that has presumed to guide me by its self-inspired thread of conviction along the Alpine path, that has indicated to me time and again, through hope and tribulation, that I am the one who is being called. Oh, I am the loser, the vanquished. With all my titles, doctor of laws, man of aspiration, husband, I have been inexpressibly ineffectual. While earlier the saps and juices of abundant youth watered the fruits of wellspring, I rattle like dry bones now. While earlier my resilient stride was quick and fresh, I now have nothing to record: no works, no fruits, alas, not even seed for the future.

He had been married for only six months when he wrote this. Perhaps here is proof how little love meant to him, and how little he could believe in attachment to others. Except for one: Hitler, with those deep blue eyes – and why does he say 'already piercing'? – had him in thrall. Hitler, for the rest of his life would be his '*belle dame sans merci*', as well as his Mephistopheles. It seemed that only his arrogance, his innate sense of superiority, allied as it was at this forlorn moment to national pride, could console him.

Map of the five districts of the Government General, 1942.

PART TWO

9

Mein Kampf

By the time Joseph Ratzinger, the future Pope Benedict XVI, was born in Bavaria in 1927, an important change in Germany had shifted both the economy and the political climate of the Weimar Republic into a more stable situation. During his short spell in prison Hitler appreciated that, for the moment, he needed a different tactic to terror and intimidation, so now he began once again to get into his stride as a gently persuasive 'People's Politician'. He put on sheep's clothing and used the smooth, demotic approach. On his release he pledged to conduct his party as a legal one. This was Frank's opportunity: as a successful advocate, he became Hitler's personal lawyer, defending him in over 150 suits. Prosperity was beginning to create the need for a different kind of change, and Hitler's appeal, he ensured, was as a man of peace.

The Bavarian Justice Minister, Franz Gürtner, who was sympathetic to National Socialist views, granted Hitler an early release. He lived to regret it. Before his death in 1941, he told Frank 'Hitler loves cruelty ... He had a diabolical sadism. Otherwise he could not stand Himmler or Heydrich ...' But only much later would Frank want to report this.

Hitler had spent the whole time in the Landsberg Fortress dictating *Mein Kampf*, his political testimony, consisting of 400 pages, or 200,000 words. Dictation was now his custom and from now on he hardly ever put pen to paper, leaving that to others. He had dictated first to Emil Maurice, watchmaker, his bodyguard, ex-convict and Nazi; then to his lifelong devotee Rudolf Hess. Maurice is one of those extraordinary characters who colour the Nazi story and add to the mystery of the unexplained phenomena of those years. The watchmaker suggests a man of skill and capacity for intricate detail. This killer had charm as well as literacy.

Maurice, it is alleged, had a clandestine affair with Geli Raubal, Hitler's niece, nineteen years his junior, but although he shared his apartment in Munich with her, some consider it unlikely that the affair was consummated. He was friends also with 'Mizzi' Reiter and Eva Braun in the 1920s. His father Alois' first wife had been fourteen years older than him, while Klara, Hitler's mother, who was Alois' niece, was twenty-three years younger. It is believed by many that the Führer fell passionately in love with Geli, and remained unmarried and pining for her the rest of his life. He remarked: 'A girl of eighteen is as malleable as wax. It must be possible for a man to leave his mark on every girl. That is all women want.' Of young women he said, 'Around them I become happy and jovial, and if I listen to their silly banter for an hour – or if they just sit near me – then all tiredness and apathy disappears.'

Speer claimed later that Hitler used Eva Braun 'to regulate his hormone balance', but while no one doubted he loved the company of beautiful women and needed a degree of eroticism, no one has found evidence to trammel a wide range of speculation (which included a missing testicle and an injured penis). That he was married to Germany was certain, and that crowd ecstasy brought him satisfaction was true, but he successfully suppressed knowledge of his private life from his people which, given the scrutiny he was under, suggests that there was nothing to hide.

Geli Raubal committed suicide on 18 September 1931. Her death is widely believed to have somehow prompted Hitler's subsequent lifelong abstention from meat; a bizarre connection if true.

A Catholic monk, Father Bernhard Stempfle, an ex-Hieronymite and anti-Semitic journalist, had also aided Hitler by straightening out the tortured syntax of *Mein Kampf*, and endeavouring to clarify some of the meaning. He crossed out passages he convinced Hitler were objectionable, such as 'Nature watches the craving, crude form of Darwinism freeing its force … the death of the weaker supplies the life of the stronger …' This is only one example; there are many more.

Emil Maurice, the first scribe, figured prominently as a hitman in Röhm's later purge, together with horse dealers and cabaret bouncers. He also led the gang that murdered Stempfle, who had the misfortune of becoming a party to Hitler's passionate love for Geli and therefore knew too much about her suicide. Stempfle was found in Haslaching Forest near Munich with a broken neck and three bullets in his heart.

The frustrated, obsessive genius had made good use of his time in the fortress: his patriotic fervour so impressed the prison governor that he allowed him to keep his lights on until midnight. The von Kahr regime in Munich again began to scheme to have him repatriated to Austria, because until 1930 he was still an Austrian, but this was blocked. During the Röhm purge in 1933 von Kahr's body was found in a swamp near Dachau, smashed by pickaxes.

Max Amann, Hitler's Nazi publisher, printed a first edition of only 500 copies of *Mein Kampf*. The sales of Hitler's testament, which some consider teeters on the rim of insanity, and which he wanted at first to call *Four and a Half Years of Struggle Against Lies, Stupidity and Cowardice,* mirrored the fortunes of its author and his party over the following years.

Mein Kampf was prophetic, insofar as it detailed with uncanny accuracy the chain of events Hitler intended to realise. Amman had wanted, it seemed, little more than a typical misery memoir showing Hitler's rise from rags to world celebrity, with a personal account of the sensational failed Beer Hall Putsch. Hitler hardly mentioned this fiasco, which, in time, would become a key heroic saga in Nazi mythology. No more naked statement of intent could be made than in *Mein Kampf*, Hitler's 'bible'. To a young man such as Frank, and, to begin with, to thousands of ordinary young German men and women in the years that immediately followed, Hitler's aims were never covert, nor were the means by which he intended to achieve them hidden.

Until 1927 Hitler was forbidden to speak publicly in most parts of Germany. Until 1928 he was banned from Prussia, where over half of the German population lived. Amann boasted that *Mein Kampf* sold 23,000 copies in 1925, and sales continued to increase in the years following, but this was a lie. From 1925, the sales dropped from 9,473 to 3,015 in 1928; but then, as the Nazi Party began its ascendancy, and with cheaper editions available, sales rose sharply. By the time Hitler became Chancellor, in 1933, they had risen to a million, making Hitler the best-paid author in Germany. By 1940, when displaying ownership of *Mein Kampf* was a token of loyalty to the Führer, sales had risen to 6 million copies.

In the elections of 1924, and in the aftermath of the failed putsch, the ultra-nationalist right was humiliated. As the Weimar Republic enjoyed expansion and stability on an unexpected scale, the Nazi Party's influence sank. But *Mein Kampf* went on gradually fomenting a kind of subversion in 'spreading its abominable ideas among a dedicated and growing minority across German society', for, as Upton Sinclair's Lenny Budd notes, 'German nationality was only for Germans to understand.'

The bullying, the bloodshed by the Brownshirts in the streets, the murder of Blackshirts and intimidation of political opponents, endorsed by that sense of nationality that only Germans could understand, did not stop. Hitler, who had unified and cemented differences at the head of his party, now made his subordinates in his re-founded party submit themselves to him unconditionally. Now a statesman, he distanced himself from the murder and mayhem. He and other leaders made increasing use of Orwellian euphemisms in their rhetoric. He diverted legal responsibility for violence from the party leadership, with the insistence that Röhm's paramilitary gangs acted independently of the party, and with the help of the likes of Hans Frank. This strengthened its aura of respectability. By these methods he gained support and backing from well connected Bavarians and many local farmers (as Joseph Ratzinger recalls) and further afield, particularly among Protestant figures in north Germany and Franconia.

To centralise discipline and order in the party, and resolve disputes between its bickering chiefs, Hitler set up a party court to settle conflicts and avoid washing dirty linen in public. First, Hitler appointed an ex-General, Heinemann, but he failed to grasp its essential whitewash and cover-up role. So another, more congenially disposed officer took his place in 1926, with two assistants, Ulrich Graf, Hitler's former bodyguard, and Hans Frank, who was now 26. Hitler found the court effective in its main aims of both preserving party discipline and limiting damage to himself, neither of which had anything to do with truth and justice. It advanced Frank's career.

Even so, the Nazis floundered – until the German economy suddenly collapsed. The Wall Street Crash of 1929 changed Hitler's fortunes.

Frank claimed, or positively expressed, feelings of anti-Semitism for the first time as late as 1936, by being part of Rossbach's squad and enjoying the patronage of rabid anti-Jewish propagandists such as Julius Streicher, but he shared early on the Nazi sense of racial superiority and also some of the lust for violence that infected the early Nazis. Though it is hard to judge whether he fully espoused the profound conviction of German racial superiority held by Hitler and other NSDAP leaders and not, at first anyway, just pay lip-service. Rudolff

Schottenborf, the Thule Society head, had publicly proclaimed
Judah was the deadly enemy of German blood. But Frank dis-
ingenuously spoke of the Society, to which he belonged, as an
'intellectual club', that is, not intent on or going to cause real
harm. Meanwhile he claimed, when he first heard Hitler speak,
'He abused no one – at that time. He humiliated no one – no
religion, no race, no state – at that time.' This would seem to
be true, for as we have seen, in Vienna Hitler had had Jewish
friends and mentors, and the Jewish Dr Bloch had looked after
his mother before she died.

On 15 March 1929 Hitler launched an impassioned appeal for
the German Army to think again about its rejection of National
Socialism and its support of the Weimar Republic. The year
before, in the Reichstag elections held in May 1928, the party
won 2½ per cent of the vote, while twelve deputies had gained
seats in the Reichstag. One leading Nazi, Wilhelm Frick, had
been appointed Minister of the Interior in Thuringia, the first
Nazi to hold an important state office.

'The future lies,' Hitler declaimed:

> … with the parties who carry in themselves the strength of
> the people … my dear Sirs… do you really feel you have
> anything in common with an ideology which stipulates the
> dissolution of all that which is the basis of the existence of
> an army? If the Communists [who had won more than three
> million votes in the election] triumphed over the Nazis, you
> may write 'The End of the German Army!'

This message went home. Although the Allied Peace Commission still forbade Nazi recruits in the 100,000-strong Reichswehr,
or Wehrmacht as it now became, and Nazi civilians in its armour-
ies and depots, Nazi infiltration grew as army officers were drawn
into debate and discussion with Hitler and his associates.

There is a turning point in the declining fortunes of the
NSDAP, which also contributed to the rise of young Frank's

career, that came during a case where he espoused Hitler's cause as his lawyer on 21 September 1930.

Three young officers of the Wehrmacht were on trial for conspiring to commit an act of treason. Lieutenants Ludin, Scheringer and Wendt, all of Ulm garrison, were charged with spreading Nazi doctrines and with attempting to induce fellow officers, in the event of a Nazi uprising, not to open fire on the rebels. Frank, in his most conspicuous brief to date, and another Nazi lawyer, Dr Carl Sach, were counsels for the defence. (Sach was later hanged for his part in the anti-Hitler plot of 1944.)

Hitler followed the risky tactic of having Frank summon him to the stand as a defence witness. Once in the box Hitler had his chance to work his spell, impressing the courtroom and the world press with his message that, far from wanting to replace the German Army, he intended to make it great again. He convinced his courtroom audience with masterly deceit that his movement had no need of force, and that it would come to power by constitutional means. When this happened it would form a German state in the image it considered to be correct. The President of the Court asked, 'This, too, by constitutional means?' Hitler replied, 'Yes.'

He promised further, when pressed to answer, that there would be a National Socialist Court of Justice too, which would avenge the November 1918 revolution; that 'heads would roll'. The fair-minded, thinking this a figure of speech, did not take this as literally as did the Nazi brethren. The cynics and socialist elite thought Hitler would hang himself with his own rope, if given enough. Nor did Hitler's speech actually help the accused officers, who were found guilty of conspiracy to commit treason. Like many right-wing offenders at this time, they were awarded light sentences.

The millions who thought this takeover could never happen had the shock of their lives when, in the following week's election, the Nazi Party returned 107 Reichstag deputies – among them 30-year-old Hans Frank, elected for Upper Silesia.

Frank could not have had much time for family life at this time, for as well as being a member of the Reichstag, he was busy serving the party as its leading lawyer and held other legal posts. A former tutor warned him, 'I beg you to leave those people alone! ... Political movements that begin in the criminal courts will end in the criminal courts!' He finally represented the Nazi Party in over 2,400 cases.

The various roles Frank now played began to take their toll on his handsome, youthful looks. Frank by 30 had grown heavy-jowled, his dark hair receding. He wore a grim expression. We see him in one such photograph at a Nazi meeting, in SA uniform, sitting on a bench three places away from Hitler, two from Röhm, and next to Gauleiter Adolf Wagner. There is a dark, inward-looking expression in his eyes. He is not smiling.

10

Bad Blood

'Justice: native endowment and fantastic obsession of the Germans' is one of Goethe's famous observations. Some residual conscience regarding truth and legal integrity or rectitude remained lodged in Frank, but after a little flutter, or display, he shook himself loose – out of his need for survival and self-interest. Worshipping the Christian God would have brought him nothing by way of advancement, rather the reverse: only breadline or modest survival, perhaps a little better than that of an average Bavarian lawyer or official. But worshipping the new Messiah with revivalist zeal would bring great and instant rewards.

Nazism was catching fire in the hearts of the German people. Only a week after the three junior officers' treason case had brought it wide attention and approval. With Hitler's display of mock subservience to democracy, and Dr Goebbels' masterly propaganda, the party increased its share of the popular vote to 18 per cent, winning 6.5 million votes. It was easily the second largest party in the Reichstag. The Social Democrats polled 8.5 million, the Communists 4.5 million – so virtually half the voting population was against the government.

Thus the victorious Western Allies, eleven years after the *Diktat* of Versailles, had driven 6.5 million into the arms of the National Socialists by binding the German Government to the 'Young Plan' and enslaving Germany to pay reparations for fifty-eight years. The majority of these voters, lulled into a false sense of security by a false promise of security, convinced themselves that the Nazi bark was considerably worse than its bite. They identified with the avuncular Bavarian flying ace Göring.

Frank, identifying with an ever more powerful father-figure, who compensated for the weak rogue Karl (whom he protected and indulged, covering his sexual misdemeanours and debts) was to find himself tested in two highly dramatic episodes. Both strengthened his intimate connection with his Führer.

The first came in 1930 when William Patrick Hitler, the son of Hitler's step-brother Alois, sent Hitler a letter threatening to reveal that he had discovered evidence which showed that Hitler's father was half-Jewish. If this could be proved, and then made public, Hitler's anti-Jewish agenda would be shattered once and for all.

What happened to the letter and William Hitler's presumed attempt to blackmail Hitler is unknown, but rumours of its contents spread. 'Hitler's Jewishness Confirmed by Notary' was *Wiener Extrablatt*'s headline in 1933, while the Austrian *Abendblatt* proclaimed gleefully: 'Sensational Tracks of the Jew Hitler in Vienna'. Hitler summoned Frank, whose discretion and powers of judicious enquiry he valued highly. He entrusted to him the task of researching into his family tree.

The story Frank found was thus. The prosperous Jewish Frankenburger family employed Hitler's grandmother Maria Schicklgruber as a cook. The Frankenburgers had a son who, it was believed by Hitler's nephew, had, aged 19, got the 42-year-old Maria pregnant. She bore his child. The Jewish family paid for the support of that child, Alois Schicklgruber, until he was 15. He grew up to become Adolf's father.

An independent source that Frank consulted, consisting of a plentiful exchange of letters, showed that not only did Maria threaten to sue the Frankenburger family (with a paternity suit), but also that they bought her off, thereafter enjoying a cordial relationship with her and Alois. It does seem unlikely that the Frankenburgers would have supported and continued to support Alois, and write letters to his mother (who had by now been remarried for ten years) out of a sense of altruism for their cook's child, had it been fathered by a man other than their son.

Alois was clearly illegitimate. No one disputed this. But it was later claimed that he was the natural child of a second cousin of Maria, Johann Georg Hiedler, a vagrant miller who married Maria five years after Alois' birth. This would have meant that Hitler had no Jewish blood.

This child, Alois Hiedler, Hitler's father, grew up to work as a minor Austrian customs official, changed his name to Hitler, and married three times. Hitler was the third son of his mother Klara, who was Alois' second cousin, so an Episcopal dispensation had to be issued for the marriage.

So did Hitler have Jewish blood or not? It seems unlikely that Johann Hiedler, a wandering miller, could have fathered Alois – and the apparent fact that Maria was well-looked after by the Frankenburgers when he married her does not seem to make sense if he was the father. But many distinguished commentators, notably Hitler's foremost biographer, Ian Kershaw, reject the Jewish ancestry theory.

It was the Hiedler version Frank decided that it was politic to supply to Hitler, without mentioning the money the Jewish family supplied. It must have relieved the Führer and calmed his upset sensibilities to hear that the main reason Frank purported to find no truth in the allegation was this: 'From his entire demeanour, the fact that Adolf Hitler had no Jewish blood coursing through his veins seems so clearly evident that nothing more need to be said on this.'

From this time on enterprising journalists tried to dig up what they could about Hitler's origins, discovering for the first time the Schicklgruber name and connection, until they were silenced by arrest and intimidation. There were numerous reconstructions of the non-Aryan descent of other leading Nazis.

Investigation established the illegitimacy of Hitler's father, and
his early connection with Czechoslovakia. None of this pleased
Hitler. Albert Speer:

> On a trip from Budweis to Krems in 1942 I noticed a large
> plaque on a house in the village of Spital, close to the Czech
> border. In this house, according to the plaque, 'the Führer
> lived in his youth'. It was a handsome house in a prosperous
> village. I mentioned this to Hitler. He instantly flew into a
> rage and shouted for Bormann, who hurried in much alarmed,
> Hitler snarled at him: How many times had he said that this
> village must never be mentioned. But that idiot of a Gauleiter
> had gone and put up a plaque there. It must be removed at
> once. At the time I could not explain his excitement, since he
> was usually pleased when Bormann told him about the refur-
> bishing of other sites connected with his youth around Linz
> and Braunau. Apparently he had some motive for erasing this
> part of his youth [his illegitimacy].

The first reported version of any affair always became established. Speer pointed out that Hitler never liked to change a
view once he had formed it, or expressed it:

> One example of this was pertinent, namely how hard it is to
> recognize a madman … Hitler would also talk about the stric-
> tures of his upbringing. In 1942 he described Alois as 'brutal,
> unjust and inconsiderate. He had no respect for anybody or
> anything … [He] played the part of the bully and whipped
> his wife and children who were unable to defend themselves.
> Even the dog comes in for his share of this sadistic display …
> My father often dealt me hard blows. Moreover, I think that
> was necessary and helped me.' Wilhelm Frick, the Minister of
> the Interior, interjected in his bleating voice: 'As we can see
> today, it certainly did you good, *mein Führer.*' A numb, horri-
> fied silence around the table. Frick tried to save the situation:

'I mean, *mein Führer*, that is why you have come so far.'
Goebbels, who considered Frick a hopeless fool, commented
sarcastically: 'I would guess you never received a beating in
your youth, Frick.'

No one would have dared suggest that the genes of a rich Austrian Jewish family may have supplied some of Hitler's unusual
gifts and qualities, which emerged in distorted and grotesque
form. In *Mein Kampf* Hitler described uncouth Jews seducing
innocent Austrian girls. He pursued his 'nightmare vision of
the seduction of hundreds of thousands of girls by repulsive,
crooked-legged Jewish bastards'. Did this imagery come, as psychologists have suggested, from his virginity and tortured sexual
envy, or some confused idea of his own origins?

In 1945–46 in his Nuremburg cell, and in *Facing the Gallows*, Hans Frank changed the conclusion he gave Hitler of his
research into Hitler's origin and the likelihood of his Jewish
blood. On the basis of what Frank told Dr Gilbert, one explanation of Hitler's anti-Semitic crimes was credible. Expressed in
extreme form, he was killing the Jew in himself – presumably
the power of empathetic, emotional reason and those qualities in
the Jewish people he once knew and had contact with – and his
own sense of being a victim.

Ron Rosenbaum, a psychology professor, describes the conclusion he was led to by his research. He points out that no one
disputes the Führer's grandmother was Maria Schicklgruber:

> When she gave birth to Hitler's father, Alois, the space for
> the father's name on the birth certificate was left blank. Some
> people later spread the story that Hitler's grandfather was a
> Jew named Frankenburger.

Rosenbaum could not find any firm evidence to support such a
claim, but found it noteworthy that Hitler wanted the story
quashed. He even went to the extent of destroying the town

of Doellersheim, where his father was born. In response to investigations into his background, he is said to have ranted, 'People must not know who I am … They must not know who I come from.'

Frank's confessor, Dr Gilbert, believed the story Frank uncovered and told him about Hitler's lineage was true. Ron Rosenbaum had heard a taped interview Gilbert gave to John Toland, a Hitler biographer:

> Gilbert sees that moment in 1930 when Hans Frank purportedly told Hitler he had come upon documentary proof that his father was fathered by a Jew 'as a profound turning point in the evolution of Hitler's anti-Semitism. Especially when [Hitler] was already committed to being a violent anti-Semite with his whole ego structure depending upon this.'
>
> Gilbert told Toland, 'the idea that [the Jewish grandfather story] could have been true could have been resolved in his sick mind only by showing, as Frank said, that he was the worst anti-Semite in the world, so how could he possibly be a Jew?'

But as Dr Gilbert reveals in his diary, Frank's confessional mood came and went. Often self-interest became the driving force:

> Frank's lack of integrity comes more and more to the fore … I asked him whether the discovery of [Hitler's] partially Jewish ancestry had anything to do with his enmity toward Hitler. He was already growing vague on that subject, and answered rather evasively.

More important than the fact that Frank believed in Hitler's partial Jewish lineage, is the indication that Hitler too, in his paranoia, feared it, and believed it could be true. Even while Frank voiced anti-Nazi statements and behaved in a way which clearly Hitler disapproved of, Hitler protected him. He repeatedly refused to sack or remove him. Maybe he was frightened that *'mein lieb Frank'* might spill the beans. But no definite proof of Hitler's Jewish blood has ever been found. Just after the Austrian *Anschluss* the German Secret Police searched for and destroyed every document mentioning Hitler's ancestors and family. William Hitler, unsuccessful in his blackmail attempt, escaped to the United States, where he gave interviews on the theme of 'Why I hate my uncle.' Changing his name, he married and fathered three sons, none of whom ever married or had children; one changed his name to Adolph Hitler, and now lives on Long Island. William Hitler died in 1987 at the age of 78.

It seemed this closeness to Hitler's ancestry served as protection for Frank. It gave Frank power over those Reich leaders who later became his enemies, – Himmler, Hans Lammers and Martin Bormann. This investigation in 1930 had perhaps given Frank a crucial piece in the chess game for survival.

After Frank had quashed the rumours about Hitler's Jewish blood, advancement came rapidly. 'Ambition drove us on – all of us – me too,' he told Gilbert. But even with such dizzyingly rapid promotion, or because of it, Frank never remained entirely secure. He claimed that Oswald Spayer predicted in 1934 that the way Hitler was carrying on, the Third Reich would not last ten years. In the same year, Frank consulted a fortune teller, as he told Gilbert:

> Did I tell you a gypsy predicted in 1934 that I would not live to see 50? See that line on my hand? It does end abruptly, doesn't it? Yes, she said there was something about a big trial – which didn't seem strange, since I was a lawyer – and then she said I wouldn't live to see 50.

Like so much else, is this story to be believed? 'Do you see? I was a man of destiny' is the implication.

11

Not Far from the Vienna Woods

On 25 February 1932, Hitler became a German citizen; on 10 April 1932 he polled 37 per cent of the popular vote and on 6 November 1932 the Nazi Party returned 196 Reichstag deputies in the Reichstag elections, 33 per cent of the vote. Following a secret meeting between the Reich Chancellor von Papen and Hitler on 4 January 1933, at which Hess and Himmler were present, the latter now the head of Hitler's SS, von Papen moved over. On 30 January he appointed Hitler Chancellor.

It was a cold grey Sunday, but Berlin became a 'seething, red, clear burning sea of torches' as thousands chanted *Sieg Heil*, a 'compound of triumph, aggression and strange, exultant relief'.

'At last we are saved,' Hitler said in his first broadcast. He promised to preserve basic principles: 'Christianity as the foundation of our national morality, and the family as the basis of national life.' Church belfries were adorned with swastikas, crosses draped with Nazi flags. There would be a new priesthood, 'storm troopers of Jesus'; racial purity and holy martyrdom were one and the same.

The holy mission of Hitler has been conveniently forgotten, especially by the Roman Catholic hierarchy. In an NSDAP speech of 1921 he had said, 'We may be small, but one man once also stood up in Galilee, and today his teaching rules the entire world.' At Christmas, seven years after leaving Pasewalk, where evidence later confirmed he had been treated for psychotic hysterical symptoms, he claimed he wanted to make 'the ideals [of] Christ a reality. The work that Christ had begun, but had been unable to finish [Hitler] would complete.' He was, as he said constantly in his speeches, the tool of destiny, acting 'in the spirit of Providence' and embodying 'Divine Will'.

He fulfilled Pacelli's belief in him as a fervent anti-communist. Just over a month after he became Chancellor, Nazi agents planned to set fire to the Reichstag and blame it on the Communists. By chance, one of the latter possibly did carry this out, a young Dutch Communist called Marinus van der Lubbe was arrested inside the building. But it is unproven whether the fire was a false flag operation by the Nazis or set by the Dutchman. The reign of terror against Communists could begin again, with the excuse of the fire.

By the end of 1933, so complete had the seduction and coercion of the German people become that 92 per cent of the 96 per cent of registered voters who cast their ballots did so for the single Nazi list for the Reichstag, while 95 per cent endorsed German repudiation of the peace treaty. 'On an eleventh of November the German people formerly lost its honour,' said Hitler in an election speech at Breslau; 'fifteen years later came a twelfth of November and then the German people restored its honour to itself.' The *Diktat* of Versailles was dead.

'The most dangerous moment,' declared Napoleon, 'comes with victory.' Hitler shrewdly realised that while the party had benefited from and relied on the brutality and sadism of the SA, now was the moment to divorce from it. Though Hitler could dissociate himself from the SA in public, claiming he had no control over it and was not responsible for its warring factions, its notorious homosexual feuds and sexual jealousies, it was time for change. While making use of their support, he disliked brawling homosexuals like Edward Heines, leader of the Munich SA, who was a convicted murderer. His own murderers,

ideally, were faithful married men with families, if possible
abstemious and nicotine-free.

He had appointed the eminently respectable – at least outwardly – loyal and meticulous Himmler to form and lead the
Schutzstaffel, the SS, and ultimately the Gestapo and police.
Hitler, thought Himmler, was 'a truly great man and above all
a genuine and pure man'. His first job for the SS security service in Munich was to run the section dealing with ecclesiastical
questions, gathering information on the activities of the Catholic Church. By now he had moved away from the faith of his
parents, considering Catholicism too doctrinaire and 'hyper-
catholic', whatever that might mean, although he still attended
mass. But his need for and belief in the supernatural were shift-
ing more and more towards spiritualism and occultism.

Mild-mannered, with the air of a self-deprecating oddball,
and much involved in esoteric cults, Himmler bred chickens in a
village near Munich. As his loyalty and dedication to Hitler was
rock solid, his zeal absolute, and his organisational power and
grasp of detail unrivalled, Hitler had made an important decision: to purge Röhm, who had been instrumental in his rise, but
who now, according to Hitler's instantly summonable paranoia,
had 'begun preparations to eliminate me personally'.

Hitler wheeled and dealt, manoeuvred masterfully and played
every trick in the book in those crucial weeks of 1933 to make sure
his takeover as sole dictator of Germany was complete and triumphant. Fundamental basic rights, by virtue of a Decree for the
Protection of the People and the State, for example the freedom of
the press, of speech and assembly, as well as privacy of post and telephone, were abrogated, and 'preventive detentions' introduced.

Aware not only of Napoleon's *obiter dictum*, but of
Machiavelli's too – the most dangerous moment may come with
victory, but the first thing you do when you have it is remove
those who helped you to it – he planned his next move.

He needed obedient subordinates, no longer unruly rebels.
He had the German Army on his side. He had the ever-more

powerful SS. He had the German people. One may wonder how so utterly intolerant a man could have countenanced so many reprobates and immoral lowlifes helping him achieve power in the first place. Not only blackmailers, pimps, embezzlers, murderers, alcoholics and sexual deviants found in Nazi land their Utopia, but the prim and respectable as well. Speer acutely observed of the Führer that his temper tantrums, his rantings, were always under his control in this period, and that his decisions, while all around him were in turmoil, were based on ice-cool judgement. He carefully staged his hysterical outbursts, Speer said, and his pretended fits of passion forced others to yield. 'In general, self-control was one of Hitler's more striking characteristics.'

Hitler had honed to perfection the facets of the demotic 'Nostromo': he was ahead of his time, the prototype of the late twentieth-century popular politician. He lived modestly, was a vegetarian, didn't smoke or drink, patted children, and loved dogs. His one personal luxury was the latest supermodel car, always a Mercedes-Benz. His followers were unaware of his many faces, and saw only the façade he presented to them. He permitted each individual to project upon him that type of personality which the individual most respected and admired: with Göring he was friendly, outspoken and blunt; with Dönitz he was simple, intellectual and quiet; with Baldur von Schirach he was a dominating authority; and with Ribbentrop a father and a master. With Frank he was Messiah-like and affectionate, talked philosophy and music, and played the gentle and forgiving guru to his deferential disciple.

In addition to these personality assets, Hitler's eyes, which almost everyone spoke of as having a hypnotic effect, cast their *Walpürgisnacht* spell. He had learned the knack of actually staring down opposition. On women he lavished 'southern' charm and friendliness. The general run-of-the-mill men he took in with his 'knowledge', namely a spectacular display of superficial information and astonishing feats of memory. They interpreted these as true education and brilliance.

Frank and his wife never belonged to Hitler's entourage, although Frank liked to believe he was close. He was like many latter-day celebrities in this respect, always emphasising his connections. He flattered and aped his master. Brigitte breathlessly reports an occasion when with other *Reichsdamen* she stood next to 'Herr Hitler' in the foyer at Bayreuth. She dropped her programme. 'Just imagine! Herr Hitler bent over and picked up the programme, kept it for himself, and gave me his own to keep. The Führer was such a gentleman!'

But Hitler showed another face to Frank when he decided the time had come to eliminate Ernst Röhm.

In 1933 Frank began his feud with Himmler, which was to last ten years. The new government, having dismantled opposition parties and annulled the power of regional governments, enacted laws imposing the death penalty for 'crimes against the public security', which meant they had a free hand to do whatever they wanted. Hitler gave Himmler sweeping powers to quell and eliminate opposition. He started in Bavaria, setting up a prison to interrogate and torture political opponents in Munich, in a street where he had once lived as a student. He then set up the first concentration camp at Dachau, 20km north-west of Munich, on 20 March 1933. There was no right of appeal and in April and May 1933 twelve prisoners were murdered.

When an SS unit killed a number of Jews in Aschaffenburg, Frank, whom Hitler had appointed as Bavarian Minister of Justice on 12 March 1933, just after the bloody takeover of Munich, authorised their arrest, but their superiors claimed the SS was not subject to civil jurisdiction. Frank disputed this, but could do no more than ask his Bavarian President to take the matter up with Himmler and Röhm. He got nowhere.

Another of his initial attempts at legality and justice came when the SS killed a Jew and two 'Aryan' inmates of the new concentration camp at Dachau. He wanted to bring charges against those involved. Himmler forced Adolf Wagner, the Bavarian Minister of the Interior, to make it clear to Frank that it was a party and political matter, and that he should stop legal proceedings. Then a Munich lawyer Frank knew, Dr Strauss, was murdered at Dachau. Frank attempted to investigate the case, but in the background as previously; this time Hitler interceded and overruled his 'meddling, pettifogging lawyer' – but did not, it seemed, bear him any ill-will personally. For a while Frank complained about illegal arrests: one entry in the record of a meeting of ministers of 4 April 1933, reads: 'The Minister of Justice Designate Frank states there is a compelling need to regulate the whole question of protective custody ... the prisons and labour camps are overcrowded.' Better, Hitler seems to have thought, to have an influential person on the inside of the tent pissing out, than one on the outside pissing in.

Perhaps Hitler was sharp enough to know Frank's opposition was token, done to salve his legal conscience. It was valuable to have Frank, who was now in the exalted positions of President of the Academy of German Law, the *Partei Reichsleiter*, the Founder of the Institute of German Law, and President of the International Chamber of the Law, preaching a confused doctrine of supremacy of the law, so long as it did not conflict with Hitler's own will.

It was a perfect example of having one's cake and eating it. Frank would go on pandering to the innate German love of justice, and preaching this to fellow lawyers. The German state would continue to be a state based on law; at the same time, co-existent with this, would be an authoritarian state implementing the *Führerprinzip*, the will of its absolute leader, the apparent legal probity a sop for fools who wanted to believe in it, at the same time a blueprint for absolute corruption. 'The law and the will of the Führer are one' were Frank's much quoted words; a perfect formula for split personality double-think.

After a lightning pre-purge worthy of a Hollywood fast-edit montage, Hitler and his men descended on Ernst Röhm and his debauched SA cohorts at a luxury hotel in Wiessee on the shores of Lake Tegernsee. According to some sources, Hitler had tried, prior to acting, to gain Röhm's compliance under his leadership and his agreement to change his debauched lifestyle by 'liquidating' his male harem. Up to the very last moment, Hitler was apparently prepared to forgive his weaknesses. But Röhm was unrepentant.

His number two, Edmund Heines, 'a girl's face on the brawny body of a piano mover', was snatched from his bed with his lover, both taken outside and summarily shot on Hitler's order, their blood splattered over the walls. The Führer erupted into Röhm's bedroom, berated him for his insubordination and ordered him to be brought back to Munich to be lodged in Stadelheim Prison.

Bertolt Brecht satirised what became known as the 'Night of the Long Knives' in *The Resistible Rise of Arturo Ui (Der aufhalt-same Aufstieg des Arturo Ui)*, written in 1941 but not staged until 1958) as an outrageous shoot-out between rival gangs in Chicago. But the reality was more complicated. The top brass of the SA were brought to Stadelheim Prison, which was under Frank's jurisdiction, by SS troops under the command of SS officers Sepp Dietrich and Prince Waldeck. Frank visited the cells, reassuring his old friend and comrade Röhm he was safe from the SS, because he was in the 'palace of justice'.

Dietrich and Waldeck told Frank they had Hitler's order to shoot the men on Hitler's list. Frank refused to allow the order to be carried out. Dietrich called the Führer and spoke to Hess, Hitler's omnipresent deputy, who passed the telephone to Hitler, who then told Frank: 'These men are in your prison because I have no other secure place to put them. They are merely your guests. I and the Reich have full power over them.'

He ordered Frank to carry out the killings. Frank stalled once more, calling Hess again, complaining the prisoners had been hauled from bed without weapons or signs of any conspiracy against Hitler, or of preparing an uprising, while some were the most decorated officers of the First World War. According to Frank, Hitler contacted the Reich President, still Hindenburg, and got him to authorise the death of 19 of those 110 taken – not including Röhm – who planned to rise against Hindenburg and kill Hitler.

Informed of the list, Frank challenged Hess a second time on the legal grounds of the condemned men's alleged crimes. When this was relayed to Hitler, the furious leader reached for the telephone. In Frank's own words:

> There was a brief pause. The Führer was back on the phone and spoke to me loudly these words: 'What are you asking Hess? I'll tell you that the legal grounds for everything that happens is the very existence of the Reich! Do you understand?' His voice was like a hammer. And I, fearful that he might fall back to his initial position, said merely, 'Yes, your command will be carried out!' Then I handed the nineteen over to the SS and calmed down the others.

The prison director, Frank claimed, then told him he had 'saved' the rest of the original detainees, and that he had 'acted under the most frightful compulsion and in utter powerlessness', thus avoiding a terrible backlash.

Two of Hitler's subordinates left a loaded pistol in Röhm's cell, reportedly with the message that he had ten minutes to use it on himself. Röhm refused to oblige with the *coup de grâce*. The two SA officers returned and one shot him dead at point-blank range.

This, according to both Frank and, later, his son Niklas, was his final test. It was the last point at which he could have turned back and behaved with legal integrity. Frank later said, 'I have the traces of some terrible wound within me.' Was it, as his son claimed, self-inflicted, and was it not the same wound the whole German people were complicit in, and inflicted upon themselves?

It was without doubt at that explicit and well-defined moment when Hans Frank became, albeit with reservations, a Nazi criminal. It was the same moment, in dramatic fiction, when Macbeth, on the orders of his wife, murders Duncan, and becomes steeped in blood so far that 'returning were as tedious as going o'er'.

Hans caved in and carried out his leader's will. In the process he had saved his own skin. 'From that point on, you were co-opted, you had blood in your throat, on your hands, in your soul, on your conscience. You sat there with your good director like some bloody afterbirth of yourself.' (Niklas.) He had, like some of the German people, sold his soul to the devil.

Of the death of the nineteen, he added, 'The firing squad was pushing me, drawing my attention to the fact that twilight was fast approaching, that it was rapidly "making the execution very difficult".' The matter-of-factness regarding life and death was extraordinary, but was to become commonplace.

When Hans next met his beloved leader, the latter joy-fully clapped him on the back, laughed, and cajoled him with, 'What a fine Minister of Justice you are, my dear Frank, talk-ing about paragraphs when they wanted to kill me!' Hitler knew human nature.

⁓

Now, after the Night of the Long Knives, there followed the purging of homosexuality and sexual impropriety from the higher echelons of the Nazi leadership; as well as anybody else who had been a nuisance. Hitler and Goebbels justified this mass murder portraying it as the 'moral cleansing' of the Nazi ranks. Later the Nazis prosecuted homosexuals and sent them to concentration camps, though this did not happen with the thor-oughness of the destruction of Jews, Catholics, intellectuals, opponents of the regime, and the disabled. As Elie Wiesel makes clear, it was almost exclusively the homosexuals who failed to live up to the ideals of 'masculinity' who were the victims arrested and sent to the camps, while in the camps themselves there were many examples of homosexual slave overseers and guards dominating the inmates.

But while Hitler outwardly tried to allay public suspicion about the sexual tastes of his inner circle, in fact he still retained some of his homosexual associates, among them notably Rudolf Hess, Reinhard Heydrich, Walther Funk, Baldur von Schirach and Julius Streicher, and he was aware of it.

The schools at the same time were targeted to de-Christianise young children. Mandatory prayer was stopped from 1935 on, and from 1940 religious education for 14–15 year olds was eliminated. The Nazi Party's open campaign against Christianity was paving the way for extreme anti-Christian atrocities in Poland. 'Christianity has infused our erotic attitudes with dishonesty,' claimed Goebbels. Brigitte, Frank's third child, was conceived and born during this tightening up of Nazi 'morality'. Was Hans trying to reassure the leadership of his normalcy?

From now on, or at least for some years, Hans behaved as Hitler's captive legal apologist – although somewhat inexplicably, and perhaps shielded by the fact that he apparently guarded Hitler's genealogical secret – with the occasional lapse into honesty and truth. Off the public platform, as ever in the history of many public servants of the Reich, Frank pursued his path of private and venal corruption, avidly supported by his materialist and status-hungry wife.

While Bavarian Minister of Justice he took fat fees and bribes while continuing his private legal practice. He reinstated the twice-debarred Karl in his practice: the Frank family now had everything they wanted, and with the various crises or stepping stones of the Nazi rise to power successfully negotiated, the good Aryan wife Brigitte could turn from supporting her man to adding to the repopulation of the Reich. Now over 40,

Brigitte gave birth to Brigitte (1935), Michael (1937) and Niklas (1939), all born in Munich.

Frank's star remained in the ascendant. Here is Dr Hans Frank telling his fellow jurists and the judiciary in 1936 how to be rid of all Jews and those whom Nazism deemed questionable:

> The National Socialist ideology is the foundation of all basic laws, especially as explained in the party program and in the speeches of the Führer … There is no independence of law against National Socialism. Say to yourselves at every decision which you make: 'How would the Führer decide in my place?' In every decision ask yourselves: 'Is this decision compatible with the National Socialist conscience of the German people?' Then you will have a firm iron foundation which, allied with the unity of the National Socialist People's State and with your recognition of the eternal nature of the will of Adolf Hitler, will endow your own sphere of decision with the authority of the Third Reich, and this for all time.

Germany was no longer a society based on laws; as Frank proudly proclaimed, 'The law is the will of the Führer.'

12

Kirchenkampf

We are the jolly Hitler Youth,
We don't need any Christian truth
For our Leader Adolf Hitler, our Leader
Always is our interceder.
Whatever the Papist priests may try,
We are Hitler's children till we die;
We follow not Christ but Horst Wessel.
Away with incense and holy water vessel!
As sons of our forebears from times gone by
We march as we sing with banners held high.
I'm not a Christian, nor a Catholic,
I go with the SA through thin and thick.

With apologies for the last forced rhyme, this was sung by Hitler Youths at the 1934 Nuremberg rally. They were 3.5 million strong. 'Once I have settled my other problems,' Speer reported Hitler as saying, 'I'll have my reckoning with the Church. I'll have it reeling on the ropes.'

The intellectual roots of the Third Reich, as much as the garbled philosophical thinking of its theorists like Alfred Rosenberg, were for the most part secular and atheistic. The starting point or original influence was Arthur Schopenhauer, whom Hitler read and studied (Frank reports discussing

Schopenhauer's *The World as Will and Representation* with
Hitler). But above all, Nazi logic, such as it was, stemmed from
Friedrich Nietzsche and Charles Darwin, who dominated Nazi
thought, and more than most others today dominate Western
European culture in the 'post-Christian society'. With particular regard to religious belief, Nietzsche might be said to have
written a rough early draft of *The God Delusion*. 'The one great
curse,' he called Christianity, 'the enormous and innermost
perversion ... I call it the one immortal blemish of mankind ...
This Christianity is no more than the typical teaching of the
Socialists.' If you ally this with Nietzsche's prophecy that 'God
is dead', and his modernist teaching on Truth ('There are no
facts, only opinions'), which has been adopted in literary circles and in politics, then the belief that Nazi totalitarian theory
survives today (in less brutal form) has some credibility. Take
away 'The law is the will of the Führer,' and certain classes,
the political class in particular, believe that they have superior
entitlement, and are not answerable to the law – unless it is
changed in their favour. The Nazi Party, the political class, had
a similar superhuman complex. In Hitler's words:

> Nietzsche prophesied the coming elite who would rule the
> world and from whom the superman would spring. In *The
> Will to Power*, he writes, 'A daring and ruler race is building
> itself up ... The aim should be to prepare a transvaluation
> of values for a particularly strong kind of man, most highly
> gifted in intellect and will. This man and the elite around him
> will become the "lords of the earth".'

Hitler's view of Christianity could on occasions become sarcastic
and contemptuous. It is also intriguing to note that he would align
the German superman dream and world domination with Islam:

> Distinguished Arabs told him that when the Mohammedans
> tried to penetrate beyond France into central Europe, in the

8th century, they were driven back at the Battle of Tours. Had they won this battle the Western World would be Mohammedan today. For they believed in spreading the faith by the sword, and subjugating all nations to that faith. The Germanic peoples would have become heirs to that religion. Such a creed was perfectly suited to the Germanic temperament. Hitler said that the conquering Arabs, because of their racial inferiority, would in the long run have been unable to contend with the harsher climate and conditions of the country. They could not have kept down the more vigorous natives, so that ultimately not Arabs but Islamised Germans could have stood at the head of this Mohammedan Empire.

Hitler concluded this historical speculation by remarking:

You see, it's been our misfortune to have the wrong religion. Why didn't we have the religion of the Japanese, who regard sacrifice for the Fatherland as the highest good? The Mohammedan religion too would have been much more compatible to us than Christianity. Why did it have to be Christianity with its meekness and flabbiness?

It is remarkable that even before the war he sometimes opined: 'Today the Siberians, the White Russians, and the people of the steppes live extremely healthy lives. For that reason they are better equipped for development and in the long run biologically superior to the Germans.' This was an idea he was destined to repeat during the last months of the war.

Allied to Hitler's studied usurpation of Catholic religious functions and symbols to his own aims was his belief in science as a basis for all personal and social action. Hitler believed in a world ineluctably ruled in the future by the Darwinian survival of the fittest, by competition, in the interests of the human race no longer adhering to the former God, but to a struggle embodying pure race maintenance and the aristocratic principle of nature between races and individuals. In the evolution of consciousness he would take the place of Jesus Christ. 'People of Germany,' he proclaimed in 1936, 'I have taught you faith, now put your faith in me.' But he never once dropped the religious frame of reference. Keeping close followers trapped with him in the collective and by then psychotic delusion, he was to say, even at the end, that he was absolutely sure he was fulfilling 'the natural laws that a God has created' and that he would 'finally receive the blessings of Providence'.

In the day-to-day running of the Reich he encouraged friction between departments and rivalry between competing systems – 'institutionalised Darwinism,' he called it. 'Friction produces warmth, and warmth is energy,' he said. He called lawyers 'deficient by nature or deformed by experience', and called his aristocratic foreign minister 'an intellectual garbage heap'.

Above all, Hitler believed in propaganda, in the power of the magic spell to achieve the mastery of the stronger will over the lesser will, and for swaying the masses. Schopenhauer and Richard Wagner both shared this view, emphatic that suspension of thought was a precondition for action by the un-owned, universal Will. Wagner consciously set out to achieve this state by means of music, while for Schopenhauer, in his belief that all human desire and action was futile, illogical and directionless, there was a necessity for the state and state violence to check the destructive tendencies innate to our species.

At the beginning of the Nazis' rise in 1919, Bavaria was one of the most devoutly Catholic areas in Europe; at the moment Hitler became Chancellor in 1933 there were roughly 20 million Catholics in Germany, or a third of its people. The primate of Bavaria, Cardinal Michael von Faulhaber, who was Archbishop of Munich for thirty years and who ordained Joseph Ratzinger, the future Pope Benedict XVI, in 1951, had, together with the

Christian Democratic leaders, effectively opposed Hitler's failed Beer Hall Putsch in 1923.

A staunchly conservative Catholic, Faulhaber was dining with Franz Matt, Vice-Premier of Bavaria, and Archbishop Eugenio Pacelli, the papal nuncio, when news came of the putsch. He had played his part in preserving the *status quo* and promised Catholic support when Matt, not counting on decisive action from von Kahr, started to plan to set up a rump government-in-exile in Regensburg. The Catholic Church's influence was powerful in Bavarian politics, so powerful it could have been the decisive factor in stopping Hitler's rise. It had not yet been mortally threatened by the concordat concluded between the Vatican and Hitler when he came to power.

The Führer's words about the meekness of Christianity being more foreign to the Nazi ethos than Islam remained broadly true. Like millions of other Germans, indeed like Hitler himself, Hans Frank dropped the Roman Catholic Church when he became a Nazi, but observed some superficial lip-service through family life, for example through the christenings of his children. Since his marriage in 1925 he had not restrained Brigitte from practising regularly, nor did he object to the presence of priests in his home and he would still sometimes describe himself as 'Old Catholic'. He even encouraged his employees to attend mass and say prayers for himself and his family. It kept them respectful and obedient.

In the crucial years of Nazi growth in the 1930s, the Catholic Church and the other churches potentially offered the strongest and toughest ideological opposition to Nazi principles. But the powerful Catholic and Lutheran churches of Germany failed to show right at the very beginning uncompromising hostility to the Reich on more than a narrowly religious front, which for the most part could be ignored by the Nazis. In fact, many fanatical Lutherans supported the Nazi doctrines. Their leader, Ludwig Müller, Hitler's friend, backed by SA and Gestapo intimidation, became the first 'Reich Bishop', with dictatorial powers to unite all Protestants in one great Reich Church.

The Catholic Church, and even the majority of moderate Protestants, both conservative in politics, had long had a tradition of anti-Semitism, but blundered in seeing in Nazism a protection against Bolshevism and the Soviets. Hitler could see all the churches were prone to, even riddled with, fear and superstition and in awe of magic and hidden forces. Because of their doctrinal differences they failed to unite. While uneasy and defiant they could be lulled, manoeuvred and forced into substituting the ideology of the Nazi German state which 'would last a thousand years', for the Christian belief in the immortality of the soul. Hitler knew that to win the battle against the churches would be to confer unanimous Nazi-hood on the German people.

Massacres of priests in the Spanish Civil War by the Falangists were widely reported. So, alongside the motivation of a guarantee of physical security, there was support for the Nazi position on cultural decadence, support of the family, public order, cleanliness and so on:

> Wherever you drove you saw perfect order. The people were clean and appeared well fed; they were polite and friendly – in short, it was a charming country, a pleasure to visit, and how was anybody to credit these horror tales? Irma was in a continual struggle between what she wanted to believe and what was being forced upon her reluctant mind.

Society was scrutinised and overseen by Dr Joseph Goebbels, master of Germany's intellectual life:

> 'His' word could make or break anyone in any profession; an invitation to his home was at once a command and the highest of opportunities. Men bowed and fawned, women smiled and flattered – and at the same time they watched warily, for it was a perilous world, in which your place was held only by sleepless vigilance. Jungle cats, all in one cage, circling one another

warily, keeping a careful distance; the leopard and the jaguar would have tangled, had not both been afraid of the tiger.

But they were civilized cats, which had learned manners, and applied psychology, pretending to be gentle and harmless, even amiable. The deadliest killers wore the most cordial smiles; the most cunning were the most dignified, and the most exalted. They had a great cause, an historic destiny, a patriotic duty, an inspired leader. They said, 'We are building a new Germany,' and at the same time they thought: 'How can I cut out this fellow's guts?' They said: 'Good evening, *Parteigenosse*,' and thought: '*Schwarzer Lump*, I know what lies you have been whispering!'

Above all, Goebbels controlled a weapon as important for arming the Reich as bombers and tanks: 'Never get boring,' he told his radio programme directors. 'Never let things drag. Never give the listener the message on a plate. Never imagine the best way to serve the national government is to play rousing marches evening after evening'. German technology swung into action to make sure the nation had the best broadcasting equipment in the world.

The first test of the Christian churches regarding the Jews, the 1933 boycott of Jewish businesses, evinced no religious response from either bishops or synods. Further, on 24 April 1933 the Premier of Bavaria reported to Frank and other ministers that 'Cardinal Faulhaber had issued an order to the clergy to support the new regime in which he (Faulhaber) had confidence' [parenthesis in original].

Faulhaber further pronounced in a letter addressed to Cardinal Pacelli, now promoted from Germany's nuncio to the Vatican's Secretary of State:

We bishops are being asked why the Catholic Church, as often in its history, does not intervene on behalf of the Jews. This is not possible at this time because the struggle against the Jews would then, at the same time, become a struggle against the

Catholics, and because the Jews can help themselves, as the sudden end of the boycott shows.

Although Faulhaber has been portrayed as a famous and fearless opponent of the Nazis and an icon of inspiration by the future pope Ratzinger, when one considers how in Bavaria the Church was weakened and marginalised, and looks more closely at statements he made and the events, one questions how accurate this is.

'The Church which is married to the Spirit of the Age will be a widow in the next.' Dean Inge's judgement is often quoted today in support of Catholic traditional values. In many disastrous ways the Catholic Church in the late 1920s and throughout the 1930s was married to the 'Spirit of the Age'. Pacelli, born in Rome in 1876, was, from the time he became the Vatican's best diplomat, dedicated to the absolute leadership principle which swept Europe in the 1930s. His ideology was of an autocratic papal control and the dictatorial authority he assumed when he became pope. He loved, as did the monarchs and the dictators, the luxuries he enjoyed with his position; on his first trip to Germany as papal nuncio, this included a private rail compartment and 'a wagon with 60 cases of special foods for his delicate stomach', shocking the reigning Pope Benedict XV in its extravagance.

Moreover, in the spirit of the age, he was also antipathetic towards the Jewish race, at least to begin with, like many millions of German and Polish Catholics. During his first years in Munich, when Bolshevik revolutionary groups supported Kurt Eisner's seizure of power, Pacelli described a visit he made to Eugen Levine, the chief of one such group headquartered in the former royal palace. The scene, he said, was 'chaotic, the filth completely nauseating ... Once the home of a king, it resounded with screams, vile language, profanities ... An army of employees was dashing to and fro, waving bits of paper, and in the midst of all this, a gang of young women, of dubious appearance, Jews like all the rest of them, hanging around in all the offices with provocative behaviour and suggestive smiles ...'

This female gang's boss was Levine's mistress, a young Russian Jew and a divorcée, while Levine, aged about 30 or 35, was also 'Russian and a Jew, pale, dirty, with vacant eyes, hoarse voice, vulgar, repulsive, with a face that is both intelligent and sly'. In this statement written to his superior in the Vatican, and from other statements and actions of his, it cannot be denied that in Pacelli was an inherited anti-Judaism that paved the way for a certain insensibility in the future to the atrocities committed against Jews.

The Vatican helped Fascism in Italy in the same way it was to help Hitler. Whatever the reasons for, or advantages which accrued from, the Lateran Treaty and the Italian Concordat negotiated by Pacelli's brother, a canon lawyer, for the independence and power of the Italian Catholic Church, the sinister provisions of the terms (bishops taking an oath of allegiance to the Mussolini dictatorship, the order for clergy not to oppose or harm it, the dissolution of the Catholic Party) delighted Hitler. 'The fact that the Curia is now making its peace with Fascism shows that the Vatican trusts the new political realities far more than it did the former liberal democracy' (*Völkischer Beobachter*, 22 February 1929). Fascism was 'justifiable for the faithful and compatible with the Catholic faith'.

The Concordat agreed between the Vatican and the Third Reich hardly differed from that signed with Mussolini. The German Church had no say in the matter, and Pacelli lied over and over again to Faulhaber when he had agreed to conditions, saying they were still under discussion. Some bishops, such as Cardinal Bertram, vehemently opposed certain aspects of the treaty when they became known, but they were ignored. On 26 April 1933, just before its signing, Hitler met the Catholic bishops and declared his undying support for Christianity, insisting on how much Germany needed its religious and moral foundation. He pointed out that National Socialism and Catholicism fundamentally agreed on the Jewish question, as the Church had always regarded the Jews as parasites and banished them into the ghetto. His outright lies were swallowed by the bishops, the pro-Nazi Bishop Wilhelm Berning of Osnabruck in particular, who reported him as saying 'We need soldiers, devout soldiers. Devout soldiers are the most valuable, for they risk all. Therefore we shall keep the parochial schools in order to bring up believers.'

Hitler could and did boast privately that he had tapped the deep well of Catholic anti-Semitism. For a long time there had been ambivalence, impulses to protect as well as respect Jews, but now bishops had to swear loyalty to the Reich and the state and there would be no more safeguards.

Moral ambivalence, and its relation to music, is a theme Mann explores in his depiction of German cultural hubris. He claims the relation is strong. 'Music turns the equivocal into a system,' says the composer Adrian Leverkühn in Mann's *Doctor Faustus*: 'Take this or that note. You can understand it so or respectively so. You can think of it as sharpened or flattened, and you can, if you are clever, take advantage of the double sense as much as you like.'

After the Concordat was signed Hitler more than tripled the subsidy he paid the Catholic Church between 1933 and 1938, which might accurately be called blood money, as it bought silence about the increasing numbers of atrocities. He left the Roman Church the richest landowner in south and west Germany. He demanded of France, Britain and America 'What was your subsidy to the Churches?' In that same summer of 1933 Faulhaber sent Hitler a hand-written note:

> What the old parliaments and parties did not accomplish in sixty years, your statesmanlike foresight has achieved in six months. For Germany's prestige in East and West … this handshake with the papacy, the greatest moral power in the history of the world, is a feat of immeasurable blessing.

But it was not long before Article 31 (Protection of Catholic organisations and freedom of religious practice) and Article 32

(Clerics may not be members of or be active for political parties) were either flagrantly ignored or abused. As already mentioned, in the schools mandatory prayer was stopped in 1935, and religious education for 14–15 year olds was eliminated in 1940. Now any cleric criticising the Reich or Hitler could be accused of breaking Article 32. From now on any Catholic who opposed Hitler was committing a sin, while every war the Reich fought would be a just and holy war. Catholics flooded to join the Nazi Party, as they believed it had the support of the Church, and German Catholic Democrats had their voice and leadership silenced. The Centre Party, the powerful Catholic party of middle-class democratic Germany voluntarily 'disbanded' itself. Pacelli seemed doubly culpable as he had so sedulously wooed Hitler to achieve his delusion of a great Vatican triumph. Hitler could still make his signature dependent on the Centre Party's voting for the Enabling Act, which gave him a dictator's power both to muzzle Catholic resistance and a free hand to persecute and finally liquidate the Jewish race. The Concordat, designed by Cardinal Pacelli, later Pope Pius XII, to strengthen the Church, had the opposite effect. 'This was the moral abyss into which Pacelli the future Pontiff had led the once great German Catholic Church.'

That Pacelli temporised and capitulated can be seen in his comments. At one stage he felt a pistol had been held to his head, he said, and he was 'negotiating with the devil himself'. He claimed, quite falsely, that he had to choose between 'an agreement and the virtual elimination of the Catholic Church in the Reich'. But surely the point is that the Church didn't, or mustn't, negotiate with what it saw as the devil. Anyway, the devil won hands down. Just after the Concordat, at the time of the Night of the Long Knives, the Vatican made no protest over the murder of Catholic leaders and intellectuals. The comment of the anonymous priest who wrote to Cardinal Magline may serve for the whole Reich: 'I wonder just which bishops have asked the Holy Father to remain silent. According to your Eminence, they did so out of fear of aggravating the persecution. But the facts prove that with the Pope being silent, each day sees the persecution becoming more cruel.'

Pacelli, like Chamberlain at Munich, was under Hitler's spell. He had thought that by making concessions, by severing the links between Church and the Centre Party, he would increase the Church's influence with Hitler. Even in the previous month, when Catholic youths at a Munich rally were attacked by SA thugs, beaten up and chased off the street and a planned open-air mass was cancelled, he failed to see that by surrendering Catholic political power he was playing right into Hitler's hands and committing German Catholics to obey the Nazis.

In line with Pacelli, Faulhaber imposed a ban on youth organisations and stopped his priests from speaking out or engaging in political activity. Pacelli thought he was centralising power in the Papacy; in fact, he was giving the green light to the SA and SS to crack down on the Church and the Bavarian People's Party. This meant the subsequent murder or arrest and deportation to concentration camps of those Catholics, especially clerics, who did not fall in with the terms of the Concordat as interpreted by the Nazis. From 20 July 1933 newspapers were forbidden to call themselves Catholic; from September the state police in Bavaria under their Chief of Police Himmler, and approved by Hans Frank, banned all activities of Catholic organisations with the exception of youth groups, charities asking for money, and church choirs holding rehearsals. Protests were made, but the general inaction meant one thing: appeasement.

In October 1933 Archbishop Gröber in Freiburg said, 'I am placing myself completely behind the new government and the New Reich.' The latter selected a few notable Catholics here and there to be murdered, but on the whole Himmler's softly-softly approach was to spread fear, not take draconian action. The weak Catholic leadership fell in with this tactic, believing it could lessen the harm done to the Church by co-operation with the Nazis.

Cardinal Faulhaber did sometimes attack the Nazi position; once, without being explicit, in his popular Advent sermon of 1933 he said: 'It is my conviction that a defence of Christianity is also a defence of Germany. An apostasy from Christianity, a relapse into paganism, would be the beginning of the end of the German nation.' He drew a vivid picture of life in Germany before the advent of Christianity. Taken from the Roman historian Tacitus, early German gods, fashioned after the likeness of men, were idealised portraits of what a German hero or house-wife were conceived to be. 'They offered human sacrifice to the Gods; they indulged in savage superstitious rites as well as savage warfare; they practised vendettas as a moral duty. They had slaves, whom they put to death at will; they drank heavily and became murderous ... They were loyal to their comrades, monogamous and faithful ...'

Nobody seemed to get the picture. It was too late in any case. Faulhaber's words, which could be read two ways, became more a prediction than a warning. Faulhaber delivered other speeches and sermons criticising the Nazis from 1933 onwards and in 1935 some Nazis called in an open meeting for Faulhaber to be killed, and his house was shot at. But these were mere gestures. On the persecution of Jews and the political violence, the German churches, with notable exceptions, remained tragically silent; only the Jehovah's Witnesses were firm in their hostility, willing to be martyred. Himmler was impressed by their fanaticism and held it up to his SS men as an example.

Particularly sinister was the Nazi reaction when, after too long a silence, and in spite of Pacelli, Pius XI, his predecessor as pope, issued his fiery encyclical, *Mit brennender Sorge* ('With burning concern') in March 1937, prompted by five German cardinals and bishops who had broken ranks. The encyclical excoriated Nazi hatred and calumny of the Church. But even in the encyclical there was no explicit condemnation of anti-Semitism. Göring fulminated and vowed reprisal, but under Pacelli's influence most Catholic bishops softened in their support of the encyclical. Again, it was too late. The Catholic hierarchy in Bavaria had allowed Hitler to insert the thin end of the wedge, while German Catholic independence had been paralysed.

In response to the encyclical, Goebbels intensified propaganda against the Church. Fifteen monks were arrested and tried, accused of sexual abuse of minors and financial misdemeanours. And still Faulhaber unctuously continued the official Catholic approval of Hitler:

> The Führer commands the diplomatic and social forms better than a born sovereign … Without doubt the Chancellor lives in faith in God. He recognizes Christianity as the foundation of Western culture … Just as clear is his conception of the Catholic Church as a God-established institution.

In his New Year's Eve sermon in 1938, Faulhaber congratulated Hitler's government: 'One advantage of our time: at the highest levels of the government we have the example of an austere alcohol- and nicotine-free life-style.'

Kristallnacht and a week of murder, arson and pillage of Jewish people and property, swiftly followed. Unleashed by Heydrich, Himmler's number two, it created horror and devastation on a scale hitherto unimagined. The list of activities and places proscribed for Jews included German forests. This provides a chilling yet extraordinary insight into the way the Nazis had aestheticised politics (similar to the way we have sexualised it today), and become what the Surrrealists had called for: 'a government of artists'.

A short while after this week of atrocity, Frank and Brigitte were at a dinner party with Hitler. The Nazis loved cruel, heavy-handed jokes, and we shall hear some of Frank's later, because he had to keep in with the crowd. To Goebbels' demand that the Jews be forbidden to enter forests, Göring replied, 'We shall give the Jews a certain part of the forest and the Alpers shall take care of it so that various animals that look damned much like Jews – the elk has a crooked nose like theirs – get there also and become acclimatised.'

The effect of early forest romanticism should never be underrated – for the German, as Canetti writes in *Crowds and Power*, 'army and forest transfused each other in every possible way ... The parallel rigidity of the upright trees and their density and number fill the heart of the German with a deep and mysterious delight ... What to others might seem the army's dreariness and barrenness kept for the German the life and glow of the forest.' Jews, keep out!

In gratitude for his invitation to the dinner, Frank sent a fulsome telegram: 'My life is and remains service to your work. Heil to you my Führer.'

Pacelli's attitude to *Kristallnacht* was the same as Faulhaber in 1933: public silence and private indifference. The Jews must look after themselves. And all through this time Brigitte Frank christened her children as Catholics and attended mass. They had a decent family priest, and Brigitte admired Faulhaber, with whom they had personal contact now she had a title and insisted on being called 'Frau Minister'. During the week-long pogrom following *Kristallnacht*, when she and Hans were at Munich Station, she turned to him and asked, 'Hans, what's going on with the synagogues and Jewish shops? Did you have anything to do with it?' 'No, Brigitte, really no,' Hans reassured her. 'I give you my word.' She too loved the official dinners with Hitler, such as the one they were invited to soon after, on 17 January 1939.

When at last, in 1938, Faulhaber did condemn the racial murders of *Kristallnacht*, a mob stoned and broke the windows of his episcopal residence. The weakness of the Nazi response suggested it was not taken as a serious challenge.

For now it seemed, Hitler was content to take a back seat, as the German Catholic Church's defeat could be taken for granted. He did not want to risk universal outrage by murdering the Catholic hierarchy. Fear and intimidation were enough to instil obedience. He left the dirty work to Bormann and Himmler, but allowed himself the luxury of the occasional intemperate outburst against Christians, one Lutheran in particular:

> He had another such fit of rage at Pastor Niemöller in 1937. Niemöller had once again delivered a rebellious sermon in Dahlem; at the same time transcripts of his tapped telephone conversations were presented to Hitler. In a bellow Hitler ordered Niemöller to be put in a concentration camp and, since he had proved himself incorrigible, kept there for life.

But while Hitler seemed to proceed carefully, his henchmen did not want Hitler to postpone his 'reckoning' with the Church.

Brutally direct himself, Bormann was vexed by Hitler's prudent pragmatism. He took every opportunity to push his own projects. Even at meals he broke the unspoken rule that no subjects were to be raised which might spoil Hitler's humour. Bormann had developed a special technique for such thrusts. He would draw one of the members of the entourage into telling him about seditious speeches a pastor or bishop had delivered, until Hitler finally became attentive and demanded details. Bormann would reply that something unpleasant had happened and did not want to bother Hitler with it during the meal. At this Hitler would probe further, while Bormann pretended that he was reluctantly letting the story be dragged from him. Neither angry looks from his fellow guests nor Hitler's gradually flushing face deterred him. At some point he would take a document from his pocket and begin reading passages from a defiant sermon or a pastoral letter. Frequently Hitler became so worked up that he began to snap his fingers – a sure sign of his anger – pushed away his food and vowed to punish the offending clergyman eventually. He could much more easily put up with foreign indignation and criticism than opposition at home. That he could not immediately retaliate raised him to a white heat, though he usually managed to control himself quite well. Meantime at a grassroots level the reckoning with the Church went on:

... Watching a young Hitler Youth member enter a classroom in August 1936, Friedrich Reck-Malleczewen observed how his glance fell on the crucifix hanging behind the teacher's desk, how in an instant his young and still soft face contorted in fury, how he ripped this symbol, to which the cathedrals of Germany, and the ringing progressions of the *St Matthew Passion* are consecrated, off the wall and threw it out of the window into the street ... With the cry: 'Lie there, you dirty Jew!'

Nazi symbols took the place of the traditional Church symbols. For Himmler, who had the personality and conviction of a religious fanatic, the swastika was redemption on earth. As his SS plan put it in 1937: 'We live in an age of the final confrontation with Christianity. It is part of the mission of the SS to give to the German people over the next fifty years the non-Christian ideological foundations for a way of life appropriate to their own character.'

Subjugation of the Catholic Church ranked as one of Hitler's greatest early successes. But he still somewhere respected the churches, and felt they were necessary to help him fulfil his mission. Even after 1942, Speer reported, he maintained that the churches were indispensable in political life, and that it was impossible to replace them by a 'party ideology'. A new party religion, Hitler said, would only bring about a relapse into the mysticism of the Middle Ages.

13

'A Humble Soldier' and *Il Duce*

'Truly,' wrote Brecht, 'I live in a dark period.'

> The innocuous world is stupid. A smooth forehead
> Is a sign of insensitivity. The man who laughs
> Has merely not been told
> The terrible news.
> What kind of a period is it when
> To talk of trees is almost a crime
> Because it implies silence about so many horrors?

Brecht reasons that he had been spared by chance. Not true, strictly speaking, because after his first outspokenly Communist work *Die Massnähme* (translated as *The Step*), German's leading playwright had decided to leave Berlin in 1933. All publications and productions of his work ceased before he fled to Sweden. His *Mother Courage*, written in 1939, though set in the Thirty Years' War, is prophetic of the war to come in its savage, continually scatological, and almost pornographically violent parody of the devastation caused by war and the murder of innocence. Brecht is derivative of Shakespeare, and his *Wars of the Roses*, which adapted the latter's *Henry VI* parts 1–3 and *Richard III*, shows war as a self-perpetuating monster. For Shakespeare, as for Brecht, war cruelly satisfied mankind's deepest instincts for profit, conflict and the selfish exploitation of others. But here they differed, because Shakespeare opposed Christian and humanist values to war, while Brecht saw war as part of a necessary evolution in the struggle between classes.

In one scene Brecht apotheosises 'Hate' as the supreme generator of energy and progress, but also interpolates into further speeches and action Nietzsche's sentiments from *Thus Spake Zarathustra*:

> You shall love peace as a means to new war – and the short peace more than the long. You I advise not to work, but to fight. You I advise not to peace but to victory … You say it is the good cause which hallows even war? I say unto you: it is the good war which hallows every cause. War and courage have done more great things than charity.

Brecht became an ardent supporter of left-wing dictatorship and later embraced hard-line Ulbricht East German Communism. In spite of the dramatic skill of his anti-Nazi sketches in *Mother Courage*, in *Fear and Misery in the Third Reich* and his satire on the putsch mentality in *The Resistible Rise of Arturo Ui*, he missed the point about Hitler, who had the masses on his side.

Thomas Mann left Germany in the same year as Brecht, warned by his daughter Erika while on holiday in Ascona that if he returned to Munich the Nazis would be out to get him. He remained silent for three years to protect his German assets and members of his family, and then donned the mantle of the spiritual leader of artists quitting the Reich. Believing German tradition and culture brought Hitler about as an inevitability, he showed that his rise was irresistible because it was endorsed by a majority who were complicit with it and were carried away by it. Brecht became, in his didactic views, and his abrasive, ranting style almost a mirror image of the target figure of his unremitting hatred. Which of these two great Bavarian writers was right?

For most Germans, the views of Brecht and Mann mattered little. Apart from those who were persecuted, terrorised or driven out, they enjoyed an unbroken growth and prosperity hitherto unimaginable. The price they paid was silence, and looking in the other direction. Praising the good times the Third Reich had brought, they had little desire to pay attention to dark prophesy. The subtle ways Hitler provoked and lied to justify and legalise the war he was about to begin, and more important to convince everyone to follow him, were legion. The Führer argued that the greatest spirit had to have its revenge when the body in which that spirit lived was beaten to death with rubber truncheons. Those sixteen members of the National Socialist Party who died in the failed Beer Hall Putsch of 1923 were the true martyrs of the nation, the *Herrenvolk* who aspired to rule all others on earth.

Hans Frank had been there in the vanguard – or just behind – and ten years on, at the commemorative turn-out in 1933, he had marched in the front rank at the head of thousands of storm troopers. This now happened every year. The martyrs of the *Blutfahne* (the blood flag) now had honour temples (*Ehrentempel*) constructed in their memory. Their bodies had been re-interred, eight each in two communal sarcophagi. Passers-by were obliged to give the Hitler salute. All over Germany from now on, remembrance ceremonies were obligatory. The four Bavarian policemen who died were forgotten.

Up to the invasion of Poland on 1 September 1939, Hans Frank, Germany's foremost legal brain, knew, to express it as Brecht would have done, which side his bread was buttered. Satan, or Lucifer, the most brilliant and intelligent angel of all, had dethroned God and set himself up in Europe, promising rewards and temptations to his loyal acolytes, promising endless pleasure domes of sex, wealth and power in the form of conquered territories. Frank saw his chance. Seeing how Hitler's mind worked, Frank once again took up his pen to record his adoration on 10 February 1937:

> I return now to this diary. I intend to resume my writing at this point, so that it may be witness to the unity of my expectations, faith, hope, knowledge, and battles. So that I may describe how it was that the young fellow with conflict and hesitation in his heart and in his life became the Minister of Justice, for Adolf Hitler.

He remembers how he first fell under Hitler's spell in December 1918; he then basks in his self-congratulatory CV:

> I was part of the movement beginning in 1919. From then on I revealed layer after layer of myself: from university student, to SA man, to law clerk, lawyer, assistant in jurisprudence at the law seminar of the Munich Institute of Technology; in 1930, Reichsleiter; March 1933, Bavarian Minister of Justice; June 1933, President of the Academy for German Justice, which I founded. Also in 1933, Reich Commissioner for Justice. In 1927, Reichsführer of Jurists. December 1934, Minister of the Reich ... Thus has been the course of my life; thus has been my active career.

But like every celebrity with his heart on his sleeve, Frank knew where his limits lay:

> And in order to demonstrate that even with all the grandeur of my titles and offices I think of myself as a humble soldier and servant of the communal whole – a knight of the order of the National Socialist German Workers' Party. I hereby swear my fidelity to the task. Down to the very last and most secret fibre of my being, I belong to the Führer and his glorious enterprise. Even a thousand years from now each German

will proclaim the same. I herewith make my confession of my faith. To serve Germany is to serve God. No Christian confession, no Christian faith, can be as strong as our conviction that if Christ were to reappear on earth, He would return as a German. In truth, we are God's weapon for the destruction of the evil powers on Earth. We battle in God's name against the Jew and his Bolshevism. May God protect us!

Even then, Hans goes on to pray directly to God to receive his sacrificial tribute, that of using the law as a weapon to secure his people's communal life: 'Our law stands forever – and it stands engraved in eternal bronze … The Party and the Reich must be as spirit and body to our nation.' He concludes, 'The night is silent round about. My path has brought me hither, where now I dwell – where now I meditate. I am aglow for you, my Germany!'

He joined enthusiastically in the bread and circuses. In October 1935 Mussolini had invaded Ethiopia, and not much later, in March 1936, Hitler had marched troops into the Rhineland, the Bavarian State and government had been absorbed into the Reich and Frank's post no longer existed. Hitler had no more need of spurious legality. He was the law. So he appointed Hans as Minister without Portfolio and gave him one or two other high-sounding legal positions. As he had fled to Italy after the Beer Hall Putsch and learnt Italian, Frank became an integral part of Hitler's wooing of Mussolini. In April 1936, ostensibly to lecture at Rome's Academy of Science on law, Frank met Mussolini on Hitler's order. Hitler's first meeting with the Italian fascist in June 1935 had gone badly; a pitiful spectacle in dirty raincoat and battered hat, he had felt humiliated by Mussolini's pomp and splendour:

Firmly erect, swaying from the hips as he talked, his Caesarean head might have been modelled from the old Romans, with its powerful forehead and broad, square chin thrust forward under a wide mouth. He had a much more vivacious expression than Hitler when his turn came to thunder against the Bolshevists or the League of Nations. Indignation, contempt, determination and cunning alternately lit up his highly mobile face, and he had the histrionic sense native to Latins. At particularly eloquent passages his gleaming dark brown eyes seemed ready to start from his head. He never said a word too much, and everything he uttered could have been sent straight to the printers.

This was Hitler's interpreter talking, who caught the contrast in their styles:

There was little about Hitler that fitted in with the popular conception of the typical German. When he got excited the much-caricatured lock of his long black hair fell over his receding forehead, giving him an untidy Bohemian appearance. I noticed his coarse nose and undistinguished mouth with its little moustache. His voice was rough and often hoarse as he flung out sentences full of rolling *r*'s either at me or at Mussolini. Sometimes his eyes blazed suddenly, and then equally suddenly became dull as if in a fit of absent-mindedness.

While Mussolini's laugh was liberating, showing he had a sense of humour, Hitler's always retained a flavour of derision and sarcasm. Frank, smoother and more cultured than Hitler, and of a much softer, warmer Bavarian temperament, hit it off with Mussolini at the Palazzo Venezia, where he also met King Emmanuel III. The two began an intense friendship, or so Frank believed, which fostered the common interests of the two countries.

Frank was lost in awe and admiration for the *grundsätzlionguter Mensch*. Mussolini invited Hans and Brigitte to attend a performance of *Tristan and Isolde* – 'Mussolini personally fetched my wife and me at the hotel,' he gushed.

Comic opera pursued Mussolini when Hitler invited him
to visit in September 1937 and appointed Frank his seneschal
and guide. He caught the special train. It was waiting at the
border town of Kiefersfelden on 25 September with the guest
of honour:

> The Italian had ten large saloon, dining, and sleeping cars, and
> two Miropa sleeping cars were attached to it for the Germans.
> Mussolini and Ciano greeted Frank heartily, he was one of
> the few in the German party whom they already knew. The
> Germans and the Italians were all wearing gorgeous gold and
> silver braided uniforms. Conversation between the Italian
> guests and the German reception committee, which included
> two Reich Ministers, Hess and Frank, was not exactly hearty.
> In Mussolini's swaying saloon the Germans and the Italians
> contented themselves with sickly smiles at each other.

The train took Mussolini to Braunes Haus, the House of
German Art, the Krupp Fabrik, and to see the army on manoeu-
vres at Mecklenburg. They hunted together as guests at Göring's
mountain retreat. On the rail journeys there were men stationed
every 200 metres who presented arms as they passed. And then
they arrived in Munich:

> At the Central Station, completely transformed by all its
> banners and decorations, Hitler stood surrounded by a
> vast entourage, all in uniform. He held out both hands to
> Mussolini, who was standing at the carriage window. The
> music of bands, the roll of drums and the yells of 'Heil!' and
> 'Duce!' echoed back from the station roof, and the tumult
> continued as we made our way to the exit along a red carpet
> which stretched right through the main hall.

The friendly contact between Frank and Mussolini continued
unbroken into the war. Later Frank wanted, but was forbidden, to

help Mussolini when he fell from power in 1943. But Hitler valued Frank's diplomatic and handling skills. He was going to send him to Moscow instead of Ribbentrop on 14 August for secret discussions with Stalin, but he decided on Ribbentrop instead.

14

Faustus at the Feast

On 7 September 1937 Hitler announced the Treaty of Versailles was dead. In a secret meeting with Göring and his top planners he announced plans for the domination of Europe by force. Replacing parliamentary democracy in a mass society by propaganda, manipulation and 'mythic fictions', which had nothing to do with truth in order to be creative and dynamic, Hitler had achieved the NSDAP dream: the subordination of truth and the individual to the exigencies of the community and the power of those who controlled the new state.

History and tradition were but dead nerves that needed root-treatment to stop any future infection. The cultural pre-barbarisation of Germany was complete; that barbaric underworld latent in civilisation, in the view of Thomas Mann in his *Doctor Faustus*, had conquered, and Nietzsche's idea, in debased form, had become more real than is perhaps imaginable from his more speculative militant psychology and triumphant vitalism, his worship of energy. Justice, as symbolised in its leader Frank, no longer had any regard for truth, but had to judge, according to fashion, in favour of what was false but fruitful. Subjective 'freedom' was now obligatory but under conscious management, a figment of propaganda, to create the appearance of natural flow. Both Brecht and Hitler considered the individual and originality dangerous and threatening. Creative management, an oxymoron at the best of times, was in these circumstances harnessed to criminality, which was about to strike.

Hitler kept up the cult of himself as the supernatural leader in whom the supreme being was manifest. 'I believe my life is the greatest novel in the history of the world,' he wrote to a Munich acquaintance in 1934. Under his enormous photograph at the Nuremberg party rally in 1937 was: 'In the beginning was the Word.' 'A new authority has arisen as to what Christ and Christianity really are – Adolf Hitler,' declared Hanns Kerrl, the Reich Minister for Church Affairs. 'Adolf Hitler is the true Holy Ghost.'

The Germans had already begun deporting thousands of German Jews to Poland. On 7 November 1938, the young son of such a deportee shot and mortally wounded the German Embassy Third Secretary in Paris, Ernst vom Rath, in place of the intended ambassador. Vom Rath was being shadowed by the Gestapo at this time as an anti-Nazi and, ironically, had never been an anti-Semite.

Following the Munich Pact of September 1938 and the Nazis' continuing successful military takeovers and partitions, on 14 April 1939 the Democrat President of the United States sent a personal message to Hitler and Mussolini (now since October 1936 Hitler's ally). Roosevelt asked for a promise that Germany would not invade the independent nations of Europe and the Near East. When Hitler read the letter aloud to the Reichstag the deputies laughed.

On 20 April 1939 for his fiftieth birthday the NSDAP presented Hitler with a small lodge on the Obersalzberg at the peak of the 1,834-metre Kehlstein Mountain near the village of Berchtesgaden where he had first visited Dietrich Eckart in 1923. On 23 May, Hitler again declared in secret to his inner circle that he meant to begin war, as recorded by his adjutant General Rudolf Schmundt:

The national-political unity of the Germans has been
achieved, apart from minor exceptions ... Further success cannot be obtained without the shedding of blood ...
We are left with the decision to attack Poland at the first
suitable opportunity ...

On 22 August, at Berchtesgaden, Hitler told his military leaders:

I will give a propagandistic cause for starting the war, never
mind whether it is plausible or not. The victor shall not be
asked, later on, whether we told the truth or not. In starting
and waging a war, it is not the right that matters but victory.

All through the years of peace since Frank had made his gesture
of support to Röhm, Hitler knew he no longer needed Frank's
spurious legal endorsement of his power.

It was a blow to Frank when the older and more old-
fashioned civil servant Dr Hans Lammers took the post of top
German lawyer as Head of the Reich Chancellery. With legality
and constitutional procedure abandoned, Lammers as State Secretary maintained a semblance of legal day-to-day order with a
staff of fifty to deal with mail. Hitler eschewed documentation,
did not sign any directives if he could avoid it, or write anything
down. He worked and constantly journeyed like a mediaeval
monarch and gave spoken orders, enjoying the spontaneity in
his decision-making of an artist before a canvas. Lammers was a
steady presence, which the voluble Frank could never have been,
and a cold reserve developed between the two lawyers to Frank's
disadvantage, something Goebbels relished.

We get a good picture from Frank's 'Year Calendar' of the
extent to which he enjoyed Hitler's favour socially. Entries such
as 'Führer invitation to supper', 'General discussion of the situation', 'Führer meeting, meaningful talk with small circle' occur
in 1935 five times, in 1936 only twice – on 17 June, 'with Brigitte, supper at the Führer's' – and three times in 1937. Similarly,

official encounters with Hitler grew scarcer. From now on Goebbels records such observations as: 'Führer spoke sharply against Frank and the "Right's" safeguards. Dr Frank II – no church light' (May 1936). 'Dr Frank tells me of his quarrels with the Ministry of Justice. Mostly he is right, but he gets dressed down in his clumsiness. Freisler [Roland Freisler, later Hitler's hanging judge] the absolute answer' (March 1937). 'Independence and undismissible position of the Judge got rid of, that is the only means. Appropriate laws of the Führer set up. I work to this end. These feeble-minded lawyers feel they are the heads of the state. We must chuck them out' (September 1937). '… Dr Frank obviously is very unpleasant' (April 1938).

When sharply feeling his decline in fortune and seeing it in men's eyes, Frank found consolation in music, from the long list of works he loved and went out of his way to attend, especially opera. *Rosenkavalier*, *Fidelio*, *Eugene Onegin* in Munich; *Tannhäuser*, *Rigoletto*, *Siegfried*, *Othello* in Berlin; socialising with Richard Strauss – music and discussion of music always took pride of place in those morally empty caverns which integrity had long vacated, filling them with glorious and uplifting passion. The energy and power of the great composers enabled him to bounce back and rejoin the fight. Music represented for Frank the same thing as for Hitler, who felt so close to his favourite composer (in his own mind) that he used him all the time to recharge his batteries.

The immense drama approached its climax, and Hitler was well aware of the high stakes. Earlier, in spite of his boast that he would have the Church on the ropes, he had taken his fears and concerns to Bavaria's spiritual leader Cardinal Faulhaber, with whom he was closeted in a long and close discussion at Obersalzberg in November 1936. He had emerged soberly from this:

Afterward Hitler sat alone with me in the bay window of the dining room, while the twilight fell. For a long time he looked out of the window in silence. Then he said pensively:

'There are two possibilities for me: To win through with all my plans, or to fail. If I win, I shall be one of the greatest men in history. If I fail, I shall be condemned, despised, and damned.'

We have passed quickly over Frank's meteoric increase in earnings and privileges, and the accumulation of titles and honours over the nine years during which he advanced to the top of the slippery Nazi legal pole. In spite of the setbacks he remained proud, showing this in his repetition at every possible occasion of his titles and achievements. Now he had reached the point where he could go no higher. He had reached a tipping point.

In the autumn of 1939 Hitler chose Frank to rule Poland as despot. In his first major military conquest of a sovereign state, why Hitler should want Frank to run his first model colony of slaves may at first appear a mystery. But what mattered to the pure Nazis were race, culture and ideology, and here the vision of Mephistopheles and his Doctor Faustus was shared. So this was to be Frank's great Faustian reward for those accumulated years of obeisance to the devil, combined, as it had been, with his zealous worship.

On the Nazi Party postcard, alongside Frederick the Great, Bismarck and Hindenburg, stood Hitler, with the caption: 'What the King conquered, the Prince fused, the Field Marshal defended, the Soldier saved and unified.' This was the *credo* of most Germans. It was persuasive. It appealed to the Nazi impulse that is perhaps in most of us to some degree or other, and which prompted Sir Thomas More, when seeing a murderer led to the scaffold, to say, 'There, but for the grace of God, go I.'

Hitler's sharp perceptions of Bismarck's war, or *Kulturkampf*, with the Church had brought him to the resolution that to assault the Church directly would only make martyrs. While he turned Pacelli's subtle and diplomatic approach upside down and

ran rings round him, he also knew that 'one doesn't attack pet-
ticoats or cassocks'. When it suited him and he thought it politic,
he could be careful with the Catholic lay population too. When,
for instance, in June 1941 Gauleiter of Upper Bavaria, Adolf
Wagner's order for the removal of public crosses produced anti-
Nazi demonstrations and the signing of petitions, the signatories
including Catholic soldiers at the front, Hitler ordered Wagner
to rescind the order.

In the 1933 Concordat, provision or concession had been
made for the Church to continue to educate and train seminar-
ians, although this training soon became indoctrinated with
Nazism, so that future priests would endorse the Reich's ongo-
ing legitimacy, as did the Vatican treaty. Even more cleverly, in
a secret annex to the Concordat, Hitler agreed to grant Catholic
priests exemption from any conscription imposed on German
males in the event of universal military service. This provision
was important, Hitler told von Papen, for it showed the world
the Vatican's tacit acquiescence before they began the campaign
for total rearmament. The payback for the Reich was that the
German Catholic bishops and the Vatican endorsed the Nazi
Party, the SS and any future acts of military aggression.

We should not disguise the fact that the vast majority loved
the new order: most of the country, at least until late 1941,
expected the party to win, as it had now for its eight years of
unbroken victory. The American journalist William Shirer, who
as eye-witness had chronicled the Reich since its beginning and
only left Germany in late 1940, wrote:

> Though their minds were deliberately poisoned, their regu-
> lar schooling interrupted, their homes largely replaced so far
> as their rearing went, the boys and the girls, the young men
> and women, seemed immensely happy, filled with a zest for
> the life of a Hitler Youth. And there was no doubt that the
> practice of bringing the children of all classes and walks of life
> together, where those who had come from poverty or riches,

from a laborer's home or a peasant's or a businessman's, or an aristocrat's, shared common tasks, was good and healthy in itself. In most cases it did no harm to a city boy and girl to spend six months in the compulsory Labour Service, where they lived outdoors and learned the value of manual labor and of getting along with those of different backgrounds. No one who travelled up and down Germany in those days and talked with the young in their camps and watched them work and play and sing could fail to see that, however sinister the teaching, here was an incredibly dynamic youth movement.

The young in the Third Reich were growing up to have strong and healthy bodies, faith in the future of their country and in themselves and a sense of fellowship and camaraderie that shattered all class and economic and social barriers. I thought of that later, in the May days of 1940, when along the road between Aachen and Brussels one saw the contrast between the German soldiers, bronzed and clean-cut from a youth spent in the sunshine on an adequate diet, and the first British war prisoners with their hollow chests, round shoulders, pasty complexions and bad teeth – tragic examples of the youth that England had neglected so irresponsibly in the years between the wars.

Frank knew, and could communicate to his Führer, that he would shape for him a crucial building block, even the cornerstone, for his racial Utopia out of occupied Poland.

PART THREE

15

To Poland

If you were a German, intoxicated by the brilliant media management of Doctor Goebbels, you could not fail to be thrilled by the way the Nazi armies scored victory after victory from 1 September 1939 onwards when Germany invaded Poland, made a secret pact with Russia, then marched triumphantly to avenge its defeat in 1918 in Western Europe.

The immediate *casus belli* of Hitler's invasion of Poland was a fake attack by a Polish military force on the Reich broadcasting station in Gleiwitz (Gliwice). This 'attack', in Hitler's speech to the Reichstag on 1 September 1939, became the direct excuse for launching hostilities against Poland in the interests of German security. 'Organised' by the Gestapo and code-named Operation Himmler, some 150 Germans dressed in Polish uniforms ('a Polish military force') seized the station, from which a Polish-speaking German then broadcast a speech to the effect that the time had come for conflict between Poland and Germany. The 'attack' was then 'repulsed' by German forces leaving twelve or thirteen dead 'Poles' behind (they were in fact condemned and executed 'criminals', concentration camp victims). These bodies were then photographed and extensively spread far and wide in the press by Goebbels' propaganda machine.

The invasion or *Blitzkrieg* on 1 September was a 'counter attack'. On the same day, Hitler issued a decree that condemned all incurable mentally ill persons to death, a curious instance of the Führer's 'displacement activity' – presumably from anxiety over the invasion, and maybe also from his own background of post-war instability, he needed the emotional outlet of a more predictable outcome.

The brutality that swiftly followed the defeat of the heroic and encircled Polish armies by the 1.8 million advancing German troops and 2,600 tanks was on a scale of vengefulness rarely recorded. Conquering Poland was an especial triumph, and even better for the German *amour-propre*, the Poles resisted fiercely when they could, charging down Panzer tanks on horseback and refusing in particular to capitulate in Warsaw. The *Diktat* of Versailles had robbed the Germans of their army. As Canetti wrote, 'The prohibition of universal military service was the *birth* of National Socialism.' Germany was united as never before, the Prussian North and the Bavarian South spoke with one voice and embraced with love and mutual regard.

There was another boost to the camaraderie, one that often sat well with occultism. The advancing Germans, who would stop at nothing, were fuelled by *Panzerschokolade*, a pill called Pervitin based on crystal methamphetamine, a stimulant to keep them alert, producing heightened self-confidence. An estimated 200 million pills were given to the Wehrmacht and Luftwaffe during the course of the war. Later, it was alleged, Hitler's physician, Dr Theodor Morell, injected him with methamphetamine.

―

The way Warsaw held out beggars description and angered by the unexpected setback the Wehrmacht High Command decided on 15 September to pound the stubborn citadel into submission. In round-the-clock raids bombers knocked out mills, gasworks, power stations, then carpeted the residential areas with incendiaries. One witness, passing scenes of carnage, enumerated the horrors: 'Everywhere corpses, wounded humans, dead horses

... and hastily-dug graves ...' Food ran out finally, so that famished Poles, as one man put it, 'cut off flesh as soon as a horse fell, leaving only the skeleton'.

On 28 September, Warsaw Radio replaced the 'Polonaise' with a funeral dirge. Hans Frank wrote in his diary on this fateful day:

> I received instructions to take over the administration of the occupied Eastern territories, accompanied by a special order to exploit this sphere ruthlessly as a war territory and a land of booty, to turn it, so to speak, into a heap of ruins from the point of view of economic, social, cultural and political structure ... Today the territory of the Government General is viewed as a valuable constituent part of German living space.

On 5 October Hitler visited the subdued capital, stood on a podium and took the march past of Field-Marshal von Rundstedt's Eighth Army, which lasted two hours, during which an assassination attempt on his life by a student was foiled. He made a fleeting visit to the Belvedere Palace. He doesn't seem to have been too happy – unlike on his triumphant visit to Paris in May 1940 to celebrate the German victory. Five days after the Warsaw visit, Goebbels noted:

> The Führer's verdict on the Poles is damning. More like animals than human beings, completely primitive, stupid and amorphous. And a ruling class that is the unsatisfactory result of mingling between the lower order and an Aryan master race. The Poles' dirtiness is unimaginable. Their capacity for intelligent judgement is absolutely nil ...

Frank embarked with great zest on his pursuit of gratification with untrammelled hedonism and cruelty, marked by the ostentatious consumption of a Renaissance prince. Hitler and he appeared to perform in a kind of deadly symbiosis, for he was to report to and receive his orders directly from the Führer. Comparing his previous thirty-nine years of life with the next five, one sees a remarkable transformation as the power he had been granted now enabled him to throw off the shackles of conventional bourgeois behaviour – his Mephistopheles had always been and remained anti-middle class. As Mann wrote of his Faustian composer's demonic lust:

> Was it not also love, or what was it, what madness, what deliberate, reckless tempting of God, what compulsion to comprise the punishment of the sin, finally what deep, deeply mysterious longing for daemonic conception, for a deathly unchaining of chemical change in his nature was at work, that having been warned, he despised the warning and insisted upon possession of this flesh?

He started to create for himself out of the, in many ways, dull and ponderous, heavy-humoured Hans Frank of real life this preposterous public figure, 'King Stanislaus of Poland':

> ... much greater in scope, dimension and cruelty than many a stage character of that tragic time. He began to live as a self-invented tyrant. As he later told the brilliant Dr Gilbert ... 'Ah, I am a unique specimen – a very peculiar sort of individual. Hah!' He burst into his high-pitched laugh. 'Have you ever seen a specimen like me? Extraordinary, am I not, to say such things!'

Having internalised the fantastic, confused, corrupt world of his early years, and combining it with the madness of the Third Reich, he now had the chance to turn both into direct action by forging the perfect model colony to please his master. Hitler's closest followers remained bewitched. Himmler defined their master's place in the pantheon: 'Goethe was such a figure, Bismarck in the political sector, the Führer is such in all areas, political, cultural and military'. Such backing constantly endorsed Hitler's belief in himself: 'I cannot be mistaken. What I do and say is historical.' That irrationality is a driving force in history that should never be underestimated. Frank was central to the collective delusion, which is why his master would never abandon him.

By the time Frank took over the Government General he really was dedicated to implementing a laboratory of Nazi radical ideology – analogous to Faust's alchemical obsession with turning baser metal into gold. The ideal of a purification, of transmutation, runs through all of Frank's administration, his decrees and his directives from the moment he stepped into Wawel Castle. And it never stopped: his litigious zeal ran wild. Frank never let up originating and extending Nazi state control to every aspect of the rule of his slave colony.

'The creation of the Government General,' he announced in his 26 October 1939 Proclamation:

> … marks the end of a historical episode the responsibility for which entirely falls on the deluded clique of the Government of the Former State of 'Poland' and the hypocritical warmongers of Britain.
>
> The advance of the German troops has restored order in the Polish territories; a new menace to European peace, provoked by the unjustified exactions of a State built upon the imposed peace of Versailles, which will never revive, has thus been eliminated forever.
>
> Polish men and women!
>
> As Governor-General for the occupied territories I have received from the Führer orders to take energetic measures to ensure peaceful conditions in this country and that the neighbourly relations of the Poles with the mighty world of the Reich of the German nation shall develop organically. You will lead a life loyal to the customs cultivated by you for a long time, you will be allowed to preserve your genuine Polish character in all the manifestations of collective life.

However, this country, completely ruined through the criminal fault of those who governed you until now, needs your strength and energetically organized labour. Liberated from the constraint exercised by the adventurous policy of your intellectual governing class, you must do your best to fulfil the duty of general labour and you will fulfil it under the powerful protection of Greater Germany.

Any attempt to oppose the promulgated orders and peace and order in the Polish territories will be crushed with merciless severity … by the powerful arms of Greater Germany …

But those who obey the just commands of our Reich, which will be entirely consistent with your character, will be able to work without any risk. They will free you of many of those abominable abuses which you still have to bear as a consequence of incredibly bad administration by those who have governed you until now.

Draconian decree followed decree at a truly amazing speed. Massacres of men, women and children became commonplace. The Nazi authorities put up a poster depicting 'Warsaw in View', with a wounded Polish soldier in the foreground pointing out the devastation to Neville Chamberlain, who, eyes averted, stands to one side, with the caption 'England, behold your work!' When a brave young woman named Mlle Zahorsa tore it down, she was shot dead on the spot. A dozen or more persons were executed every day in Warsaw, and it was the same elsewhere. Here is an account of two other such episodes, as reported later in 1941:

On December 26, 1939 – three months after the occupation of the country … inhabitants of the town of Wawer, near Warsaw and of the neighbouring summer resort of Anin were massacred.

In the former town, two German soldiers were killed in a small restaurant by two common criminals, fugitives from justice attempting to evade arrest.

Two hours later, a battalion of *Landesschützen* arrived at Wawer. At two o'clock in the morning soldiers went from house to house, rousing the innocent inhabitants from sleep and dragging them from their beds, though they knew nothing whatever of the affair. Some of them were given no explanation whatever; others were told that as a punitive measure every tenth inhabitant of Wawer and Anin would be shot ... In some houses, where there were several men in the family, the women were ordered to choose who should go; in one case, a mother had to choose between her two sons; another had to choose between her husband, brother and father. From other houses all the men were taken, including old men over sixty years of age, and boys of twelve. Despite the thirty-six degrees of frost, many of them were dragged out of their homes in overcoats thrown over their shirts. In addition to Wawer and Anin, this raid embraced the neighbouring villages of Marysinek and Wawerski and Zastow.

... All the men who arrived by train from the direction of Otwock, to report for work, were held up at the Wawer railway station. These men and those taken from their homes – in all about 170 persons – were assembled in a railway tunnel and were obliged to stand in the frost for several hours, with their hands above their heads. At six o'clock a dozen or so were detached from the group and led out of the tunnel; a few minutes later the noise of machine-guns was heard. Every few minutes a fresh group of a dozen or so men was led out and conducted to a place where already there were heaps of bodies, lit by the lamps of the police cars. The unfortunates were placed with their backs to the machine-guns, and ordered to kneel.

The last group was not shot, but ordered to dig the graves of the murdered men, who numbered 107 in all. Among the victims were two doctors, one of whom, sixty years old, was the physician of the Hospital of the Felician Sisters; also a boy of fourteen, with his father an engineer, etc. Thirty-four were less than eighteen years of age, and twelve were over sixty. There were two American citizens, a man named Szczygiel, and his son, the latter sixteen years old. Mr Przedlacki and his two sons and a twelve-year-old boy named Daknowski were also shot.

Mr. Bartoszek, the proprietor of the restaurant where the original incident had taken place, was hanged and buried. Not long after, his body was exhumed by the Germans and hanged again.

In the second episode, an eyewitness reported:

On February 14, 1940, after three p.m. a crowd of Jews with shovels was driven to the place of execution. Forcing them along with butt-ends and whips, the Germans ordered them to dig nine holes. When the holes were ready the Jews were driven over a little rise, kicked and bawled at as they went. Then a group of Gestapo-men conducting nine prisoners came from the direction of the Sejm building. One of them was in the uniform of a customs official, two were in police uniforms, without belts and hats, the others were civilians, without caps, overcoats, coats and probably braces, in threes. They were escorted up to the holes and came to a halt at the order of an officer who walked, carrying a document case, behind the group. The officer took a sheet of paper no larger than the size of a scribbling pad from his case, and, after reading something from it, turned and went off. The Gestapo men made the first three men stand in line. Six soldiers armed with revolvers went up to them; the revolvers were fitted with a muffling device. Aiming at the condemned men's chests, the soldiers fired without any word of command. The three men fell. Jews were then summoned, and were thrown bayonets to cut the bonds fastening the dead men's hands; then they were ordered to throw the bodies into the first three holes, and cover them with earth. The Jews were driven over the rise again, and the next three condemned men were drawn up for execution.

These were not isolated cases. They took place with Frank's knowledge and approval. His bureaucracy of death had got off to a vigorous start. His attitude towards it seemed almost cavalier, if not directly sadistic:

> My relationship with the Poles is here like the relationship between ants and aphids. If I treat the Poles reasonably – so to speak tickle them in a friendly way – I do this in the expectation that the work they do will benefit me. This is not a political problem but a purely tactical and technical one ... In cases where, in spite of all these measures, performance does not increase, or where the slightest act gives the occasion to intervene, I shall actually not hesitate to take even the most drastic measures.

Direct military rule of Poland ceased in late September 1939. SS atrocities ordered or overseen by Himmler continued unabated. He was now Commissioner for consolidating German territory, and he and Heydrich planned to extend SS power into Poland, for instance by murdering or arresting the Polish intelligentsia and clergy, even though that meant coming up against Frank's marginally more circumspect civil administration. It served Hitler well to have subordinates divided and at war.

There were still a great number of German front-line units in the country. In February 1940 General Johannes Blaskowitz complained about the SS atrocities of the *Einsatzgruppen*. Frank intervened and personally requested from Hitler Blaskowitz's removal. Von Rundstedt, the commander of the German invasion forces, also demanded an end to anti-Jewish measures and resigned his command. He was moved to plan and then execute the forthcoming invasion of France. Hitler was loath to lose one of his best military minds.

As an aid to understanding the attitude of the German people as a whole to the Polish invasion, it is perhaps useful to consider not the mindset of the Nazi fanatics but of a different and ostensibly anti-Hitlerian figure. What the young aristocratic officer, Claus von Stauffenberg, a staunch Catholic who served in Poland with his 17th Cavalry Division, made of the wholesale slaughter of Poles and Jews is unknown. He, too, remained in Poland only a short while. He is portrayed in popular mythology (for example, in the 2008 film *Valkyrie*), as a true military prince, a man of principle who put Germany before Hitler, who preserved the heroic tradition of old world family and aristocratic honour.

But he supported the occupation and the Nazi regime's use of Poles as slave workers. He believed, in common with many of his class and background (and indeed many of the lower German classes), that the Polish lands partitioned by Poland in Russia and handed back at Versailles in 1919 should be colonised, in line with what the Teutonic Knights did in the Middle Ages. He called for a 'systematic colonization of Poland', and believed it would happen. He approved and endorsed the tyrannical occupation. In 1944, just weeks before the bomb plot, he demanded a new partition of Poland, or in other words, the frontiers of 1914.

While he approved of the racial principles of Nazism, he did after some time believe that they had become excessive and exaggerated, and that the shooting of Jews *en masse* was criminal. His wife Nina said after his death:

> He let things come to him, and then he made up his mind …
> one of his characteristics was that he really enjoyed playing
> the devil's advocate. Conservatives were convinced that he
> was a ferocious Nazi, and ferocious Nazis were convinced he
> was an unreconstructed conservative. He was neither.

Up until the German invasion of Russia, when Hitler assumed the role of supreme commander, von Stauffenberg had been favourably impressed by Hitler's military success. It was not until 1942 that he finally became convinced of the need to rid Germany of the Führer. Had military success continued, would von Stauffenberg have gone on to lead the conspiracy? Was von Stauffenberg a figure of true integrity, or was he someone who was true to the mystical, racial aristocrat principles of the post-First World War German movements – like the Thule Society – and therefore, morally speaking, a 'situationist' and an opportunist? He could see that, by getting rid of Hitler when he was losing, he could preserve German national pride, keep the German Army intact and 'honourable' and possibly prepare for the rebirth of military nationalism in another form. Would he have fought to avoid the unconditional surrender that actually came nearly a year after the plot? Many others, when the tide turned, were ready to desert the sinking ship.

While his plotting and self-sacrifice – he was willing to risk his life – won post-war German approval, a further question hangs over his 'staunch Roman Catholicism'. It, too, was very German, nationalistic and anti-Jewish. He would have approved, as did the Catholic hierarchy in Germany, of racial laws and measures against the Jews. It stopped short of physical violence and extermination.

This and other moot points are glossed over in *Valkyrie*, which makes little of von Stauffenberg's aristocratic elevation, his particular Roman Catholicism, his anti-Semitism, or his wife Nina's later assessment.

If Hans Frank turned a blind eye to the daily scores of dead Polish men, women and children, with his flurry of impressive sounding decrees with their cosmetic air of legality, his drooling subservience to and imitation of his master emerged in some quaint ways. He quickly took up Hitler's animal rights quirk. Hitler's law forbidding hunting on horseback with dogs had come into force around the same time as the Night of the Long Knives in 1934. As part of 'eternal nature', animals were to be protected from 'degenerate' or 'unnatural' life, which meant people with disabilities and of course Jews. Anti-hunting protestors would have approved of the alacrity with which, within three months of arriving in Poland, Frank signed these new laws:

It is forbidden (1) to shoot at hoofed game with buckshot or with coarse lead-shot (2) to use steel traps, self-firing devices, or night-time lures of any kind or sort whatsoever (3) to poison game …

Hunting of game is to cease 'immediately and entirely' with the exception of black deer, but including (1) other hoofed game of all sorts (2) beavers (3) marmots (Decree of 26 October 1939).

In any territory under German rule all acts whose purpose is to torment animals of any kind is an impossibility … I forbid immediately all so-called *schlächten*, the torturing to death through blood-letting of animals, whose purpose is the consumption of so-called *meat*.

While protecting beast and fowl, Frank set about immediately feathering his own nest from state funds (the Polish Government General budget, which he alone controlled): 'Dress shirts, half a dozen each, in white, silver, gray, and brown, at 7.80 marks each, were delivered, together with 156 metres of dress-shirt material and 42 metres of pyjama material at 42 marks.'

This attested to the amount of time he liked to spend in the bedroom. He charged up bars of chocolate at 50 pfennigs a bar. 'Come join me, my love,' he wrote to his wife Brigitte, now elevated to 'Queen', and indeed, *Königin von Polen* soon became her nickname. He wrote to her from his Royal Seat, Wawel Castle, that it was 'fabulous. You should see all the gold leaf around the windows, in all the rooms, the treasures here are magnificent.' He insisted, even to his powerful police chief, Himmler's deputy

Friedrich Wilhelm Krüger, that he was absolute ruler, 'at his disposal at any time – convenient to me'.

If he took a *laissez-faire* attitude towards the murder of Poles and Jews by Gestapo death squads, he placed the whole world of Polish art treasures under his personal protection. The glorious symbols of Polish cultural life were confiscated from thirty public museums and hundreds of private collections.

Hitler personally made a present to Frank of Count Potocki's chateau at Krzeszowice, name of which was changed to Kressendorff. It became the Franks' summer country residence. Frank immediately stuffed it to the ceilings with plunder from the Barycz collection of Krakow's National Museum. While many historic churches and collections were simply destroyed, Frank hijacked the leading art historian and museum director Dr Kajetan Mühlmann, dispatched to Poland to hunt out choice artworks for Göring's private collection (the number two art preservation connoisseur), and sent him all over Poland to build his own private collection.

From the famous art collection in Warsaw Castle, hundreds of precious artworks including twenty-five views of Warsaw by Canaletto, arras and Gobelin tapestries, bronzes, rich collections of porcelain and historic pieces of furniture were seized, mainly for Frank's own personal use, but also for his officials and Nazi Party functionaries. Procured for him by another art historian, Dr Posse, the director of Dresden Art Gallery, Frank also took into his 'safe-keeping' – to hang in his Wawel Palace office – Raphael's 'Portrait of a Youth', believed to be a self-portrait, and Leonardo's 'Cecilia Gallerani, or Lady with an Ermine'. With the antennae of these super-qualified PhDs alerted to art treasures, and under Frank's legal aegis, the Government General became an *Unterlebensreich* almost overnight in the last months of 1939, as Frank always called it, where larceny, black marketeering, bloodsucking, murder and execution thrived.

'Dr Frank', as the Nazi leaders always addressed him, the man who once lived with chickens in his father's flat, now took his

baths in a monstrously grand tub in the Royal Castle. On his first
visit to Warsaw Castle he tore off the silver eagles from a royal
bedchamber canopy and put them in his pocket. After desecrat-
ing and destroying ancient churches everywhere in Poland, Frank
satisfied his own private love of religious art. In specially targeted
areas, he went so far as locking hundreds of devout Poles and
Jews into revered seats of worship, such as the cathedral in Czestochowa, shrine of Poland's Black Madonna, without food or
toilets for two days and nights so that they should be irreparably
profaned. All over Poland, hospital chapels were turned into gyms
or drinking dens for German troops. Local people were forced to
smash wayside shrines and crosses. Frank brought to his palace,
and established in his music room – where he played Chopin and
Beethoven – the Czestochowa Madonna, a beautifully carved
sixteenth-century wooden statue venerated in the Church of
Our Lady in Krakow. There, German soldiers, during one mass,
also ripped out the Wit Stwosz Gothic altar, and looted nineteen
sixteenth-century paintings by Hans Suess. He dispatched chalices, pyxes, monstrances, and pitchers as gifts to flatter Hitler, who
then generously gave them to General Franco of Spain.

Frank did place the monastery of Czestochowa under his
'personal protection', although priests were terrorised and in
some cases shot, and the faithful who came to pray before the
now absent Madonna were threatened and intimidated. Frank
would in time boast how he had 'preserved' it. Otherwise,
the minority Ukrainian Orthodox faithful were incited to
violence against Polish Catholics, and later, when Germany
invaded Russia, Ukrainian Orthodoxy was supported against
Russian Orthodoxy.

This interval of Polish rape and exploitation was a honeymoon period for Frank and his wife. They were in their element.
They attended concerts and operas, entertained and supped with
all the visiting dignitaries to whom they showed off their fine
palaces and the treasures they contained, and, feverishly busy as
he was, Frank even organised chess tournaments.

He was full of himself, chubby and expansive, living richly off the land he ruled; just like a mediaeval tyrant, he even composed light-hearted lyrics of triumph. One was the 'Song of the Germans at the Lowering of the Polish Flag in the Land of the Vistula, 1939':

> *So holen wir die Flagge nieder*
> *Wie stolz and hoch sie auch geweht –*
> *Und Freiheit zeigt sich fröhlich wieder*
> *Denn alle Tyrannei vergeht –…*
>
> *Nie wieder wollen zu Sklaven werden*
> *Nie wieder beugen uns dem trügend Gaukel treiben*
> *Nie wieder dulden, dass auf deutscher Erden*
> *Die deutschen Herzen sollen Opfer bleiben!*

'Behold, we lower the flag now, no matter how proud and high above it may once have waved. And Freedom shows its happy face again, for all tyranny comes to an end … Never again shall we endure slavery, never again bow down to deceitful trickery, never again suffer German hearts to be victims on German soil!'

He depicts the conquest of Poland as a release of Germans from slavery. Below is part of a list of those whom Frank considered 'political instigators', 'shady profiteers' and 'Jewish exploiters'. This is one of twelve pages of murdered, imprisoned or deported Poles published in London in 1941–42:

Pelczyński, Ryszard; shoemaker – murdered
Perliński, Mieczyslaw; – murdered
Perylman, Natan; prisoner of war – murdered
Piach: Mayor of Śmigiel – murdered
Piątka, Felix; curate – murdered
Piech, Casimir Dr.; Prof. of Kracow – deported
Piechocki, Andrzej; – imprisoned
Pieczynis, Jerzy; – murdered
Piekara, Arcady, Dr.; Asst. Prof. of Kracow – deported
Pieszowicz, Ignacy; – pursued

Pietrzak, Wincenty; – murdered
Piętka; student – deported
Pigoń, Stanislas, Dr.; Prof. of
  Kracow – deported
Pijanowicki, Stanislaw; – murdered
Pikula; - imprisoned
Pinecki; Professor – hostage
Piotrowicz, Louis, Dr.; Prof. of
  Kracow – deported
Piotrowski, Pavel; – murdered
Pirog; Curate – arrested
Piwarski, Casimir, Dr.; Asst. Prof. of
  Kracow – deported
Plebanek; lawyer – murdered
Plichcińska, Helena; (girl) –
  imprisoned
Plutowski, Julian; tram-conductor –
  imprisoned
Platkowski, Lejba; – murdered
Plonka; Father – arrested
Pobożny; Prelate – imprisoned,
  deported
Podlarski; merchant – murdered
Poduchowski, Kazimierz; – murdered
Poduchowski, S; – murdered
Polaczek; Polish Sejm Deputy –
  imprisoned
Polednia, Paul; Parish Priest – died
  in prison
Poleszewski, Jan; – imprisoned
Pomorski; Dean – deported
Ponikiewski; landowner – murdered
Poniński, Edward; landowner –
  murdered
Poniński, Count; landowner –
  murdered
Popielewski; – imprisoned
Posmyk; Curate – deported
Potworowski; Madame – deported
Potworowski, Edward; Papl
  Chamberlain –murdered

Prawocheński, Roman, Dr.; Prof. of
  Kracow – deported
Prądzyński; Prelate – arrested
Pruchniecki, Waclaw; – murdered
Przedlacki, Józef; – murdered
Przedlacki, Mieczyslaw; – murdered
Przedlacki, Stanislaw; – murdered
Przepiórkiewicz, Ryszard; – murdered
Przepylski, Wladyslaw; – murdered
Przybysz, Katarzyna; (woman) –
  murdered
Przybysz, Stanislaw; – murdered
Puchalski, Julian; – murdered
Pulawski; Papal Chamberlain –
  murdered
Putz, Narcyz; Parish Priest –
  arrested, maltreated
Raba; Father – arrested
Racik, Czeslaw; – murdered
Raszewski; General – tortured
Raszkiewicz; Curate – murdered
Rataj, Maciej; former Sejm-Marshal,
  leader of the Peasant Party –
  tortured
Ratajczak, Józefa; (woman) –
  murdered
Ratajczyk, Ludwik; – imprisoned
Regowicz, Louis, Dr.; – deported
Reiter; Father – maltreated
Reszkak; chemist – murdered
Robel, John, Dr.; – deported
Robik, Józef; labourer – imprisoned
Robota; Parish Priest – died in
  prison
Rogaczewski; Father – died in prison
Rogoziński, Felix, Dr.; Prof. of
  Kracow – deported, tortured to
  death
Roksi, Michael; Dean – murdered
Romanowski; – murdered
Rosenberg, Leon; – murdered

Rospond; Suffragan Bishop –
   arrested, deported
Roszak; – murdered
Rosenberg, M.; – murdered
Rozental, Jan; – murdered
Różalski, Adam; Father – murdered
Różański, Adam, Dr., Prof. of
   Kracow – deported, tortured to
   death
Ruciński; Canon – imprisoned
Rybarczyk, Jan; – imprisoned
Rymer, Edward; – murdered

Ryng, Antonan; (woman) –
   imprisoned
Ryszke, Tadeusz; – murdered
Rzadki, Anthony; Professor –
   murdered
Rzetelski, Ignacy; – imprisoned
Saenger, Alojzy; – imprisoned
Salamucha, John; Father – deported
Samolewicz; merchant – murdered
Sarna, Sigismun, Dr.; Prof. of
   Kracow – deported

Resentment, described by Roman Catholics as a deep sin, and envy the root of all evil, were, it seemed, enthroned. But at no point does one detect unforced or genuine contentment in Frank with the self-gratification he now enjoyed.

Later he would confess, as he did to Dr Gilbert on 7 November 1945, that he was 'in league with the devil from the beginning'. At the time he seemed to exult in the two spirits of Goethe's *Faust* that dwelt in his breast, happily co-habiting. As Brecht put it:

> You have the rival spirits
> Lodged in you!
> Do not try to weigh their merits,
> You have got to have the two,
> Stay disputed, undecided!
> Stay a unit, stay divided!
> Hold to the good one, hold the obscener one!
> Hold to the crude one, hold to the cleaner one!
> Hold them united!

This expresses perfectly what Frank, the self-styled entrepreneur for the profit of and expansion of the Third Reich, set out to do in his exploitation of Poland.

Yet in this shameless self-indulgence, both in his egotistic aping of Hitler in his decrees with 'I' or 'we' frequently mentioned, and in his sexual licence with servants, even on one occasion with a 'Polish countess in Warsaw' there was, from the start, one problem which obstinately stuck in his gullet and provoked his greatest anger.

Dr Hans Frank (left) in SA uniform, shortly after Hitler became Chancellor of Germany in 1933.

Above: German soldiers marching into Poland, 1939.

Child in the ruins of Warsaw, 1939. The suffering of that benighted city was not over.

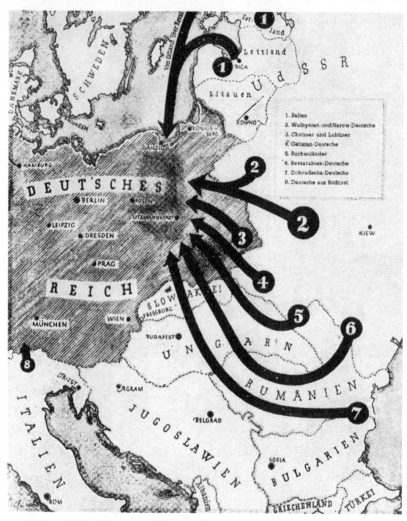

The resettlement of the Polish territories denuded of Poles by Germans (1940).

Beauftragter für den Vierjahresplan
   Der Generalbevollmächtigte
   für das Generalgouvernement
       Polen

     G B 1/40

                           Streng vertraulich !

      An

den Leiter der Dienststelle
für den Vierjahresplan,
Herrn Generalmajor Bührmann

oder Vertreter im Amt

    in   K r a k a u
         Lenartowicza 13

      Zur Durchführung der Aufgabe, die Wirtschaftskraft des
Generalgouvernements im Rahmen des Vierjahresplans planmäßig
in den Dienst der deutschen Wehrwirtschaft zu stellen, gebe
ich nachstehende

         R i c h t l i n i e n :

1.) Jm Hinblick auf die derzeitigen wehrwirtschaftlichen Be-
    dürfnisse des Reichs kann vorerst im Generalgouvernement
    grundsätzlich keine Wirtschaftspolitik auf lange Sicht
    getrieben werden. Es ist vielmehr erforderlich, die Wirt-
    schaft im Generalgouvernement so zu lenken, daß sie binnen
    kürzester Frist Leistungen vollbringt, die das Höchstmaß
    dessen darstellen, was zur sofortigen Verstärkung der
    Wehrkraft des Reichs aus der Wirtschaftskraft des General-
    gouvernements herausgeholt werden kann.

2.) Es werden von der Gesamtwirtschaft des Generalgouvernements
    insbesondere folgende Leistungen erwartet:
    a) Jntensivierung der landwirtschaftlichen Produktion vor
       allem bei den größeren Betrieben (über 100 ha) und
       planmäßige Verteilung der zu erfassenden Nahrungs-
       mittel zur Sicherstellung des durch die derzeitige
       Produktion noch nicht voll gedeckten notwendigen Be-
       darfs der Truppen, Verbände und Dienststellen sowie
       der einheimischen Bevölkerung.
    b) Weitestgehende Ausnützung der Forsten, unter vorüber-
       gehendem Verzicht auf nachhaltige Forstwirtschaft mit
       dem Ziel, etwa 1 Mill. fm Schnittholz, 1,2 Mill. fm
       Grubenholz und bis zu 0,4 Mill. rm Faserholz ins Reich
       zu liefern.

Part of an order issued by Governor-General Hans Frank on behalf of Göring concerning the economic exploitation of Poland. The demands are quite specific: 2b) for example calls for 'the utmost exploitation of the forests … with a view to supplying to the Reich 1 million m3 of sawn timber, 1.2 million m3 of pit props and up to 0.4 million m3 of pulp wood'.

The merciless execution of Polish civilians.

The Germans hang their victims in public squares. To their bodies are attached white sheets of paper on which their alleged crimes are written.

Nazi conquerors in silent Warsaw. On 5 October Hitler flew to Warsaw to take the salute at the march past of his victorious troops. The route was carefully chosen to avoid those parts of the city that had been devastated by aerial bombardment, and the streets were lined by Nazi troops to keep the crowds in check. This precaution, however, seemed unnecessary since Warsaw's population stayed indoors and the procession made its way through almost deserted streets.

Forced labour for Polish Jews. This photograph was published on 12 October 1939 in the *Illustrierter Beobachter*, less than a fortnight after the end of the Polish campaign.

The official Nazi photograph of Hans Frank (taken shortly after the war began), intended for gifts and presentations.

Below: SS Reichsführer Heinrich Himmler and Governor-General Hans Frank – dinner at Wawel Castle, Krakow. United States Holocaust Memorial Museum, No.15074

Polish civilians were subjected to on-the-spot searches as the occupying German forces sought to destroy the last vestiges of Polish resistance.

Home Army (AK) wireless operators – possession of a set was punishable by death. Muzeum Armii Krajowej

A Nazi firing squad at work in Poland.

ANGLIO! TWOJE DZIEŁO!

The famous poster, which appeared on the walls of Warsaw after its capture by the Germans, depicting a wounded Polish soldier showing a scene of destruction to Chamberlain. The caption reads: 'England, your work.'

Wawel Castle, Krakow, today; a fortified complex built over many centuries.

The Renaissance courtyard of Wawel Castle. It is believed that many of the Castle's art treasures looted by Frank have never been returned.

Governor-General Frank in the Polish town of Sanok. The 14th SS-Volunteer Division Galizien was founded here in 1943, made up in the first instance of Ukrainians. The word 'Volunteer' is misleading in that service was mandatory for wide categories of the mostly Ukrainian population.

'German snipers rarely missed' – running the barricades during the Warsaw Rising.

The last days of the Rising – an AK soldier is pulled out of his sewer refuge.

The British forged a stamp in 1943 featuring Hans Frank's head. It was to be used by Polish resistance groups to disrupt and embarrass the mail service.

Reinhard Heydrich (right), head of the Central Office of Reich Security, was responsible for imposing the Nazi regime of terror by the police in occupied Europe. In this early photograph from 1934, he is seen talking to his colleague, Alfred Naujoks.

Auschwitz – SS officers from the camp singing at their retreat at nearby Solahuette. Front row: Höcker, Höss (leaning back), Baer (arms folded), Kramer (behind Baer's left shoulder), Hoessler, Mengele (immediately left of accordionist). United States Holocaust Memorial Museum, No. 34739

About 2 miles from the original Auschwitz camp, the real 'death-factory' – Auschwitz-Birkenau – was erected.

The undeniable evidence of genocide: human ashes at Majdanek camp on the outskirts of Lublin, where the Jews of the Government General were sent to be murdered. The camp was taken almost intact by the Soviets in 1944.

The capture of Rudolf Höss, the commandant of Auschwitz. Höss would be hanged at the former Auschwitz I camp on 16 April 1947. 'I have inflicted terrible wounds on humanity. I caused unspeakable suffering for the Polish people in particular.'

Hans Frank (in dark glasses) during a recess at the Nuremberg trials.

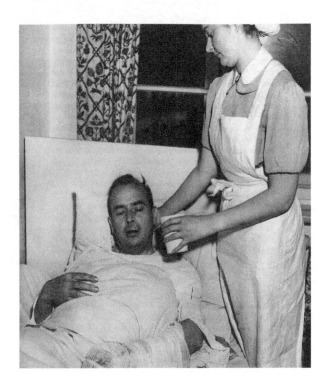

Hans Frank after his suicide attempt in May 1945, following his arrest by US troops.

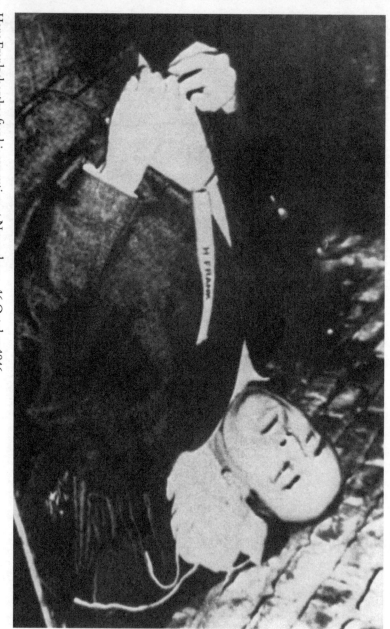

Hans Frank shortly after his execution at Nuremberg, 16 October 1946.

16

Warsaw – 'From Which Everything Harmful Flows'

> To Sonne's mind, history was eminently the area of guilt. We
> should know not only what happened to our fellow men in
> the past but also what they were capable of. We should know
> what we ourselves are capable of. For that, much knowledge
> is needed; from whatever direction, at whatever distance
> knowledge offers itself, we should reach out for it, keep it
> fresh, water it and fertilize it with new knowledge.
>
> E. Canetti, *The Play of the Eyes*

While Frank made the Royal Castle of Wawel on the hill overlooking Krakow the seat of his despotic power and the centre
of his administration, with Hitler's full enablement, his first
priority was to destroy its rival, the Royal Castle of Warsaw,
as it symbolised everything that stood for Poland. No stories
of historic buildings in Europe since the thirteenth century
in any nation evoked such loyalty and reverence in the hearts
and minds of its citizens. It was central to the often-fractured
identity of the Polish nation. In the rebirth of the country as a
republic since 1920, the Royal Castle, as the seat of the President
of the Republic, signified resurrection.

During the seizure of Warsaw in September 1939, Stuka
bombers dropped incendiaries on the Royal Castle, while heavy
artillery shelled the walls, killing Casimir Brold, chief custodian

of the art collection, as he tried to rescue paintings. The roof of the Great Ball Room collapsed, destroying the famous Bacciarelli ceiling and the magnificent stucco ornamentation. Immediate restoration was at hand, Polish conservators and architects were feverishly eager to commence work.

This was only until 18 October, when Frank visited the castle. In the Throne Room he 'ordered silver eagles from the back of the baldachin to be taken off for his own use'. The conservation work was halted; the green light given for systematic pillage.

The day before, Hitler had delivered his guidelines for future Polish policy. As well as Frank and Himmler, Rudolf Hess, Bormann, Frick, General Keitel and Heinrich Lammers, head of the State Chancellery, attended. The Government General was to 'clear the old and the new territory of the Reich of Jews, Polacks and riff-raff'. Polish living standards were to be kept low: 'All we want there is a reservoir of labour.' Himmler provided his programme for this: to put the population 'through a racial sieve', pluck racially valuable individuals out of the hotchpotch and send them to Germany to be assimilated.

No more restoration or preservation, then. The German building firm Rudolf, awarded the contract by Frank, employed several hundred Jewish workers to demolish the castle's interior and reduce the frescos, wood and marble panelling to rubble thrown out in the yard to be ruined by rain and frost. A further Bacciarelli ceiling in the Audience Chamber, which had survived, and which depicted the triumph of science and art, collapsed when the contractors cut out the floor beams. Several thousand electric light fittings were removed.

On Thursday 26 October Frank and Reichsführer Himmler visited the castle again to check on the thoroughness of its destruction. Frank noted in his diary, on 4 November, that the Führer 'approved the work of Governor General, especially the destruction of the Royal Castle in Warsaw' in a personal meeting with him. Five days later German Army sappers prepared for the *coup de grâce* by boring two rows of holes 75cm apart at a height of 1.5m from the ground to blow up the castle walls, an operation fixed for the end of December 1939. It all had to be very neat, complying with Nazi thoroughness, but the operation was never carried out.

When, in early 1940, Schlösser, Economics Chief of the Warsaw district, pointed out that Warsaw had an industrial role in the Government General, Frank defined what the limits should be. 'The principle,' he answered:

> ... to be followed is that Warsaw should never become any sort of capital and that it should not play any leading part in the struggle against the Germans. There is always present the great danger that Warsaw might become the centre of the area, at any rate in the sense of a great political force. This also has always been the Führer's opinion. According to him the ideal picture of Warsaw would be that of one great factory, one great station and one great port. If once more hundreds of Poles are able to find work and bread, and a certain stabilization takes place as far as living conditions are concerned, we would then have to pay for this with a certain amount of political anxiety. People who are hungry are forced to use up a lot of their energy in trying to satisfy their hunger. But if that hunger is satisfied then energy is released once again for other matters. At any rate it must be obvious that the so-called Polish leadership should not be allowed the slightest opportunity of declaring Warsaw the capital. If, then, we talk about Warsaw as the economic capital of the Government General, this is music for all Polish ears, but sounds a grim note in German ears, which have heard of these Polish political aspirations. There is nothing easier than building up a centralized movement from economic foundations. A city like Warsaw with its huge masses of workers provides Communism with a fruitful field for its propaganda ...

During the rest of his rule of the Government General, Frank distanced himself from Warsaw as much as he could. His last visit there was in September 1943, he recorded this in his diary, and he subsequently referred to it in his speech to Luftwaffe officers on 14 December 1943:

> In this country there is one source from which everything harmful flows: this is Warsaw. If we did not have Warsaw in the Government General we would not have four-fifths of the difficulties with which we have to contend. Warsaw is and will be a hotbed of agitation and a point which is the source of all disturbance in this country.

The logic of the *Führerprinzip* extended perfectly to the treatment of Polish prisoners of war and indeed to all Poles. The French satiric comedy *Ubu Roi* jokes that the play is set in Poland – 'That's to say Nowhere'. In November 1939 the German foreign ministry informed the neutral Swedish legation in Berlin that the Polish state no longer existed, so Sweden's mandate for protecting Polish POWs (numbering 694,000) no longer held. The following spring these Polish POWs were 'released' so they could now be treated as slave workers.

The Germans had three principal methods of terror. First, they took hostages to ensure good behaviour: for example, to prevent any outward display of Polish independence, when Krakow citizens displayed posters on 11 November, they first took one man from each house displaying a poster and shot him, then took 120 hostages to make sure it never happened again. In Warsaw they impounded prominent citizens:

> Next they employed the *lapanka*, the mass round-up, encircling blocks of houses and flats and sending tens of thousands of men under 40 to forced labour in Germany, and women between 17 and 25 to agricultural labour in East Prussia. Finally, imprisonment and execution after interrogation

in the new concentration camps, which at first were filled by Polish Christians, then, only after the German invasion of Russia and the implementation of the Final Solution, by Jews. And as Poland became the centre of this endeavour, not just the estimated 3.5 million Polish Jews.

17

Anni Mirabili of the Reich, 1940–41

Hitler was the new Napoleon, and now he was conqueror of France and Paris. He had devoured his former enemy, he had buried the *Diktat* of Versailles with rallying cries of 'dishonoured humiliation', 'broken promises and perjury'. Revenge was total, and to pay for the upkeep of German occupation the reparation was fixed at 400 million francs a day.

Admiration of Hitler was widespread, even outside Germany, not only among the French who collaborated, but even those who hated him most. After the capitulation of France, on 7 July 1940, French Nobel prize-winner André Gide wrote, Hitler was the 'sole master of the circus ring, whose sly and hidden smartness surprises that of the great captains'. He noted wryly:

> And we shall continue to accuse Germany of 'being short on psychology!' …
>
> The thing seems to me to have been prepared with consummate cleverness: France and England are like two puppets in the hands of Hitler …
>
> And what I wonder at the most is perhaps the variety of his resources. Since the beginning of the war (and, indeed, since long before) everything has taken place exactly as he had foreseen it, wanted it; even with no delay; on the appointed

day, for which he can wait, letting the engines that he has wound up and that must not explode beforehand act stealthily. No historic game is known or can be imagined that is more skilfully engineered, that involves so little chance … Soon the very people he is crushing will be obliged, while cursing him, to admire him. He does not seem to have been mistaken in any of his reckonings; he correctly evaluated the power of resistance of each country, the value of individuals, their reactions, the advantage that could be drawn from this, with everything involved …

One awaits with breathless curiosity the next chapter of this great drama he had so minutely and patiently elaborated.

I should like to be told which of his insults that made us call him a monster, which of his contempts has not been found, and proved in practice, to be motivated. His great cynical strength consisted in not deigning to take account of any token values, but only of realities; of acting according to the prompting of an unhampered mind. He has never taken any but others in with fine words.

So here he was in Paris on 21 June 1940. Heinrich Hoffmann, bright blue-eyed and with a sniffer nose, Hitler's lapdog with a Leica, scurried here and there, snapping his leader giving the Nazi salute at the Arc de Triomphe to the *Guerrier inconnu*, a change from the Führer scoffing his vegetables crowned by a poached egg, or affectionately cuffing his German Shepherd dogs. The crowd would see the victorious commander, modest in his sartorial grey, a symbol of his proletarian solidarity.

Then, at the climax of that visit, he entered Les Invalides to pay homage or crow over the red porphyry tomb of the other law-maker who had written a code for Europe to last 1,000 years. He had forgotten that Beethoven had torn up the dedication of his *Eroica* symphony to Napoleon when he was crowned emperor. Surrounded now by the twelve massive figures, each a representation of the Corsican corporal's twelve victories, the retreat of Napoleon's armies from Moscow must also have slipped his mind.

He stood there in silent deference to the greatest figure in his own internal pantheon. He entered into mystical communion, no doubt inspired by the thought that while Napoleon had failed, he now had the resources for total victory. 'New order in Europe: Change modern conditions! New Code.' There was only one decisive factor. Success. He was now the most powerful leader in the world.

While Hitler was communing, his most ardent disciple in the Government General presided over the management and recycling of the racial and indigenous slave refuse, to extract from it the maximum value and resources for the Reich's use. Frank, as everyone said, had great business sense. Poland was to be one vast recycling plant. The exemplary Nazi Reinhard Heydrich, Himmler's No. 2, blond, blue-eyed, well-bred and turned out, had outlined Frank's policy, as agreed with Hitler:

About the development of former Poland, the trend of thought is that the former German districts will become German and in addition a foreign-language district will be set up with Kracow as its capital ... The solution of the Polish problem, as has been repeatedly explained, will be carried out by distinguishing between the stratum of leaders [Polish intelligentsia] and between the lowest stratum, that of the labourers. Of the political leaders in the occupied territories, at the most 3 per cent have remained. These 3 per cent must also be rendered harmless and they will be brought to concentration camps. The operational groups [*Einsatzgruppen*] will prepare lists of outstanding leaders and also lists of the middle class of teachers, clergy, nobility, legionnaires, returning officers, etc. ... The care of the souls of the Poles will be placed in the hands of Catholic priests from the West [i.e. Germans], but these will not be allowed to speak Polish.

The primitive Poles will be included in the labour forces as nomadic labourers and in time they will be evacuated from the German-language area into the foreign-language area ... Commanders of *Einsatz* groups ... must weigh how, on the one hand, to include the primitive Poles within the framework of labour and how, at the same time, to evacuate them. The aim is: the Pole is to remain a seasonal labourer – the eternal nomad. His permanent place of residence must be in the vicinity of Kracow.

One of those nomadic labourers was Karol Wojtyla, the future Pope John Paul II, who worked in a quarry and chemical works for four years.

With hindsight but somewhat naively, one of Hitler's constant companions, his press chief Dr Otto Dietrich, wondered why his leader could not have contented himself with Danzig, the Polish corridor and territory predominantly inhabited by German elements. He should have given the Poles 'a magnanimous solution', although this would have been somewhat tempered by the Russian occupation of east Poland – soon to be ended. Hitler could never be magnanimous in victory.

In 1940 and the first six months of 1941, Hitler's armies, navies and air force tightened their hold on Norway, Denmark, the Netherlands, Belgium and Luxembourg, and Mussolini declared war on Great Britain. No resistance to the Axis Powers, joined by Japan on 27 September 1940, seemed possible. Italy invaded Greece towards the end of October, Germany Romania, then in April 1941 Yugoslavia and Greece. The culmination of all this came when on 22 June 1941 Hitler tore up the Molotov–Ribbentrop Pact, and sent his Panzer divisions to Moscow; at first they were hardly opposed. These were heady days for the Third Reich.

In Poland the killing and confiscation of property, together with mass deportation of able-bodied Poles to work in the Reich until they dropped, went on relentlessly. To defy or oppose Frank was to defy the Führer, and the Führer was Germany's law. *Ergo*, Frank's word in the Government General was law. He put his personal stamp on everything, as can be seen from his diary entry of 15 February 1940: 'All transactions between the Reich and official departments of the Government General should be conducted only through the Government General. Direct instructions from authorities in the Reich to official departments in the Government General are expressly forbidden.'

And at a conference on 8 March 1940, held in the Mining Academy:

> One thing is certain: the authority of the Governor General as the representative of the Führer and of the will of the Reich in this area is indeed strong and I have never left it in doubt that I would not allow anyone to trifle with this authority. I had all authorities in Berlin informed of this again, particularly after Field Marshal Göring had – on the 12. 2. 40 from Karin Hall – forbidden all Reich departments, including the police and including even the Wehrmacht, to interfere in any way in the official affairs of the Government General. The same applies to the attempt which the SS made once on the 15th or 16th December, when the Reichsführer of the SS wished to decree – with effect for the Government General too – that all art treasures and other works should be promised to the SS. This decree was cancelled following my protest.
>
> As far as the Jews are concerned – and this I shall tell you quite openly – they must be done away with in one way or another. The Führer once said: Should united Jewry again succeed in unleashing a world-war, it will not only be the peoples who have been egged on into war who will shed this blood, but the Jews in Europe will have their end. I know that many of the measures now being taken in the Reich against Jews are being criticized. Conscious attempts are continually being made – as can be seen from the reports on morale – to

speak of cruelty, harshness, etc. Before I continue, I should like to ask you to agree with me on this formula: as a matter of principle, we shall have pity only for the German people and for no one else in the world. The others did not have any pity for us either. And I must say, as an old National Socialist: should the Jewish brotherhood in Europe survive the war, whereas we had sacrificed our best blood to save Europe, this war would only be a partial success. My attitude towards the Jews will therefore be based only on the expectation that they should disappear. They must go. I have entered into negotiations for their deportation to the East. A big conference on this question is taking place in Berlin in January, to which I shall send Secretary of State Dr Bühler. This conference is to be held in the Reich Security HQ with SS *Obergruppenführer* Heydrich. At any rate, a great Jewish migration will begin.

He went on to say, in his closing address to the conference, that the Jews were 'particularly harmful gluttons', that there were 3.2 million of them, maybe more, and they could not all be shot or poisoned, 'but [we] will nevertheless be able to intervene in ways which will lead in some way to successful annihilation'.

Frank spoke these words in March 1940, but it was not until that fatal date of 22 June 1941 that Hitler began the war he had long dreamt of, large-scale genocide marching hand-in-hand with 'eastern clearance'. When Himmler discussed the aims of the invasion of Russia, he stated it was 'to decimate the Slav population by thirty million'. By November 1941, when Hitler promised the imminent fall of Moscow, *Einsatzgruppen* extermination units had already murdered half a million Russian Jews. Meantime, in the summer, Auschwitz Commandant Rudolf Höss had been experimenting with a new lethal gas, Zyklon B, using 500 Soviet POWs as guinea-pigs.

Auschwitz was 80km from Frank's Wawel Castle, an hour's ride. As although in Poland, it was not part of the Government General, but in territory directly controlled by the Reich. No mention of it was made by Frank, who stuck to his lofty ideals. A visitor to Wawel Castle records:

> Before me sat Frank, on his high stiff-backed chair in the old Polish royal palace of Wawel in Kracow, as if he were sitting on the throne of the Jagiellons and Sobieskis. He appeared to be fully persuaded that the great Polish traditions of royalty and chivalry were being revived in him. There was a light of innocent pride on his face, with its pale, swollen cheeks and the hooked nose suggesting a will both vainglorious and uncertain. His black glossy hair was brushed back revealing a high, ivory-white forehead. There was something at once childish and senile in him: in his full pouting lips of an angry child, in his prominent eyes with their thick, heavy eyelids that seemed to be too large for his eyes, and in his habit of keeping his eyelids lowered – thus cutting two deep, straight furrows across his temples. A slight film of sweat covered his face, and by the light of the large Dutch lamps and the silver candlesticks that ranged along the table and were reflected in the Bohemian glass and Saxon china, his face shone as if it were wrapped in a cellophane mask. 'My one ambition,' said Frank, thrusting himself back against his chair by propping his hands against the edge of the table, 'is to elevate the Polish people to the honour of European civilization.'

The visitor might well have mentioned, too, the presence of Cecilia Gallerani, the Rembrandt portrait, and the fourteenth-century Madonna with Child, all of whom kept Frank company. Had the visitor stayed to dinner he would have reported how Frank kept the best table in Europe, with the choicest food and wines, and afterwards showed him his fine, confiscated art collection: a codex of Balthazar Bens; pearl decorated ornamental vestments, a gilded chalice and ivory chest from Krakow's Wawel Cathedral and portraits by Gerard Don, Amy de Vois, Terbach, and Pinturicchio. He didn't go quite as far as Goebbels, who, in his sumptuous residence, had painted on the ceiling in his bedroom a large, luscious and naked Europa signifying the German conquest of Europe.

During this first phase of the Nazi terror in Poland there were complaints by high-ranking Christian German officers which the Führer quashed by threatening to put SS and Gestapo men in each of their military units. But, to understand a little more deeply the morals of German officers, they were not exactly *against* the Polish 'house cleaning', that is, the wiping out of Jews, intellectuals, clergy and nobility; they merely wanted it to be 'deferred' until they left Poland and could no longer be held responsible.

Frank did not mind. On the day he heard that Baron Konstantin von Neurath, the 'Protector' of Bohemia and Moravia – dismissed by Goebbels as 'a weak sneak', but defended by Hitler for being considered in the Anglo-Saxon world 'a man of distinction' (and as such he would not deprive Czechs of their racial and national life) – had put up posters in Prague announcing the execution of seven Czech university students, Frank told a Nazi journalist that, 'If I wished to order that one should hang up posters about every seven Poles shot, the forests of Poland would not be sufficient to manufacture the paper.'

While Himmler and Heydrich concentrated on the liquidation of the Jews, Frank turned his hand to liquidating his own kind, the Polish intelligentsia. The code he thought up for this was 'Extraordinary Pacification Action' or 'AB Action'; by the time Paris fell and the French signed the Armistice with the Reich at Compiegne, 'AB Action' was going with a swing. Roughly 2,000 men and several hundred women had been seized and 'summarily sentenced' – in other words, murdered. These were joined shortly by another 1,500.

We can go on cataloguing these horrors *ad infinitum*. They continued unabated and increased, with fluctuations, through his fiefdom. Yet, in that first winter of Nazi victory, desperately severe and full of heavy blizzards, more Poles and Jews died

from the effects of the weather and starvation during deportation than from firing squads and gallows. Who would not feel
pity for Himmler when he brought attention to the 'tough job'
he and his henchmen faced?

> It happened in Poland in weather forty degrees below zero,
> where we had to haul away thousands, tens of thousands,
> hundreds of thousands; where we had to have the toughness –
> you should hear this, but also forget it immediately – to shoot
> thousands of leading Poles – Gentlemen, it is much easier in
> many cases to go into combat with a company than to sup-
> press an obstructive population of low cultural level, or to
> carry out executions or to haul away people or to evict crying
> or hysterical women.

New relief was at hand promising deliverance from these trials.
German industrial efficiency, ever to the fore, ever to the rescue!
Rudolf Franz Höss, a former convicted murderer and then
prison jailor, not far off the same age as Frank, arrived on the
Polish scene like a shining knight in armour, with the rank of
colonel. Handsome, debonair, a family man, his zeal was boundless, his mind and judgement cool and deliberate. Hitler had
found yet another alter ego and *doppelgänger*.

The leading, respectable and good Christian manufacturing
company of I.G. Farben, with unlimited slave labour at its disposal, had detected the hot scent of huge profits to be made in
the marshy hinterlands of a former Austrian Cavalry barracks.
Russia would capitulate and Jewish mass extermination would
begin together in early 1942.

Hans Frank's interior life, and what really made this master Nazi
criminal tick, now comes vividly to the fore. Truly extraordinary is how, as carnage and murder multiplied, Frank began in

a curious way to diverge from the Satanic force and purity of his idol and mentor – as if he could not quite hold it all together in the way the Führer managed. There were two phases to his 'unravelling'.

The first took the form of a kind of galloping corruption of a very mediaeval and venal nature: greed and lechery. And what is perhaps even more extraordinary is that Brigitte, Frank's exemplary Aryan, Roman Catholic wife, with her later connections with Cardinal Faulhaber after the summer of 1945, the highest spiritual power in Bavaria, should now join him in black-marketeering and confiscation and enjoy the deluxe lifestyle, as well as a nepotistic salary from the Institute of German Law.

A further indulgence in Brigitte's unbelievable conduct included the pre-war affair with Frank's colleague, Dr Karl Lasch, ending at latest in autumn 1938, whom Frank had appointed Governor of Galicia since it had been relinquished by the Soviets in their withdrawal and added to the Government General. She used an official car to send her husband's officers to find art treasures in the Netherlands – carpets, pictures, sculptures, linen, food – and use its official status to evade customs and bring them back to Wawel Castle. Lasch smuggled on his own and he had at one time four cars for personal use: a Buick, a LaSalle, a Studebaker and a Packard. A former mistress betrayed him to Krüger. Brigitte had no interest in him, the only man she guarded was the husband who opened to her the doors to a life of luxury.

18

Himmler Reacts

Reichs Frank ist Frankreich.
Typical, heavy and somewhat pointless pun; literally means
'Germany's Frank is France' or a rich man (*reich* also means rich)

Now well-established as 'Satrap' of the Government General,
Frank had his private nest well-feathered and supported. He
ran (naturally) a Mercedes-Benz with an SS driver, a private
railroad car, two, if not more, palatial castles, an estate in
Bavaria, a villa in Berlin, and enjoyed unlimited food, wine
and the tobacco the Führer hated. Until he was arrested, the
Government General became his private theatre where he
could script, resource and exact backers, cast, prepare and dispose, license and play out all the themes that had made him
what he had become. He also had two stenographers at his
beck and call, taking it all down as a record of his life, fulfilling
his desire to preserve his life for posterity.

He put money aside for the future: 5,200 marks, his son reports,
into his private account at Munich's Merck and Finck Bank.
Reciprocal favours fell into his lap, for example seventy bottles of
three different vintages of Durkheimer wine from the Bavarian
Minister-President Siebert. But, as too often happens, the appetite stemming from power grew and grew and he could not resist
breaking the bounds of such restraint as cold-blooded killers like

Himmler with their quasi-divine mission imposed on themselves. And he did not exactly have a Lady Macbeth by his side. Brigitte did not 'screw his courage to the sticking place' to commit more murder. Her attitude would seem to have become, after her objection to *Kristallnacht*, similar to that of most Germans, especially the women, who so devotedly supported their spouses – not so much that she didn't want to know what was going on, but that she positively wanted *not* to know. Difficult when, like many German women, she lived in such proximity to it.

Her Polish slaves boiled up the whole fruit harvest of Kressendorf Castle, filled jars and bottled it, and had it transplanted to the Schoberhof where her five children lived for most of the time. As well as 'military provisions' loaded on to official transport, a stockpile of provisions, much aired afterwards in accounts of Frank's misdeeds, crossed the Government General's borders, as listed in one assignment: 150 pounds of beef, 45 pounds of pork, 20 geese, 50 chickens, 22 pounds of salami, 27 pounds of ham sausage. The accompanying grocery list detailed 170 pounds of butter, 105 pounds of lard, 42 pounds of coffee beans, 120 pounds of sugar, 25 pounds of cheese, and 1,440 eggs.

This was not just a one-off, but an example of a constant flow of provisions, indicative of the devastation of the slave colony. Frank reserved 1,000 eggs a month for his own private consumption. The records make reference to a preposterous 200,000 eggs Frank had preserved in lime.

Gestapolis was rife with informants, and soon Himmler, who distrusted everyone everywhere, compiled a sizeable dossier on Frank and on two of his subordinates in particular: Lorenz, Chief of the General Office of Administration in Warsaw, and Franz Lasch, the old friend of the Franks (believed to be the earlier lover of Brigitte) whom Frank had appointed Governor, first of Radow, then of Galicia.

Brigitte Frank had a passion for fur coats and for getting things on the cheap. She became quite an active visitor to the ghettos, where she could haggle for knockdown prices. Other relatives of

Frank, including his sister, followed suit, for such influential figures could buy furs and jewellery for prices fixed by themselves
(the Jews called these deals *taxatieren*, which was a prudently disguised way of saying 'confiscation'). It clearly salved Brigitte's
conscience to 'pay' for her rich trappings. On the Polish black
market a pair of boots cost 1,500 zlotys, a horseshoe nail 3 reichsmarks and 'one paint brush or a dress would buy a cow'.

One day, Frank sent Löv into the Warsaw ghetto to buy a
gold fountain pen. Or – the alternative version – Löv entered
the ghetto and bought a gold fountain pen to give his superior
as a birthday present, which he duly gave him. When this was
reported to Himmler, he had Löv arrested, for it was illegal
to trade with Jews. To save his skin, or to tell the truth, Löv
made a statement that Frank ordered him to buy the pen, at a
cost of not more than 100 zlotys. The Gestapo also accused
Löv of buying furs, presumably for Frau Frank, but this was
defended on the undeniable count that Poland's climate was
very cold in winter.

Himmler also gathered evidence to impugn Frank. One of Brigitte's brothers, Heinrich, had renounced his German citizenship
in 1934. Now living in Stockholm with Swedish citizenship he
was doing good business with his sister's colony. A second brother,
Otto, was Frank's private secretary, while the third, Marian Bayer,
acted as head trustee for the Government General textile industry. Likewise, Himmler had gathered evidence of Franz Lasch's
'gigantic corruption'.

A further factor made it imperative for Himmler to get
rid of Frank. The latter bickered and quarrelled continually
with Krüger over the chain of terror command. He repeated
in one form or another that there was no authority in the
Government General higher or stronger in influence than his.
The Wehrmacht had security functions and general military
tasks, but that was all; likewise, the police and the SS. 'There
is no state within the state here, but we are the representatives
of the Führer and Reich!' Frank also claimed that no death

sentence imposed by a summary court should be carried out without his authorisation.

But, for all Frank's blustering, police chief Krüger took his orders directly from Himmler. While Frank told his subordinate provincial governors that they, like him, had full powers, he also said they had to co-operate with the police and the SS, who were under the governors but subject to the directives of the Reichsführer SS. (It seemed a repeat of the formula by which Frank had stood up to Hitler over the murder of Röhm, then meekly obeyed.) Even so, Frank continually stood in Himmler's way, and Himmler wanted him out of it. It seemed he would get his way, with Löv's testimony against Frank, and then with Lasch's.

Hans Lammers, the Reich Minister of Justice, a much reduced function, summoned Himmler, Martin Bormann, Hitler's private secretary (nicknamed 'the typist-fucker') on whom Hitler relied more and more after Hess had gone, and Frank himself to a meeting on 5 March 1942 in Lammers' private railroad car in a siding not far from Berlin. Frank arrived from Berlin in his Mercedes; he had left behind what was known as his 'smugglers coach' in Krakow. Himmler arrived in his special train, to which Lammers' coach was coupled. Was Frank nervous at the prospect of this 'comradely interrogation'? It's hard to judge, although by this time, a slight fluttering of the eyes and twitch of the hands was already a trait. This was compensated for by 'the obscene gesture' of sticking his thumb between two middle fingers.

Lammers began the proceedings by picking up a sheaf of the complaints against Frank, including the interrogation transcripts of Löv and Lasch, which accused him, to ask for his reactions.

Frank's response, as Himmler noted in his minutes, was predictably a highly dramatic self-defence: 'Frank replied in a very theatrical way and spoke about his work and about corruption.'

Later, in his wider defence at Nuremberg, Frank complained bitterly that his struggle with the SS, with Krüger and Himmler, had been under-represented: 'No attention has been paid to the fact that when I addressed the SS and police, I was talking to my mortal enemies.'

This reeked of self-pity. His fecklessness, his conspiracy in corruption with both his wife and her lover clearly had no bounds. He had wasted no time at all setting up Lasch as a partner in plunder. Having been advanced by Frank onto the nursery slopes of legal administrative corruption, Lasch was now a medal-bedecked gangster in Lvov who aped the lords of the East, squandering state funds on Dutch limousines, which he then transported to Poland where they were illegally sold for further profit. As an example of how far a Nazi lawyer could go before hitting the Himmler buffers here is a shortened version of his CV, compiled by the historians Prag and Jacobmeyer:

Lasch, Karl, Doctor of Political Science, Doctor of Laws. Born December 29, 1904, in Kassel. Wilhelm-Gymnasium; banking apprentice, passed examinations, received his certificate of maturity. Studied economics (Cologne). June 1, 1928 in the auditing department of the Klöcker Works (Castrop-Rauxel); graduate degree, Doctor of Political Science; January 1, 1931, fiduciary for economic matters in Kassel; implicated in several civil suits on account of financial irregularities (inconclusive); March 18, 1932, oath of disclosure (bankruptcy). Winter semester 1931–32, law studies (Munich), working simultaneously for the Allianz Insurance Company. Party member (NSDAP) since June 1, 1931 (No. 547640). June 26, 1933, temporary director, and since October 1933, chief business manager, Academy of German Justice; February 12, 1934, director of the Academy. December 1934, promotion to Doctor of Laws, partially by virtue of credits earned through the irregular use of prize essays lifted from the files of the Academy of German Justice (inconclusive party-court trial). June 10, 1936, chief of the Office of Justice for the Reich. December 28, 1939, Governor of the district of Radom. August 1941, Governor of the district of Galicia; September 30, 1941, party-court trial because of various irregularities (quashed by a decree of the Führer dated April 27, 1938). January 24, 1942, committed to detention by the German Special Court in Krakow.

Lasch's deputy later commented on how 'incredibly fast' Lasch was arrested and dragged away by the SS.

It must have depressed and saddened Frank, as well as scared him rigid. Only eight years earlier, as the youngest ever Reich minister, Frank had shared a still uncompromised enthusiasm with his friend, who was three years younger, joined in mystic union with each other and the Führer:

I know why Hitler loves me. Hitler has left me alone and close to his heart, because I so appeal to Hitler's vanity. But there is a further reason. It is my secret, and it is Hitler's too. I cannot describe the ecstasy I feel, the rapture, the high peak of my emotions. This evening I am with Lasch, my colleague, and friend at the great festival concert in support of the German nation's *Winterhilfswerke* to hear Furtwängler conduct the *Freischutz* Overtures. Lasch is a handsome man, blond while I am dark; he has pale blue eyes, he is tall and lithe to my spreading frame with my pitch black eyes. In the seat beside me I am aware not only of his powerful thighs but of the German musical soul we share. These sounds cause the years of my own existence to pass me by in unspeakable emotion – this magical web of my fate strung together from point to point … And with the arousing sounds, I tremble before youth, might, hope, thankfulness. The Führer sits there too in the box with his most loyal followers, the soldier and the speaker – with Göring and Goebbels. All manner of other celebrities from Berlin are here too. Sparkling and in a mood to celebrate, the whole leadership of the Reich is present. The representatives of all lands, the bearers of names which the whole world knows. And I am among them as a Minister of the Reich –

the youngest of all. The music bears me up. Eternal Germany: now you are alive again! Wonderful Reich: now you are saved. Undying Volk: now may you remain happy! The Führer is beaming all over his face. And I am silent … lost in a dream: that he becomes us … We are identified, we are one and the same. Oh God: how fortunate you have made us, to allow this unique man, the greatest in world history, to be called ours! Generations will come and envy us, to have been our contemporaries. And what's more, I am being allowed to do my part for this man, I may call myself a colleague. Right down to the last, deepest fibre of myself, I belong to the Führer, and his wonderful movement … We are in truth God's tool for the annihilation of the bad forces of the earth. We fight in God's name against Jews and their Bolshevism. God protect us!

But saving his own skin came first. At the railroad conference, while Lasch awaited trial in Krakow, Frank denied Lasch was, or ever had been, his friend. He gave his approval, thereby asserting his authority, for Lasch to be delivered up to the court at Breslau – Himmler noted with satisfaction that 'Frank was in complete agreement'.

When at the railroad conference Bormann put in his thrust concerning Himmler's attack on Frank's nepotism, with the single (and for a Nazi, succinct) point that 'The Führer maintains the view that relatives are not to be employed by other relatives.' Frank answered that he had to express his surprise at hearing this viewpoint claimed as that of the Führer. 'That's new to me. That is completely new to me.'

He would dismiss his brother-in-law Marian on 1 August and convince him to join the infantry. In fact, Marian received a four-and-a-half-year jail sentence for black-marketeering and died soon after he started serving of a weak heart.

Frank went on giving reassurances, which apparently made Himmler 'withdraw' his reservations about him. The rapprochement, or capitulation, of Frank was such that Himmler could also report, 'Frank agreed without hesitation that henceforth and immediately a state secretariat would be established for ... Krüger for all questions relating to the police and to the strengthening of German culture.'

Although Frank had asserted in his defence that 'only a ruthless determined corps of representatives worthy of the Reich can maintain administrative authority, as a tiny minority in a land of 16 million people full of murderous animosity towards them' – perhaps a veiled assertion that they deserved what they could grab to keep them happy – he had been utterly humiliated. Even Brigitte had written a pleading letter to Himmler, to which he referred without revealing its contents.

The meeting ended with Frank inviting Himmler to Krakow to 'discuss our future common enterprise', and with an expression of his happy anticipation of the visit. While Frank had believed at one stage that he would not possibly return to his post in Krakow, the outcome strengthened his position, for it was clear that it was Hitler who kept Frank there – so Himmler would never be able to unseat him. Hitler defended his decision, which reflected the fact that the higher you are in government, the harder it is to sack you, by maintaining to Goebbels that Frank had an impossible job and there was no suitable replacement. Just to make his hold on his private kingdom even more certain, Frank now wrote to Lammers:

> Should you ever again hear the assertion that Löv bought a gold fountain pen in the ghetto under the pretext that it was for the Governor General and that it was to cost no more than one hundred zlotys, please be assured that the following are the simple facts of the case. The officials and employees of the Governor General's office wished to present me with a fountain pen for Christmas, 1940, a pen that could be used every day for signing my official correspondence ... Consequently, I have not been informed about the details of its purchase.
>
> As to the purchases made by my wife and/or my sister in the Government General, the usual regulations apply,

according to which every German from the Reich within the
Government General has been permitted to make purchases
in compliance with the general moderation demanded by the
present situation, so long as the supplies were available in the
Government General, this procedure is in line with practices
in effect in all occupied territories, in the East as in the West,
in the North as in the South.

Löv got off relatively lightly, which is to say he was never heard of
again, so was unlikely to have been executed. Not so lightly maybe,
he probably died on the Russian Front. Lasch was not so 'lucky'.
On 9 May 1942, he was charged by the Attorney General at the
Special Court in Breslau (verdict demanded by prosecution: death
sentence by reason of corruption, criminal foreign-exchange dealings, black marketeering, etc.). He wrote to his sweetheart, whom
he was shortly to have married: 'In one hour I shall be no more.
After settling all other matters I am sending my final letter to you,
so I might be with you at the hour of my death.' He continues with
a clear reference to Frank: 'I have been abandoned and betrayed
by all; in my despair, I know I have done much wrong and would
in any case have faced harsh punishment.' Did he commit suicide
or was he executed? 'How I would have loved to experience the
German Reich in all its splendour and glory after the war.'

Frank, his betrayer, recorded that he died on 6 May 1942, in
a clearly false retrospective diary entry. The true time and date
was 4.45 p.m., 3 June 1942 – 'June 3, 1942, Lasch was executed
on the orders of Himmler, without judgment having been rendered.' It could be, if it was true Lasch had been Brigitte's lover,
that Frank had no qualms about the departure of what he called
'my blond rascal'. Or had Lasch been given up by Brigitte, who
had heard of his engagement and marriage plans?

When the SS stopped Lasch's illegal traffic at the German
border they had found his father in the vehicle: 'I have forgiven
my parents,' he had added in his last letter, in the hope of their
reprieve, 'because they were only fools of fate.'

19

Redemption – The Real Gretchen

'My Lilli is back again,' Frank recorded ecstatically in his diary entry of May 1942. How they had first remade contact since the 1920s is not known. Frank, in his pompous mode, almost apologises for including this in his self-important chronicle. 'But one event seems to me worthy of note within the framework of this diary: Lilli has re-entered the realm of my psyche.' Correspondingly, she re-entered the realm of his flesh and senses:

A few weeks ago she told me in a letter that her only son was missing in Russia … He was a junior officer in a Panzer tank division. Consequently we met on May 6 for the first time in twenty years. In Bad Aibling. At her home. Immediately we burst into uncontrollable flame. We were reunited once more, so passionately that now there is no turning back. On Monday, May 11, we were truly united in Munich – and the same thing, all day long, on May 12 …

Fate or destiny is something which figures much in the view Nazi personalities had of themselves. Hitler believed in it, and so did Frank. Both had, as Frank reported, showed an early love of Schopenhauer, the Danzig-born German philosopher whose ideas on race, euthanasia, and the triumph of the will were useful and attractive to the Nazis – and could be usefully distorted.

Strangely enough, Schopenhauer's ideas about heredity also played out to a recognisably significant extent in the psychology of both Frank and Hitler, who must, if one has even only a slight attachment to Freud's influential theories of the subconscious, have been unconsciously following the pattern of their parents' behaviour. Schopenhauer, whose father had hurled himself to his death from the attic of his house in Hamburg, believed a person inherited the degree of intellect they enjoyed through their mother, and through their father the elements of their personal character. Was this true of both Hitler and Frank?

Both of Frank's parents had been more educated than Hitler's. His spirited mother had run off with a teacher while his father, a weak character, had turned in his life to venality and corruption. Hitler's father was cruel, humiliated him, and had been – although this is disputed – frustrated by him in his attempts to make contact. Hitler had displayed as a child, it seemed, distinct traits of what later became known as autism.

A further similarity linked Hitler and Frank, which also attested to the underlying and ever present influence of Schopenhauer. This was the special status enjoyed by music. Schopenhauer not only saw music as a sublimation of, or diversion from, the grim everyday reality of life, but also as a pure expression of the will itself, not copying ideas and forms as did the other arts.

Where Frank and Hitler differed in their attachment to Schopenhauer's notions, and parted company, was in their conceptions of love, which of course is the basis of Christian belief. Hitler had the Schopenhauer will-in-itself to stay alive, but it stopped in him as an end in itself, he never responded to the second part of Schopenhauer's will directive, the will to reproduce. Schopenhauer's illegitimate only child was born and died in 1819, so Hitler may have felt in good company (and both adhered to a supremacy of the will, taking precedence over reason).

Schopenhauer saw love or sexual desire as an immensely powerful force in human affairs, as Frank did, and wrote: 'The ultimate aim of all love affairs ... is more important than all other aims in man's life; and therefore it is quite worthy of the profound seriousness with which one pursues it.'

In the midst of his dire setbacks of 1942, with the hounds of Reich hell at his heels, almost sure he would come to a sticky end and aware that Nazi fortunes on the battlefront were at a turning point – he foresaw that ultimately the Third Reich would topple – Frank plunged headlong into the fulfilment of an early sexual passion.

The danger in his life was now extreme. It was the stuff of third or fifth act opera, and his vivid psyche and love of words orchestrated it as such. Frank at this time even wrote verses about himself which Richard Strauss, a frequent guest at the Wawel (who had a decade before written an open letter demanding the expulsion of Thomas Mann from the Reich), set to music.

But with Lilli, first and foremost, 'It was a solemn and transfigured reunion of two human beings who ignited one another and whom nothing could restrain for long.' Even God had got in on the act: 'May God give gracious assent to our union.'

It is just possible, however, to interpret the whole reunion in a different way:

20 April 1942

Himmler's second in command, Higher SS and Police Leader Friedrich-Wilhelm Krüger, a tall, commanding classic SS type, came to him to discuss the matter.

'Krüger, What do we do with our friend, Governor Frank? As we have shown, this evidence is not enough. Hitler will want more. Treason. A plot to eliminate him. Can we find evidence of some mental incompetence, sexual deviation, adultery maybe.'

'With all respect, simony and graft, corruption, aren't these enough, mein Reichsführer? The rampant nepotism. See here – the numerous jobs for the family. His brother-in-law is managing director of a Polish firm ... and then going back, you know how he behaved as Bavarian Minister of Justice, still practising and taking fees for his own law practice, with a father who'd been disbarred from practice.'

'Frank has promised to end the nepotism.'

'To turn to what he puts his name to and endorses in the occupied Government General. Experimental use of aborted foetuses. Jewish women for the German chemical industry. The placentas of Jewish women for I.G. Farben, used for cosmetic products to make German women beautiful. The Poles are not allowed to buy German cosmetics.'

'We all agree with that,' observed Himmler. 'The Führer believes in organic German women.'

'Then there is the Polish countess. In my investigation I found he shares her with an unknown SS officer.'

It was almost impossible for the white-faced Himmler to turn more pale.

He sank into greater inscrutability than usual.

'Who told you?'

'The concierge of the Warsaw house where they met.'

'We pass on this one. That was me. More to the point is treason: some of his recent public utterances on a lecture tour. Preaching respect for the law. Attacking the growth of police power on German soil. Giving criminals against the Reich the right to defence and to state their own case.'

'I would remind you, mein Reichsführer, that although he's a liberal, Frank is Germany's top lawyer. He drafted all our Reich laws. The Führer needed him to give the Reich its legality. His words on how the Führer's will and the law are one are enshrined forever in our history.'

Himmler took off his metal-rimmed glasses and passed a hand across his brow.

'Frank has had his uses. The Führer, who never committed a word to paper, and lived on his own divine intuition, was flattered by this legal wizard who commanded every last piece of litigation and judicial precedent in the book. I don't think he has ever been so heavily flattered by an intellectual. But there is one way to entrap Frank, to make him dance to our tune. If there is one thing our Führer will not tolerate, it is marital infidelity. Look what he did to Goebbels … He stripped him of all power, and had his mistress commit suicide. We have to make for our dear Stanislaus a honey trap: an early sweetheart, someone he has never got out of his system. Someone to appeal to his innocence, his romantic innocence and his vanity. Cherchez la femme, Krüger.'

'Lilli – Lilli Gau.'

They fetch her there, blonde, tall, still young-looking (even though her recently deceased son had been Frank's age when they first met years before) without the layers of corruption, deceit, and self-indulgence that had enlarded the Governor General into flabby dissolution.

'Herr Reichsführer, how can I help you?'

'Your son, an officer in the 42 Panzers, died a hero, Frau Gau. You are a widow. I will see to it he is suitably decorated, and that you are well provided with a widow's pension.'

'Yes? And …?'

'I have a task for you.'

Lilli wrote to Hans and suggested a meeting in Bad Aibling. He took a few days off. The answer was yes, they get on well – only too well. He was champing after many years of dutiful congress with Brigitte.

Here they are in the Hansibauer Hotel on the shores of the Tegernsee in a luxurious room overlooking the lake, where his mentor Röhm was picked up by Hitler, and Röhm's Number Two, Edmund Heines, was snatched from his bed and taken outside to have his blood splattered all over the balcony. For him it is a first, an unexpected departure from having sex with Brigitte in marital fidelity to provide the Reich with good Aryan stock.

'I wanted to see you again. Look at me, Hans. I'm a plant. Do you understand? Himmler has sent me here to watch you and compromise you, so Hitler will dismiss you for marital infidelity. You remember what happened to Dr Goebbels when he took a mistress. Hitler forced him to go back to his wife and family and then, well, the mistress committed suicide – whether on Goebbels' order, who knows.'

Frank laughed in that strange way that shook his whole body. 'Couldn't ask for a more delicious honey trap. Look, Lilli, they are children, and I am invincible. But why did you agree to my dear Heinrich's plan?'

'I really wanted to see you again. To make up my own mind – after so long. Also, separated from my husband and with my son dead, what do I have to lose?'

'I will divorce Brigitte.'

'The Führer will never let you.'

20

The Sex Life of King Stanislaus

She had no orgasm when you came – when I came.

She had no lofty sensation when you were lying on top of her, fat as you were – not even at the time you were siring me.

No memoir of a father, no intimate life of an important Nazi leader begins quite like the opening words of that written by Frank's fifth child, Niklas, born in 1939. His three other siblings, the two daughters and middle son, Michael, died at relatively young ages, while Norman, the eldest, more reticent than Niklas, who devoted much of his life to writing books and articles about his father, remained so deeply affected by his nefarious parents, that he did not want to have children so that 'the name of Frank should bid this world farewell'. The Frank children made a pact they were not going to recover any of their father's assets as they were 'loaded with guilt'.

Niklas piled up detail after detail, often obscene and even pornographic, in order to strip his father and lash him with the impulses of his rage and anguish. It was a desire to humiliate his father in the most public way, or was it something deeper, to atone for his own desperate deprivation of not having a father he could love and value? He had a father with whom he could not connect in any way.

Niklas becomes – to my mind with justifiable and often highly
original wit and fantasy – carried away with what must have
been almost impossible for a young, sensitive child to embrace,
the extent and horror of his father's cruelty and inhumanity.
He heroically, as an articulate and gifted adult, confronts it and
frees himself from its corrosive force in what is a splendid and
certainly shocking act of catharsis, which is to make him very
unpopular with many of his countrymen. In any attempt to
look at Frank from within, and to show at least a little sympathy towards the 'internal sovereignty' of this tyrant, we often
have to discount the emotional impact of Niklas' rejection of
his father's life and legacy. His relationship with and judgement
of his mother is not so unforgiving. In his book *Meine Deutsche
Mutter* he writes: *Ich hab sie verzweifelt geliebt. Und um ihr sattes
Leben beneidet.* 'I loved her desperately. And was envious of her
full (opulent) life.' Did Lilli know of her lover Hans' obscenities
produced for the Nazi machine and stuck in his diary or mentioned in his speeches? 'Kill without pity all men, women and
children of Polish race and language. Only in such a way will we
win the vital space we need.' Again, the force of Thomas Mann's
explanation of Nazism in *Doctor Faustus* carries conviction. We
hope she did not. Or did she know and turn a blind eye? Or did
she not want to know?

What is unbelievable is that Frank, now at the height of
the Nazi struggle for world domination, with Hitler about
to order thirty-five divisions to commence the attack on
Stalingrad, veers into an unchecked private passion, a potential
liebestod release in which he risks everything. It represents in
some ways the identification in *Doctor Faustus* of the total self-
abandonment of the German artistic soul for the hubristic folly
of the Third Reich.

How Frank, our paradigm of Nazi Germany, dealt with
this rebirth of love, brings us to the most fascinating chapter
of Frank's life. Hitler and the Nazi hierarchy are intimately
involved – even at that most crucial moment, the tipping point

of the war, when Hitler's good fortune is about to change cata-
strophically and irrevocably.

Did Brigitte Frank confront or nag Frank concerning the cruelty
and terror she saw around her on all sides? The role of women
in Nazi Germany in supporting Hitler is sometimes ignored or
glossed over. Nazism had successfully created an atmosphere of
undefined terror and every individual must have known of the
confinement of hundreds of its opponents; Brigitte had questioned Frank when *Kristallnacht* happened, and she could never
have ignored the signs everywhere of slave labour and murder.
Who could, with their eyes truly open? Primo Levi:

> In a circular dated November 9, 1941, and addressed by the
> head of the Police and the Security Services to all Police
> officials and camp commandants [in Germany], one reads:
> 'In particular, it must be noted that during the transfers on
> foot, for example from the station to the camp, a considerable
> number of prisoners collapse along the way, fainting or dying
> from exhaustion ... It is impossible to keep the population
> from knowing about such happenings.'

There is a revealing detail in the diaries of Eichmann, *Ich, Adolf
Eichmann* (which admittedly are of dubious provenance taken as
a whole) concerning Frank and the 'Jewish question':

> ... a note of 13 October, 1941, on a discussion of the General
> Governor Dr Hans Frank with Reich Minister Alfred
> Rosenberg, shows the change [in strategy towards the Jews]
> ... 'the General Governor then came to talk of the pos-
> sibility of the deportation of the Jewish population of the
> Government General to the occupied eastern territories.
> Reich Minister Rosenberg pointed out that similar desires

had already been brought to his attention on the part of the
military administration in Paris.'

This surely implies that Frank was *active* in the decision-making
process – he was second-guessing the plans in the minds of
his superiors.

Brigitte, in support of her husband, maintenance of her luxurious lifestyle and her casual exploitation of the ghettos had
also made her pact with the devil. How different was she from
millions of German women, despite the privileges she enjoyed?
The nineteenth-century Christian tradition, including both
the Lutherans and Catholics, had influenced Reich women to
remain wholly subservient to their husbands and consider them
their masters. The Reich repudiated the religion, but continued the tradition of subservience. Vanished were the women
of classical or Christian mediaeval character, who were more
independent. German women, 3.5 million of them, had joined
the NS *Frauenschaft*. Many made use of abortion on demand, in
legally prescribed circumstances according to Hitler's race laws
to curtail procreation of allegedly feeble-minded and inferior
peoples. Goebbels decreed that the 'mission of women is to
be beautiful and to bring children into the world,' a mission
fulfilled by most with zeal. Yet they were, in the truest sense,
accomplices rather than victims. At every level women operated
at the centre of Nazism, sustaining male morale. So when the SS
man came home from exterminating enemies, he entered a doll's
house of *ersatz* goodness in which he could escape from his evil
actions. The emotional work done by women contributed to
stability. How complicit they were came to be largely ignored;
when the war was over the Allied Control Commission failed
to look into Nazi sterilisation programmes and the part German
women played in them.

But, like her husband, Brigitte also played both sides of the
street, so in Bavaria she was an upright *Reichsdame*. The first children, born in 1927 and 1928, were christened shortly after birth.

The other three, born in 1935, 1937 and 1939, were baptised in the autumn of 1944 by Father Anton Haas. Their earlier family priest, Rupert Mayer, was, according to Niklas, an honest and devout man, an example of faith and integrity. He was a brave opponent of the Nazis who was silenced and banished to a monastery by Faulhaber. In the Government General, it seemed, Brigitte was a collaborator who relished every privilege she could lay her hands on – and convinced herself she was helping poor downtrodden Jews by buying goods at her own price (or extorting them). Niklas would not even allow her this much, saying she never convinced herself she was helping the Jews. She simply didn't care what happened to them. But the Jew who sold to her thought she would help them to survive.

She kept and fed her relatives in outbuildings in the Schoberhof, a Bavarian farmhouse with 5,000 square metres of land, renovated inside in pompous style. She enjoyed the free labour of chef, chambermaids, nursemaids and kitchen-maids, paid from state funds, if Germans, or imported as slaves from the Ukraine, right up to the end of the war. Two months before Frank left Krakow, his office manager wrote to Brigitte, 'I have been able to ascertain that your desire to continue employing Polish and Hungarian workers at the Schoberhof, but at the same time have them reported as being employed in Krakow, is no longer permissible,' – an example of what came to be known a lifetime later in the United Kingdom as 'flipping'.

The household held Brigitte in some contempt and defied her frustrated attempts to have them address her as 'Frau Minister'. One servant later related how, at an elegant dinner for Nazi leaders, the chef urinated into the Polish Meissen porcelain tureen, which had been filled with asparagus soup. Below stairs they fell about with laughter as it was served. Brigitte's unknowing response was 'Tell the *maître* his soup tasted delicious.'

On 18 May 1942 Frank told Brigitte 'the most gruesome things'. She wrote this in a letter to an unspecified 'correspondent' in the Reich Chancellory (Lammers, one assumes, who would have told Hitler). 'Details later, but only private … the utter abyss.'

Frank now wanted the divorce. She then went on to write in her diary, 'Dear Lord, protect him. What is our fate to be? Have we come to a great turning point?' She turned it round so that she was sorry for Frank in his predicament. A fortnight later, on 3 June 1942, in the music room of the Wawel, the following conversation took place:

HANS:	Tell me, Brigitte, how long have we been married?
BRIGITTE:	Let's see … seventeen years …
HANS:	My, that's a long time. Tell me, wasn't I always chivalrous towards you?
BRIGITTE:	You were in a position to offer me an agreeable life.
HANS:	Wasn't I always chivalrous towards you?
BRIGITTE:	You were generous, and I've been comfortable.
HANS:	Well, Brigitte, I don't love you anymore.

Brigitte continues:

I had to stop myself from fainting, my legs were weak. 'But Hans, what are you saying, that can't be true, etc. …' My diary entry reads: 'He doesn't love me anymore. The earth is opening up beneath my feet … I am unhappy beyond words.' He wants a divorce. He asks whether there isn't someone else in my life, too … was there someone else who loves me and whom I love? And then he asks whether I realize how often and with how many women he has already deceived me in our marriage.

She can't reply. 'Everything suddenly seems so disconnected, so crazy, and I truly began to doubt my husband's sanity.' So far as can be ascertained, she then threw a hysterical fit, with the result that Frank abjectly 'apologized for everything, was so charming to me, and a scene of reconciliation followed'.

White-faced, shaking, Hans next day called her into the music room and tells her Lasch has shot himself to death. Divorce is no longer necessary. 'Evening harmonious' she records. Next day, there was a new twist 'because Hans very upset with me. Said I was to blame for his unhappiness. Someone told him I was not a good National Socialist; and he made out as if they had advised him to get a divorce.' She then, ahead of the game, said she was prepared to be divorced immediately if he demanded it. 'Jan 6. Hans came and brought me a wonderful piece of jewellery as a talisman to make up for all the suffering he had so inexplicably caused me.'

In this whirligig of fearful emotions, Frank, recovering some of the purer, more innocent feelings of his youth, now returned to the idea of legality and defence of the law that from time to time stirred his conscience. He gave four lectures in June and July in Berlin, Vienna, Heidelberg and Munich, the theme of which was the defence and security of the law within the state. This flurry of intensely championing the law needs to be seen not only in the context of his newfound passion for Lilli, but also against a backdrop of a rapid deterioration of internal security and administrative competence in the Government General itself. This is as far as his crusading zeal went; but it was something, presumably at least in the eyes of his paramour Lilli:

> The idea of a state without law or against the law has always
> been unthinkable. The state and the law, as the history of the
> world shows, form a whole ... I believe it is possible to recon-
> cile an authoritarian system of government with the security
> of the law in its widest sense.

This was delivered in the huge auditorium of Berlin University. At once it invited intervention from Bormann, secretary to the Führer. Niklas reconstructs this:

BORMANN: The Führer heard about your speech yesterday.
FRANK: *Jawohl*.
BORMANN: The Führer does not find it proper for you
          to be delving into abstract ideas about justice
          during this serious period.
FRANK: *Jawohl*.
BORMANN: You're getting me all mixed up. So then, the
          Führer ... etc. ... delving into ... Instead, he
          would like to have morale-building speeches
          from his leaders.
FRANK: *Jawohl* – although I would like to add, Herr
          Reichsleiter, that we are dealing here with
          only closed sessions at the university.
BORMANN: Do you think we don't know that? The people,
          however, are perfectly satisfied with the justice
          system they already have. The will of the Führer,
          that's their justice. It's what you said yourself
          everywhere, ten years ago. Heil Hitler, Frank.

In Vienna, however, undeterred, Frank delivered that same message, to prolonged and strong applause: 'There can be no Reich without justice, there can be no justice without judges, and no judge can proclaim justice without the genuine power that has been granted him from above.' At Heidelberg on 21 July 1942 Frank went further: 'There must never be a police state, never. Every fibre of my being rejects this.'

The consequences were that Hitler stripped Frank of his remaining legal status and posts in Germany. Henceforth, his Germanic feeling for the sacredness of law, which had no place in Poland, became an increasingly unfulfilled desire for rectitude, and later turned into a plea for forgiveness on the basis of sensitivity and moral feeling. Was it just a ploy? Was it hypocrisy, an attempt to hide a rotten soul – rather like Eichmann confessing he could never be a doctor as he hated the sight of blood?

So now Hans can be seen to be following his desires and covering his tracks at the same time: sexual fulfilment with Lilli; sublimation of will *à la* Schopenhauer with endless operatic gala evenings at the Krakow opera; face-saving barbarity and murder to keep Himmler and Krüger placated; compliant domestic behaviour with wife and family, in order not to incur the tantrums of the terrifying Brigitte (and to keep her exalted role without divorce as 'Frau Minister' – during Frank's absence on his German lecture tour she entertained Edda Mussolini at Kressendorf). Finally, more placatory noises and even minor co-operative action towards the Poles, giving more autonomy to their leaders, and fostering Polish art and music, with an eye to the future.

He now professed himself against arbitrary labour procurement, for it was clear that simply rounding up Poles at random led to sabotage. He started an inquiry into improving the wages and work conditions in his colony. In April 1942, he opposed the replacement of law courts for 'foreigners' (i.e. Poles), with SiPo (*Sicherheitspolizei*, Security Police) summary courts, writing to this effect to the Reich Chancellory. He saw himself as 'an ice-cold technician', who wanted the social machinery of warfare to function at top efficiency. By October he was delivering speeches thanking Polish farmers for their efforts with the harvest. Love was working wonders for him, but these 'reforms' counted for little.

However, he never succeeded in playing the subtle political role of appealing to all shades of Nazism. On 7 July he demanded a divorce from Brigitte, saying his physical needs were taken care of by Gertrude (the other revived girlfriend) and Lilli. When Brigitte objected and clung to him he abused her. He then, so the official records claim, tried to resign twice (later, with his usual exaggeration, he claimed this was fourteen times). Then he once again backtracked, after pointing out how much he had done for the Government General, by stating that the one and only condition on which he would remain in his post was if the Führer expressed his emphatic trust in him and his future actions. The Führer apparently did so. Frank certainly made Brigitte happy again when he told her that Hitler was letting him keep the job.

She might have thought she had won, but Frank did not stop seeing Lilli. Brigitte found his diary in which he continued to write of the affair. He made a contract of employment to take Lilli as a part-time personal assistant in Krakow. Brigitte quashed this. He continued to see Lilli, while Brigitte kept a record of her battle to keep him and avoid the divorce he repeatedly demanded. Between 28 April 1942 and 12 March 1943 he made fourteen trips in his railroad car to Germany, a total of 170 days spent for the most part with Lilli.

Brigitte found it necessary or consoling to record on 3 January 1943 that Frank had sex with her at the Schoberhof. She wrote to a specialist in racial law to find out if there were grounds for suspicion – voiced by others, she said – that Lilli was Jewish. She wrote to Lammers asking if it was true that he and Himmler – or even Hitler – had demanded she divorce Frank. She won her obsessive mission to keep her husband, 'to save [him] from [his] own unhappiness'.

Hiding the fact he was meeting with Lilli and enjoying his affair, he patched up the outward form of his marriage so he and Brigitte could keep their privileges. He had other affairs, too, during this period, not only with Gertrude, in Krakow.

It is implied, through Brigitte's appeal and correspondence, and the letter Frank finally instructed his lawyer to write to Brigitte, that Hitler and Himmler were involved:

> On behalf of the plaintiff I withdraw the petition. In the matter of the resolution of his matrimonial status the plaintiff relies for the present on the fairness of the Führer. The legal separation of the plaintiff from the respondent, however, is not affected by this decision and shall remain in effect. Nor does the plaintiff relinquish his right to an eventual divorce.

Brigitte had the last word:

> After stating in a letter that her husband withdrew his divorce
> petition of 7 June, she complained certain individuals had
> been spreading false rumours and evil statements about her
> and that her honour as a woman had been attacked. She has
> been accused in connection with Governor Lasch, and that she
> dealt illegally in furs and diamonds with him. It was, she said,
> claimed that her youngest child, Niklas, was fathered by Lasch.

She then declared – a much-quoted statement for which she is
likely to be remembered forever – 'I'd rather be widowed than
divorced from a Reichsminister.'

The 'legal separation' turned out to be a farce. She and Frank
more or less stayed together. The affair with Lilli lasted to the
middle of 1944 at least, if not longer. Faust and Gretchen had
become Tristan and Iseult, living out their adulterous and forbidden passion. Lilli wrote: 'I am constantly with you in my thoughts.
You accompany me in all my paths, in everything that makes up
my being. You, my own Hans, my happiness and good fortune, my
life. I love you, unutterably, and I am ready for any sacrifice.'

This was in the summer of 1944. Germany by then was on
its knees, with many more millions dead than two years before,
when they had resumed their relationship. 'Summer sunshine,
shimmering lake,' she writes on a card from Bad Aibling, 25km
south-east of Munich – 'Where are you? Your Lilli.'

After the final defeat, when Frank was arrested she refused, in
spite of his frantic requests, to meet him, although she attended
his trial. She became reconciled with her estranged husband,
dying in 1977 at the age of 77.

Meantime, the complications in the Government General multiplied. Frank was forced to supply 120 men from his staff to

the Wehrmacht, and now, given the decline in Government General food and industrial production, he began to temper his more homicidal policy towards Jews and Poles with conciliatory talk, such as that it was an error to murder *all* Jews on German-controlled territory while the war was still not won.

Earlier in that transitional year of 1942, and before the 'Zamosz experiment', a project for a more reliable and utilitarian means of preserving rather than destroying Polish labour, he had at least been savvy enough to realise Hitler's exploding obsession with a 'complete racial and political homogeneity' was taking precedence over military victory and both would soon be in jeopardy.

In November 1942, Rommel's armies in North Africa were in full retreat following the battle of El Alamein. The Germans invaded unoccupied Vichy France and the French Navy scuttled its fleet at Toulon. Frank claimed later that Hitler must have known by 1941 that he was in danger of losing the war.

By the end of 1942 this began to become clearer with the encirclement of General Paulus' Sixth Army at Stalingrad. Here, offered 'honourable' surrender by the Russians, Hitler refused Paulus' option of a break-out to the West, and ordered him to stay and win victory. Twenty-nine thousand German casualties had been evacuated by air, but Göring's Luftwaffe could no longer supply support, although Göring had promised it.

As a distraction, Göring invited Speer and his staff on 12 December to the gala reopening of the destroyed Berlin State Opera House with a production of *Die Meistersinger*. Hitler ordered the Sixth Army to fight to the last man on 12 January and the last phase of the battle began. The Russians opened a bombardment with 5,000 guns. When the Soviets had reduced the German Army of 285,000 men to 91,000, Paulus surrendered (of this spent force only 5,000 ever returned). With this self-inflicted defeat Hitler entered his impaired and psychopathic last phase. He ranted against Paulus: 'He should have shot himself ... Even as Varus ordered his slave, "Now kill me" ...

Life is the Nation. The individual must die anyway ... a man like [Paulus] besmirched the heroism of so many at the last minute.'

The tide had definitely turned. German radio announced the defeat with a roll of drums and the second movement of Beethoven's Fifth Symphony. Four days of mourning followed.

What would faithful disciple Frank do? Now back as Faust at the top of his game, but only with a limited span left; he had enjoyed Helen of Troy, his Lilli, as long as possible.

He had an eye to putting his own survival well above that of his nation in the deteriorating situation, which on 9 February 1943 Goebbels called for 'total all-out war'. How he set out to do that showed once again both the intellectual skill and the moral corruption of a man whose mind had been completely deformed by his satanic leader.

While in Berlin, the Reich leaders, led by Göring, jockeyed and speculated how they might take power away from Hitler and replace him, in Poland Frank set in motion his own agenda for survival. Germane to this, he had also began to recognise, or so he claimed later, that:

> ... we are the symbols of an evil that God is brushing aside ... I began to come to my senses in 1942, and realised what evil was embodied in him [Hitler]. When I protested against terror measures in public at that time, he deprived me of military rank and political power – but he let me sit as the figurehead Governor General of Poland, to go down in history as the symbol of the crimes in that miserable country.

A ridiculous episode at the time illustrates how Hitler still outranked his minion, and kept him in his place.

There were so many driving accidents during the Nazi war years that they were taking their toll of leading personalities.

Hitler, always a lover of fast cars, who preferred his beloved Mercedes to all other vehicles – he made a point of attending the annual motor show – reacted by ordering a 25mph speed limit in all towns. It became law that no car should overtake the Führer's, even if he was travelling at a snail's pace. This often caused traffic jams.

One day Frank, impatient at being stuck behind the cavalcade in a Munich street, overtook the Führer in his own Mercedes. Hitler reacted with fury. He ordered Frank's Mercedes to be confiscated on the spot, and threatened every other government and party leader with the same treatment. It should be satire, but alas it was all too real.

21

L'uomo Universale

Frank imagined himself an all-round man in the Renaissance (the new German Renaissance) spirit, a Leonardo, a Machiavelli, or, at the very least, a Goethe. The art-robber and gifted pianist was also a chess master, although he makes no mention of this in the 11,000 typed foolscap pages of his diary. Just a few chess references found elsewhere indicate his intellectual prowess in this field.

There is record of him playing in March 1936 in Berlin in a blindfold exhibition game with Fritz Samisch, at one time Austrian chess champion; they drew. Similarly documented, on the front page of the August 1937 issue of the chess magazine *Deutsche Schachblätter* ('Chess Leaves') was a meeting of chess masters in Berlin including Frank, while in December, with the caption 'Leading men of the new Germany in the great German chess league', the magazine's cover ran a picture of a preoccupied Reichsminister. When Frank was General Governor he was presented with a chess table carved by Ukrainian mountain farmers as a Christmas present in 1940. In November 1941 *Schachblätter* magazine again ran pictures of him with furrowed brow (not surprisingly) engaged in combat with the Moscow-born Dr Alexander Alekhine, who reigned many years as the fourth World Chess Champion, and who stayed in Reich territory during the war. Later, Alekhine was accused of writing anti-Semitic articles, which he claimed were forged. According to Dieter Schenk, Frank's German biographer, he received the Ukrainian top grandmaster Efim Bogoljubov, a challenger to Alekhine for the world title, at Krakow Castle. On 3 November 1940 he organised a chess congress in Krakow. Six months later he set up a chess school under Bogoljubov and Alekhine, and visited a chess tournament in October 1942 at the Literary Café in Krakow.

Frank even drew Goebbels into his chess circle, for he joined Frank in supporting a chess tournament in Munich in September 1941. But by late 1942 Goebbels' mood had changed and he considered chess a frivolity for a devoted servant of the Reich, and turned his sarcasm on Frank:

> Frank is pursuing a policy which is anything but that sanctioned by the Reich. I have been shown letters in which he orders the setting-up of a chess seminar in Krakow under Polish management. That is evidently now very important when it comes to providing the necessary basic foodstuffs for the Reich and to putting together the organization that this requires. Frank sometimes gives the impression of being half mad. Some of the incidents that have been reported to me concerning his work are simply dreadful.

But, ignoring Goebbels, Frank, whose energy – like his cowardice – sometimes seemed boundless, lost no opportunity to enhance his intellectual credentials and polish his reputation in other ways. This was particularly evident in a repeated invitation made to the 1932 Nobel Prize-winning physicist Werner Heisenberg, who developed the 'uncertainty principle' and who had been placed in charge of developing nuclear fission for a Nazi atomic bomb. When the hypothetical effects of an atom bomb dropped on Great Britain were shown to Hitler by Speer and others, Hitler beamed with unbounded enthusiasm: 'That is how we will annihilate them.' But when plans to build a cyclotron or particle accelerator in Frank's birthplace of Karlsrühe were implemented, the German physicists led by Heisenberg deemed a nuclear bomb technically unfeasible. The idea was dropped. Hitler tended anyway to consider nuclear physics as 'Jewish Physics'. German uranium stocks were subsequently diverted to the production of solid-core ammunition.

As a boy, Heisenberg had, like Frank, and the future Pope Benedict XVI, attended the Maximiliansgymnasium in Munich. He was in the year below Frank, while his brother Erwin was an exact contemporary. Heisenberg, as a *Neuespadfinder* (new pathfinder) passed through some of the same Teutonic romanticism as Frank, but was spared the grounding in political violence. Even so, he must have known what had been going on in Poland since early 1943. He was sensitive to the issue of race. Much earlier, in the 1930s, Heisenberg had been called a 'White Jew' because of his association with Jewish scientists, such as Einstein, and his refusal to accept the absurdity of Aryan 'physics'. Himmler intervened on Heisenberg's behalf and they agreed Heisenberg could use Einstein's physics as long as he did not refer to its non-Aryan source. His wife Elizabeth, in her memoir of her husband, says he addressed those who denied the reality of what was happening around them:

> I can still see my father standing in front of me. He was a man with a venerable and law-abiding outlook, who actually went into a rage when Heisenberg once showed him a report he had received from a colleague at the institute who had been a witness to the first cynical mass executions of Jews in Poland. My father lost all self-control and started to shout at us: 'So this is what it has come to, you believe things like this! This is what you get from listening to foreign broadcasts all the time. Germans cannot do things like this, it is impossible!'

He was never a Nazi, Elizabeth claimed; he had prematurely retired from his position following the National Socialist

takeover. Even so, it is a surprise that Heisenberg came to visit
Frank in Krakow in December 1943, at the height of the annihilation of the Jews in Poland:

> Here in Munich I was in school with some people who
> later became great Nazis, among them the Herr General
> Gouverneur of Poland, Frank. Frank was in the school class
> of my brother, and so naturally he knew us and *dutzen* us
> [He used the informal 'you', implying the friendship was
> close enough for this]. I had completely lost sight of him and
> thought, O.K., I will have nothing further to do with him.
> But then around September of '43, if I remember correctly,
> he wrote that I should nevertheless come to Krakow, and give
> a scientific lecture there. I felt, this is stupid, what am I doing
> there in Krakow; Frank does not concern me anyway. But he
> wrote in such a friendly way: my dear friend! Can you not …
> so that I wrote: Dear Frank! Well, I have so many other things
> to do here, unfortunately it is impossible for me to come. But
> then he sent me yet another letter, and was so pressing, and
> with implications that did not sound so pleasant, so I thought
> I do not really need to make an enemy. O.K., I will give the
> lecture in Krakow. So in December 1943, if I remember well,
> I went to Krakow where first I was his guest in his castle, then
> I gave a lecture on the innocent theme of quantum theory, or
> something like it …

Frank entertained Heisenberg in the Wurtenberg Castle,
another of his 'grace and favour' residences where he
entertained Himmler as part of his 'reconciliation with the
SS' in the last two years of the war. He had donated it, while
continuing to use it, to the SS. Polish physicists, formerly well
known colleagues of Heisenberg, were forbidden to attend the
lecture and were turned away at the door. A communiqué of
the lecture ran:

For about the last ten years, the main line of research in atomic physics became the investigation of atomic nuclei. By the use of high voltage devices and other high technology means, it became possible to transform the atomic nuclei, and thus to fulfil the old program of the alchemists: the transmutation of chemical elements.

Frank thanked Heisenberg after the enthusiastically received lecture. It seemed that even here, with the most famous German nuclear scientist fulfilling the old programme of the alchemists, we could not get escape from the myth of *Doctor Faustus*:

> ... the ideal laboratory, in which atomic transformations occur at highest energies, was presented to us by nature in the form of cosmic rays. The sources of this strange radiation in space are unknown. However, the effects of this radiation are being investigated by physicists and provide us with most interesting information about the nature of the smallest building blocks of matter.

It was fortunate for the future of mankind that for the moment the German scientist was prepared to leave the matter there.

22

Managerial Problems

With the many reverses the Germans were now suffering, life in Poland assumed a haunted, crazed complexion. The Polish patriots and the AK Army had become emboldened to attack more and more military posts and prominent figures. On 20 April 1943, at 9.45 a.m., the 'Kars-Osch' detachment of the AK Army lay in readiness to kill *Polizeiführer* and *Höhere* SS Krüger as he drove in from the outer ring road to the city centre. An observation post near the Platz Kossaka warned of his approach. In the 'mouth' of a side street two operatives of the AK Army waited in ambush and threw hand grenades at his vehicle as it passed; the rear was destroyed and Krüger escaped with light injuries. 'God be thanked without great harm!' commented Frank, who must have been extremely disappointed they had failed to kill his enemy.

Frank learned soon after that his own life was in danger from a similar planned attempt, but with the mounting defeats, and Himmler and Krüger nervously contemplating the unstoppable advance of the Soviet armies, Frank had the upper hand as he plotted to put into operation another safeguard: increased co-operation with the 'foreigners', as the Poles were labelled in their native land.

Goebbels issued a directive to all local party bosses or Gauleiters in 1943 to stop 'everything that endangered the necessary cooperation of all European peoples in the cause of victory'. Frank, who had observed that the Germans were slaughtering the cow when they wanted the milk, would later claim this was actually a genuine change of heart. But at that time he still believed, or so he professed in his diary, that Germany would win the war: 'When we have finally won … you can make mincemeat of the Poles and the Ukrainians and all the others as far as I'm concerned … What is crucial at the moment is the maintenance of order, discipline, and diligence among a hostile population.'

Governor Dr Ludwig Fischer stepped up the terror in an increasingly stubborn and hostile Warsaw. As public works were attacked, Frank issued a decree in October 1943 suppressing civil violence, which was followed by mass SS round-ups, as Norman Davies in his epic account relates:

From then on, scores of people were killed almost every day … most frequently people seized at random on the streets. The execution of hostages took place behind heavy police cordons … The manhunts were conducted with great brutality by the police and were often accompanied by the Wehrmacht, the Luftwaffe, or even by youngsters from the Hitlerjugend, who would shoot escapers or 'suspicious' passers-by. The city was transformed into a jungle, in which not just 'slave traders' and 'gangs of thugs' were at large to hand the unfortunate over. Now, nothing protected one from death – not the 'right documents', not a clean record, not a lack of contact with the Underground, not even collaborationist inclinations, neither illness nor advanced age. The inhabitants of Warsaw were turned into hunted animals, who had to go outside to live, but who were constantly on edge, lest they were pounced on. … One could see with one's own eyes the names of one's neighbours, relatives, colleagues, and loved ones on the lists of the condemned. Their blood was literally flowing in the city's gutters. The threat dominated everything. And the unseen hand had managed to write on the walls – *Mene, Tekel, Fares*.

Here again, a different aspect of Hitler Youth is revealed, and of the junior members of the Luftwaffe (which makes Joseph Ratzinger's own account in his book *Milestones* seem disingenuous).

At Auschwitz-Birkenau, where a south westerly breeze wafted the stench of death even as far as Wawel Castle, the efficient, industrialised gassing of Jews and Poles reached its peak. Even here, there were dedicated, individual acts of revolt. One of the crematoriums at Birkenau was blown up. Primo Levi:

> … a few hundred men at Birkenau, helpless and exhausted slaves like ourselves, had found in themselves the strength to act, to mature the fruits of their hatred.
>
> The man who is to die in front of us today in some way took part in the revolt. … perhaps the Germans do not understand that this solitary death, this man's death which has been reserved for him, will bring him glory, not infamy.
>
> … everybody heard the cry of the doomed man, it pierced through the old thick barriers of inertia and submissiveness, it struck the living core of man in each of us:
>
> '*Kamaraden, ich bin der Letz!*' (Comrades, I am the last one!)
>
> I wish I could say that from the midst of us, an abject flock, a voice rose, a murmur, a sign of assent. But nothing happened.

In *Kaputt* by Curzio Malaparte, the Italian writer describes Governor Frank and Brigitte on a visit to Warsaw. He writes of Brigitte, at the Belvedere Palace, kissing Frank's hands – 'those soft, white tender hands' – and then, as they entered the Jewish ghetto, for *spiel* shooting down Jewish children like game. Later, Brigitte, perhaps a forerunner of German wives in Holocaust denial, raged at Malaparte, telling her children that Frank never knew how to shoot a gun, which was untrue, as Frank had been familiar with firearms from an early age. (Here again is another echo of Cardinal Ratzinger's future disengagement from the dark side of the Reich, for he claimed no knowledge of firearms though he was a policeman's son.) We cannot know if Malaparte's accusation has any truth in it and tend to disbelieve it, based upon what we know of the Franks.

Brigitte lied that neither she nor Frank had ever been enemies of the Jews or the Poles. As a token they had Jewish workmen at the Wawel, and when they left they claimed that their Polish retinue, who were more likely to be Ukrainians than Poles from the Government General, begged to be taken with them back to Germany. This was much later, when Frank, like many others, sought to show a different face. Krüger came and removed the Jews from the Frank household, for as the possibility of victory receded, Krüger, like Hitler, believed at least that the Final Solution could still be a Nazi success.

In 1943–44 Frank was careering from one escape hope to another, though he never lost his overriding arrogance and conceit. At a meeting in January 1943, he announced to his colleagues who ran the Government General:

> We must not be squeamish when we learn that a total of 17,000 [Poles] have been shot ... We are now duty bound to hold together ... we, who are gathered together here figure on Mr. Roosevelt's list of war criminals. I have the honour of being Number One. We have, so to speak, become accomplices in the world historic sense.

At the same time he voiced regret over the deportation of Jewish manpower that was still usable (his own Wawel servants, for example). As he put it, the decision for their annihilation had been made at a higher level than his. They had to abandon a great building project, which need not have happened had thousands of skilled Jewish workers been allowed to remain at work. Here is another ambiguity: was he genuinely concerned about the project, or just trying to win his private war with Himmler and Krüger?

Security in the southern part of the Government General and in Galicia (or the Ukraine) was less tight than in the north and Warsaw. The SS General Elrich von dem Bach-Zelewski testified at Nuremberg that Himmler called Frank a traitor for objecting to the increasing SS demands for more Poles and Jews to be arrested and deported. This objection seems, however, to have been voiced primarily because Himmler and Krüger continued to go behind Frank's back.

Frank's worries were sometimes managerial, he was for example fearful of epidemics which could spread to Germans, or were for his own personal survival. He sought allies. He took the side of the Ukrainians, seeing them as potentially amenable in their hatred of the Russians and Bolshevism. He agreed in June 1943 to the re-establishment of a Polish welfare organisation, the *Polnische Haupthilfsanschluss*, to which he allocated a budget and agreed to a board of Polish directors. He attempted to form a Polish anti-Bolshevik league in February 1944, at the same time pressing on Berlin his plans to explore the possibility even of Polish military formations, new directives in educational policy, and a change of direction over property rights (or confiscation).

He got nowhere on either front. The Poles said that it was too late to press for a 'statement of the future role of the Polish people in the New Europe'. The Nazis viewed his plans as a categorical about-turn from the Lebensraum vision. Meanwhile, the resistance, growing in force and influence, was executing leaders of the 'Sword and Plough' collaborationist group.

Goebbels in the meantime pulled off his spin-doctor's masterpiece and caused major mischief with the delayed revelation that Stalin was a mass murderer responsible for the liquidation of 15,000 Polish officers in Katyn Forest. His plan was to split asunder the 'Grand Alliance' of Great Britain, the US and the Soviet Union, and while he failed in this he did achieve a fatal rupture of links between the Polish government-in-exile in London and Stalin. Poles in Poland, commented Norman Davies, when shown footage of the Katyn massacre and the corpses and skulls of their loved ones, 'were not unduly impressed by one gang of murderers exposing the crimes of another'. There were tragic consequences in August 1944, the time of the popular rising in Warsaw, when the Russians took their revenge on the Poles for not believing their lies.

On 25 January 1944, when Frank visited Berlin, an event which in typical pompous style he described as the 'Arrival of the Governor General in Berlin', and noted that the 'Governor General delivered lecture for the representations of the German press in the Pompeian Hall for the Ministry for Public Enlightenment and Propaganda'. He pointed out that in his domain, out of a population of 16 million there were hardly 250,000 Germans. Too many of these 16 million lived in Warsaw, so here the master race was very thinly spread, which meant trouble.

On 29 January 1944 a resistance unit detonated a bomb under Frank's private railroad car as he travelled from Krakow to Lvov. Frank reports:

At 23:17 hours, kilometer 22.3, there was a muffled explosion caused by the detonation of an electrically ignited device. A section of track approximately one metre long was destroyed. The explosion took place directly behind the rear axle of Salon Car 1006, which was violently shaken by the sudden air pressure. Salon Car 1001 was immediately derailed but continued to jolt and bump over the railroad ties and roadbed, as did its auxiliary car immediately behind it. The chief steward of Saloon Car 1006 pulled the emergency signal immediately after the detonation, but the locomotive engineer had simultaneously felt it and of his own accord applied the brakes at once and brought the train to a halt.

Frank was in the saloon car and was uninjured. He returned to Krakow, then took a plane to Lvov. The next day he had recovered enough to occupy the *Ehrenloge* (VIP box) in the Krakow State Theatre for a performance of *Aida*, the second of twenty attendances at major musical events in the first six months of 1944, which had begun with *Die Fledermaus* on 15 January.

Music, as we have seen, following the precepts of Schopenhauer, was a moral sublimation of the will that fed and sustained Frank's soul, as it did Hitler's. No doubt when he met Hitler on 6 February 1944 for the last time at his Wolf's Lair headquarters in East Prussia and spent two-and-a-half hours with him, they discussed favourite operas and their recent performances. Describing himself at the Führer's headquarters in conversation with Hitler, Frank presents the latter as 'a compassionate listener' to his troubles:

> The Governor General reports on the contents and course of his conversation as follows ... The Führer then inquired about Warsaw and thought Warsaw should cause me the greatest sorrow. I could only confirm to him, that Warsaw means to me the darkest point in the Government General. The Führer pointed out as absolutely right that we chose Krakow as the capital. Warsaw should be pulled down as soon as possible.

It seems quite strange, just days after the surrender of Paulus' army at Stalingrad, for Hitler to devote such time to Frank, but, no doubt, although we have no other record of it apart from Frank's subsequent report, they reminisced about the good old days, while fulminating against the Poles and Warsaw.

Frank found a pitifully reduced Führer. He no longer visited the battlefronts and he refused to boost civilian morale by appearances on the rubble following Allied saturation bombing. He suffered increasing insomnia, and rejected the advice of Dr Morell, his quack doctor, to take exercise. Just recently he had developed some weakness in his left leg and left arm, which betrayed increasing tremulousness; his left hand shook and he carried it close to his body. When questioned about it, his numerous physicians said it would stop. Later, while the July 1944 bomb plot bruised his right arm and leg, the left side recovered perfect function for eight weeks, but when the right side healed, the left-sided symptoms came back.

With his Führer, Frank was, as always, a consummate flatterer and could react effectively to the complex personality of Hitler. He piled on the good reports of how brilliantly he ran the Government General; he knew how to feed into Hitler's paranoid need for scapegoats, the main role the Poles had been given in the 1,000-year Reich. In turn, Hitler praised Frank (which the latter reported endlessly) for his administration, and for everything he had succeeded in extracting from the land.

According to Frank, Hitler blamed the setbacks in Russia on bad weather (just as Napoleon had done before him), or rather the '*difficult* weather conditions that had been characteristic throughout the length of this war. Had the weather in 1941 not been so bad, Moscow would long since be in our hands.'

The talk between them ended, as Frank recorded officially, 'in an atmosphere of friendly humour. The Führer's assessment was undoubtedly the same, and it was clearly his intention to establish a complete settling of differences between himself and his oldest battle comrades, and officially to record it in the presence of the Chief of the Party Chancellery.' (This was written for the benefit of Bormann, Frank's enemy who out-manoeuvred him on every occasion.)

Hitler's ardent desire that Warsaw should be obliterated was gratified. The rising of Polish patriots and the AK Home Army in August 1944 and their betrayal by the Soviet Army, which halted on the east bank of the Vistula, refusing to advance and support the insurrection, gave the Nazi hierarchy its excuse. It also gave Frank the opportunity to prove the purity of his Nazi soul and his absolute trustworthiness.

On 3 August he telephoned General Guderian and asked him to send help to the Nazi detachments in Warsaw. Guderian assured Frank that everything humanly possible would be done to 'help' Warsaw. Once they had regained control of the city they would pass sentence on it.

On the evening of the same day Frank telephoned Dr Bühler, his deputy in Krakow, to inform him of Hitler's decision to use every means available to suppress the uprising. On 5 August Dr Fischer, the Governor of Warsaw, telephoned Frank saying the insurrection was already feeling the effects of dive-bomber attacks. Frank noted Dr Fischer's exemplary co-operation with the Nazi military commander General Reiner Stahel. The same evening he sent Dr Lammers, the Minister of the Reich Chancellory, a telegram: 'The City of Warsaw is in flames for the most part. The burning of the houses is also the surest method of getting the insurgents out of their bolt-holes ... After this insurrection and its crushing Warsaw will be completely destroyed as it deserves.'

Warsaw was almost totally razed to the ground. Frank made no protest against the savage behaviour and reprisals of the German forces, while he agreed to take part in looting the 'movable property of the city' – by which he presumably meant more artefacts to plunder.

A telegram sent to Frank by Dr Fischer on 11 October 1944 informed him that SS-*Obergruppenführer* von dem Bach-Zelewski (the Waffen SS General) had been given orders for the pacification of Warsaw; that is, the levelling of the city. Before this happened all raw materials, textiles and furniture were to be removed from the city. This was to be primarily the job of the civil authorities. Dr Fischer stressed that he had informed Frank of all this because the new order from the Führer to destroy Warsaw was of import to the new Polish policy. So Frank endorsed in full the destruction of the capital of Poland.

What Frank also did as Governor General was to authorise a final, completely gratuitous act. He ordered German sappers to place dynamite charges in the Warsaw Castle walls, in those very same holes which had been left empty since December 1939. A Holocaust survivor, Dr Micha Tomkiewitz, who was present in Warsaw attests:

> The Germans blew up the walls of the Royal Castle in December, 1944, when they were burning and destroying on a large scale the public buildings and private dwelling places that were still untouched. I saw the Castle with my own eyes in November, 1944, when the uprising had been put down. I can state that the Castle was almost in the same condition as it had been in 1940. When the Soviet units entered the city on 17th January, 1945, the Castle was nothing but a heap of ruins.

In spite of Frank's calculated softening of attitude towards the 'foreigners' in Poland, and his now quite dedicated commitment to providing public support, within what a future generation would call 'politically correct' limits (according to the Nazi code) the Poles were not grateful. The effects of all this frantic activity were marked: he put on weight; he had to clear his throat often; he started to attend Catholic mass – celebrated by a German, not a Polish Catholic. Niklas comments in his relentlessly acerbic, but gripping memoir of his father, 'Murder Puts on Weight'.

Frank now starts to complain in his diary, as the Soviets reduce the distance between their Joseph Stalin tanks and Krakow, and his new humanitarian stance falls away:

> It is outrageous that the Government in Berlin can send only a handful of men, give them orders to exterminate fifteen million foreigners here, and then expect them to remain in this territory without additional security. When the Bolsheviks plan to annihilate people, they send at least two thousand Red Army troops into every little village where the people are to be exterminated. But to send us only ten thousand police

troops for the whole GG, and then order us to finish off fifteen million people ... it just can't be done.

During the Easter recess of 19–22 April 1946, after the testimony of the Auschwitz Commandant Höss at Nuremberg – telling of the order from Hitler to exterminate the Jewish race – Frank rather dramatically changed his mind about Hitler, as the American psychiatrist Dr Gilbert records:

'*Herr Doktor*, will history ever get over this degradation of human civilization that Hitler brought us to? There is no doubt that that demon Hitler brought us to this. If Himmler had tried to do it on his own hook, and then Hitler had found out about it and had hung him for it, it would have been different. But no, Hitler gave the order himself – he indicates it even in his "Last Testament" [in which he blames the Second World War on 'International Jewry'] – And that man wore the mask of a human being! – the head of a State! ... I am going to write you that essay on Hitler that I promised you, but do you know that he is actually repulsive to me now? Now that he is unmasked and I see what a horrible repulsive man I have been following, I am nauseated.'

He leaned on the table with his elbow, his face in his hands, with eyes squinting as if in a trance. 'It is as if Death put on the mask of a charming human being, and lured workers, lawyers, scientists, women and children – everything! – to destruction! – And now we see his face unmasked as it really was – a death's-head skeleton! *Herr Doktor* it is terrifying! – it is repulsive!'

He felt very differently when he wrote in his diary on 17 February 1944:

Last June it was 25 years since I got to know the Führer, and I have now been with him for 25 years; during many and difficult hours we were bound to each other. I belong to the circle of the few representatives of the earliest National Socialist development. I was present when the Party programme was formulated. I know the preparations for the first party meeting in the Mathäser Brewery. I know the history of the movement right from the beginning. For me, looking back on 25 years of this work is a retrospect of one of the most marvellous epochs of development of our people and today also of the history of the world.

Winifred Wagner, Richard's widow, when she read what Frank finally wrote on Hitler in the 'essay' included in his posthumous *Angesicht* (*Facing the Gallows*), commented that it was 'the best character study of Hitler I have ever read'. Three days before his visit to East Prussia, Frank had drunk deep of Goethe's *Faust* (*Part One*), that seminal work of German literature, also playing at the State Theatre in Krakow. Between the twin spirits in his breast, the split in his personality had come to resemble a chasm.

23

The Prince Archbishop

Hitler said it was the German misfortune to have the wrong religion. His devoted disciple Frank had the triple misfortune to be surrounded, as head of the 1 per cent of Germans who ruled the 99 per cent of Catholic Poles, by a population who conformed hardly at all to the Führer's idea of Catholicism as weak and feeble. It had of course been so in his native Bavaria, the German bishops led meekly into self-slaughter by the appeasement and silence of Cardinal Pacelli, later Pius XII. Hitler ordered Frank to make use of the Church to keep the Poles, 'quiet, stupid and backward'.

Himself a lapsed Catholic, Frank saw at once, more clearly than Hitler, the nature of the beast he had to subdue and keep to heel. Of course, being the man he was, with a need to intellectualise and rationalise everything, he could be quite eloquent about it:

> The Church is maintaining a remarkable aloofness. But this is only a method which has recurred constantly in Polish history. The Church, as long as there were still other centres of operation available, has always kept itself in reserve as the final nucleus of Polish nationalism. To Polish minds the Church is the central rallying-point, silently shedding a constant ray of light and in this way acting as a sort of inextinguishable

beacon. Whenever all was darkness in Poland, there was still Our Lady of Czestochowa and the Church. You must never forget this. For this reason the Church in Poland has no need to be active. Catholicism in this country is not just a religion; it is a necessity of life.

In spite of this measured statement and the almost euphemistic directives to colleagues and security police to pay attention to the activities of the clergy and 'intervene' in cases of the use of the Church for political ends, the religious community was, as already described, brutalised systematically and without mercy. Mainly the Gestapo and SS were responsible, Frank turning a blind eye to the murder and torture. And of course the repression, unlike in Catholic Bavaria (except in certain exceptional cases of very brave and defiant priests), only served to strengthen and harden Polish faith, causing Frank to bluster and threaten even more, and proclaim even harsher restrictions:

I observe in increasing measure that the Church is beginning to become unpleasant. While until now this mighty ideological bloc in Poland has, strangely enough – so to speak – been loyal, the Church is beginning here and there – apparently as a result of the stiffening of certain political situations on this continent – to become an embarrassment. I would like to stress straightaway that I shall not stop at anything here and even have bishops arrested immediately if the slightest thing occurs. I request you in this connection to take the severest steps to ensure that officials in uniform are strictly forbidden to visit Polish churches during a service.

But, ultimately, he did recognise that he had neither the resources nor the will to break the power of faith over the hearts and minds of the Polish people. It was this unwavering faith – a few thousand quislings apart – that unified the nation, even including left-wing believers, and underpinned the prevalence of instinctive, spontaneous support for the resistance. It was an underlying unspoken trust which stopped the Gestapo from infiltrating and crushing the Polish resistance. Resisters were able to serve without ever learning about the links to the unseen chain that bound them to their superiors. The Polish resistance was thus imitating the hierarchy and courage of the Catholic Church at its best, courage which it had been lamentably short of in Nazi Germany.

An anti-Nazi activist recalls how he arrived in Warsaw from London one day after narrowly escaping discovery and arrest when crossing Germany. Leaving a secret meeting in the centre of town he was stopped by a Gestapo agent. He said he had just been to visit his dentist. Pressed by the agent he gave the telephone number of the dentist, a woman who, when called, without hesitation told the agent he had just been with her.

The German cultural 'New Order', just as the 'New Soviet Man' later, was doomed from the start in Frank's 'Gestapoland'. Deeply frustrated, Frank tried out the tactic he had employed with the German legal profession in the 1930s – playing both sides of the street. He knew how faith kept people within the social order, and encouraged obedience and acceptance of authority and, in hard times, adverse fate and struggle. He published a book in 1944 called *The Cabin Boy and Columbus*, which implied he had kept a residual belief in the faith, although this may well be a further example of his religious hypocrisy. It would emerge that he still went on praying privately while he had his own German Catholic curate, Father Bürger, whom he appears to have seen often, and may even have said mass privately in the Wawel.

In public utterances and his endless Government General decrees, he waged an intensifying battle: the Nazi official line took a savage and theatrical delight in denouncing the Church: 'If, as is claimed, Catholicism is really a dishonour for a nation, then all the more Catholicism must I wish for the Polish race ... If Catholicism is a poison, then one can only wish this poison on the Poles. The same applies to other things as well.' But as the security situation worsened in 1943, he sounded almost weary when he spoke to Luftwaffe officers on 14 December 1943: 'The Polish clergy and the Polish schools are my chief enemies precisely because I have to put up with them for reasons of general policy. I am aware that the Polish priests and teachers are systematically keeping this country in a state of unrest.' On 11 February 1944, Frank spoke in similar vein to party officials: 'We cannot carry out any Church or school policy. I am intelligent enough to realize that these curates are our mortal enemies.'

Chief of these 'mortal enemies', since the Polish Primate, Cardinal August Hlond, had fled ignominiously into exile into Italy and then neutral France in 1939, was Prince Adam Sapieha, Archbishop of Krakow, whose episcopal palace lay only hundreds of yards away from the Wawel. Hlond belonged to the reactionary school of Catholic belief that still believed Jews should be blamed for the killing of Jesus Christ. Echoing his fellow bishops in Bavaria, he wrote in a pastoral letter in 1936:

It is a fact that the Jews are fighting against the Catholic Church, persisting in free thinking, and are the vanguard of godlessness, Bolshevism and subversion ... It is a fact that Jews deceive, levy interest, and are pimps. It is a fact that the religious and ethical influence of the Jewish young people on Polish people is a negative one.

While Hlond would not go as far as to endorse extermination and did later denounce Nazi cruelty and oppression in Poland in reports to the Vatican (but without mentioning the Jews), anti-Jewish persecution continued in Poland, with sporadic pogroms, in particular those instigated by Reinhard Heydrich and the German Security Police, which occurred in the summer of 1941 after the Russians had been driven out of the Lomza District and the Bialystok Region. These continued to break out, with burnings in barns, and even continued in liberated Poland in 1945, when over forty Jews were killed in Kieke.

Pius XII, in his papal state, an isolated enclave surrounded on all sides by Mussolini's fascist regime, had not condemned Hitler's seizure of Prague and Czechoslovakia in March 1939; a month later, he sent birthday greetings to Hitler.

In February 1942 Archbishop Sapieha sent a courier to Rome to inform the Vatican that prisoners in Nazi concentration camps 'were deprived of all human rights, handed over to the cruelty of men who have no feeling of humanity. We live in terror, continually in danger of losing everything if we attempt to escape, taken into camps from which few emerge alive.' He told a Knights of Malta chaplain who witnessed the Jews departing for Auschwitz from the Krakow ghetto: 'We are living through the tragedy of these unfortunate people and none of us are in a position to help them any more.' He added, significantly, 'And there is no difference between Jews and Poles.'

Beak-nosed with piercing eyes, Sapieha, a gaunt, tall man of 75 in 1942, had lost none of his iron will and natural authority. He had offered to retire several times and been refused. He now stood alone, a captive cleric, isolated from Rome. He continued to smuggle out warnings which went unheeded. Sapieha accepted hardship as a basic condition of human life. He prayed every night for an hour, alone and undisturbed in his chapel, presenting his problems to his Lord.

When inaugurated as Bishop of Krakow thirty-two years before, he had shunned the gentry who awaited his arrival and visited a poorhouse. A comparable asceticism may be detected in the new Pope Francis I, elected in 2013. Nine years spent in Rome as Secret Chamberlain to Pope Pius X had taught him everything about the Church's inner deviousness, and its predilection for gossip and politicking. He fell foul of Pius XI and lost promotion to cardinal by refusing the future pope, then still papal nuncio Cardinal Achille Ratti, permission to attend a meeting of the Polish episcopate. He despised the Vatican's obsession with style and frivolity, and ultimately its Italian snobbishness. There is little doubt that he had little point of contact with Pius XII.

In 1942 Frank's diary records that Sapieha sent him a memorandum complaining about the arbitrary arrest of priests and Catholics made by the Security Police. Frank intended to meet Sapieha then, and point out to him that it was the direct order of Hitler. But SS Brigade führer Dr Eberhard Schöngarth, a commander in the *Sicherheitspolizei* (executed for war crimes in 1946), gave Frank secret information about the clandestine activities of Sapieha and his confidant, Canon Odyl Gerhardt. Rather than having to confront Sapieha with his infringement of Nazi protocols, Frank preferred to 'postpone' the meeting. Was this strategic or outright avoidance caused by faint stirrings of conscience?

Sapieha continued to protest, in June 1943, and in November 1943. This was, according to the interpretation one might place on it, either an act of courage on Frank's part, or more likely, a desire not to stir up the Archbishop's defiance and thus be forced to make an example of him and have him arrested. He could have justified this as an act of political expediency to avoid more trouble and the potential revolt of the Poles, but there are notable examples of Hitler in Germany refusing to take action against mass Catholic defiance.

Frank's uneasy time with the Krakow Prince Archbishop continued as Sapieha made further requests for a meeting, which Frank ignored. In early 1944 Frank accused the Church, without any justification, of conspiring with the Jews and masons against Hitler's plans. He echoed the Führer's catchphrases:

That the enemies we had in Germany have organized themselves internationally and have international support, we recognize from the fact that the carrying out of the Führer's programme in the world-historical sense leads to the same enemy front which we saw as victors over us in 1918: the

Jews, the Jesuits and the Masons. These enemies of ours are
today present again in the world drama.

It may be that Schöngarth agreed with Frank's softly-softly
attitude to the Archbishop, for on 20 April 1943, Hitler's birthday, Schöngarth spoke these strange, apparently compassionate,
words – 'No people has ever before had to suffer such oppression as that being suffered by the Polish people.' One must add
quickly this was just prior to an ordinance which accelerated and
increased public mass executions.

By early 1944 Frank had decided it was no longer politic to
keep Sapieha at arm's length, but that he could make use of him
while beginning officially to claim his administration sought
a rapprochement with the Polish people. Sapieha by now was
known underground and even publicly acknowledged as the
embodiment of heroic resistance. Frank thought that, in the
increasingly ungovernable Government General, he might even
convince Sapieha to support him.

Frank believed he was cleverer than everyone else. He
could also, in those moments when he had fits of conscience,
even if only short-lived, tell himself that he had not wholly
destroyed the Catholic Church. He now conceived the idea
that in the long term, following his beloved Führer's idea that
the Reich would last 1,000 years, the Catholic Poles were a
race he could turn, with their partial co-operation, into civilised helots, make them the intelligent Greek slaves of the new
Roman Empire.

Accordingly, he instructed Dr Harry von Craushaar, another
high ranking security official (and yet another PhD who staffed
the higher echelons of the SS), to make contact with Sapieha,
letting him know that he, Frank, out of his generous consideration for the feelings of Polish Catholics, had persuaded Himmler
to release Cardinal Hlond, who had recently been placed under
house arrest in Vichy France when the Nazis took it over in 1943.
Hlond would be freed on the condition that he did not return to

the Government General. (In effect, this never happened. Hlond anyway did not return to Poland until 1945.)

Frank then discussed with Crausshaar and Wilden, a Nazi judicial functionary, the position of the new postulants in seminaries, a matter he had already taken up with Himmler. It seemed that new postulants could be accepted (and this was prior to the Warsaw uprising of 1944), provided they were not active in the resistance. To this end, as ever, the Nazis were checking names on their registers. This is important because the future Pope John Paul II, Karol Wojtyla, had already enrolled as a secret seminarian under Sapieha's urging in the Archbishop's Palace.

Frank met Sapieha for the first time on Wednesday 5 April 1944. One apocryphal but believable account has the following exchange. The Archbishop provided lunch for Frank and Crausshaar, to the glutton and hedonist Frank's obvious discomfort. Something along the lines of the following exchange took place: 'I see, Herr Governor General, you are unhappy with what you eat,' said the Archbishop.

'Beetroot preserve ... Lentils ... Potato soup. Your Grace, it is not exactly what I am used to.'

Frank had begun to feel ill with indigestion, but forced himself to remain polite.

'I do not wish to break German regulations. It is what the people in Krakow eat.'

The waiter then brought black bread partly baked with acorns. And a small portion of cheese. There was no wine. Frank appeared more and more uncomfortable.

'Are you telling me this is what you eat all the time, your Grace?'

'I cannot risk one of my staff being arrested by the Gestapo for buying food on the black market. Our rations are roughly half those which Germans receive. Germans are served first in all food queues, and generally buy up everything there is. Germans have red ration books, Poles green. I pass you the list as published

in the *Völkischer Beobachter* together with the announcement of
regulations forbidding the sale of wheat flour and its products to
Poles. In a week, for instance, Germans are entitled to 250g of
butter, Poles to only 62.5g of margarine, no flour, no fats, 250g
of meat as opposed to 500g, one as opposed to two eggs. I quote
Dr Ley, head of the German Labour Front, who states Germans
need more space and a higher quality of life than races with a
lower culture, like the Poles. A lower race, says Dr Ley, needs
less food.'

Without further ado, Frank explained his new policy towards
the Poles, which promised relief for Polish workers deported
to the Reich and full religious rights. Frank suggested that
the Church put out a statement condemning the resistance
movement and adopt an attitude favourable to the Nazis in their
conflict with the Soviet Union. He wanted Sapieha to issue a
pastoral letter 'against Bolshevism and the English'. Sapieha
turned this down on the grounds that he was no politician. He
saw the situation only as a man and a bishop. As such, he had
heard about cases of human suffering and that was why he had
sent his memorandum to the Governor General.

When Dr Crausshaar and Frank insisted that they had often
been told that the Church was the real centre of the Polish
underground resistance, the Archbishop denied being the head
of any kind of resistance, but observed that in the last five years
the Nazis had not proved themselves friends of the Polish nation.
Archbishop Sapieha went on to describe the living conditions of
the Poles in the Government General:

> The life of the entire population is rather unprotected. It has
> happened that it has been left to lower administration offices
> to decide whether to shoot Poles or not ... The deportation
> of workers to the Reich has been carried out in a bad manner
> ... In the Reich [the part of West Poland incorporated into
> Germany] the Poles have been expelled from the churches
> and this creates a bad impression in this country.

'Archbishop Prince Sapieha,' noted Frank in his diary, 'then referred to the arrest and shooting of Polish priests. He states that many of them were quite innocent. Twenty priests had already met their death in Auschwitz and a further twenty were still in gaol.'

Later the matters discussed in this interview between Archbishop Sapieha and Frank were used in his trial as evidence that the leading representative of the Church hierarchy in Poland had informed Frank of the crimes committed by the Nazi administration in the Government General.

Frank gave a one-sided account of the meeting. He maintained that Sapieha 'condemned' the killing of Germans by partisans, that he was a staunch defender of 'Polishness' and understood collaboration with the Germans would help preserve Poland's cultural and political identity. This was almost certainly not true, and the last stage of Frank's fantasist vision of his Führer's model colony. The Russians were fast approaching. There is a legend to the effect that when Sapieha handed over the keys to Wawel Cathedral, he had told Frank that one day he would be giving them back.

When the Russians were only 118km away from Krakow, Frank telexed Goebbels in Berlin with the proposal that 'the splendidly conceived memorandum on the treatment of Poland, and the interconnections between German policy and current Polish trends and concerns be sent to SS *Obergruppenführer* Kaltenbrunner'. The wilful blindness is astonishing.

24

Vogue La Galère

Frank seems to have got himself into a state of increasing spiritual confusion over religious observance. As the Russian tanks grew closer, the German garrisons grew more Christian and pious. Frank found this a 'disagreeable sight! … filling our Catholic churches with more Germans than I would ever have expected'. At the same time, he lamented the fact that every time a German was murdered, a Polish Catholic priest celebrated the funeral mass. So he set out to encourage German clergy in the Government General to perform the rites themselves, and to this end invited all the German priests and Evangelical pastors to dinner. You would have to be Voltaire to do justice to this scene.

Apparently only one turned up, a Father Burger. The Father was at pains, so Frank reported, to establish that he had no connection with his fellow Polish priests, who were, he alleged, involved in the Polish underground. The priest's main objective, and the reason he turned up, seemed to be that of acquiring an official car for his pastoral duties, so that Poles could be relieved of the duty of burying Germans.

Frank countered with a request for Father Burger to instruct German women in their moral behaviour. He had become greatly concerned at the 'enormous increase in the birth rate of illegitimate children'. Before he left, Frank, always ready to pillage more from the Wawel stores, promised robes and vestments 'so that the services in German churches in the Government General could be held in more fitting fashion'.

It is dreadful that one is tempted to show Frank in those last months of his rule of the Government General as a farcical character. But this is what he had become: a comical king. Liberation from the Nazis was for Poland in many ways just as tragic than the past five years of slavery, if not more, for now another monster in another ideological shape and costume was slouching towards Bethlehem. The Soviets were rolling back the *Wehrmacht* like a carpet, and sending the 25,000 Germans in the Government General (the 1 per cent or so often quoted by Frank) scuttling back in mortal fear of losing their lives, although heavily loaded with as much booty as they could stash away and carry.

In 1944 the main military action in Poland, namely resistance to the military advance of the Soviets, plus the suppression of the Warsaw uprising and retaliation for the mounting number of anti-German incidents, was now completely out of Frank's hands. The German generals, the SS and the Gestapo ran everything. Frank, the civil governor of a battle zone, for all his outward show and pomp, was effectively side-lined. Most of his staff left to join the diminishing ranks of the Reich Army under threat of being shot if they didn't.

Frank could now initiate that most important exercise beloved of failing rulers and first ministers: the exit strategy; and the second most important, the securing of his place in history. He wanted to be remembered as a lover of the Polish people who had battled endlessly with Hitler and the SS for justice. To this end he decreed a whole raft of new laws in which the Polish people suddenly acquired human dimensions. He opened Polish secondary schools. He instructed that the police should no longer be used to capture 'slaves'. On Hitler's birthday, he praised the Government General as the 'homeland' of the Poles and Ukrainians. At an official reception for Ukrainian

Orthodox Catholic churches he set his jaw as best he could to utter the slogan: 'Stalin is the embodiment of the denial of God on Earth. Adolf Hitler is the affirmation of God.' He held fast to promoting chastity and productivity, and the continuing annihilation of the Jews in the beautiful city of Krakow, which he dubbed 'Antisemitopolis'.

As he closed down luxury restaurants and prepared for the removal of bank notes and printing plates, he still regularly attended performances at the State Theatre. While he had paintings and *objets d'art* crated up for removal to Bavaria, he adopted a new role as saviour and protector of Polish culture. He suggested that a Krakow theatre company supply itself with clothing, stage costumes and scenery fabric, the lack of which it constantly complained about, from the Jew camps of the SS. He became an active patron of Polish music, later claiming, 'Among other things I have established a great Polish orchestra, the Philharmonic of the Government General.'

When von Stauffenberg's July 1944 attempt to kill Hitler failed (and by now most were likely privately disappointed that it had), Frank sent Hitler this convoluted telegram: 'My heartiest congratulations and words of blessing for your divinely inspired deliverance from the hideous peril of the criminal attack on your life.' Later that month he conceded that his realm and kingdom had suffered 'decisive losses in power and space'. This is, after all, what the Third Reich was all about: 'power and space'. He so loved the phrase *Ostluft mach frei* – 'the air of the East makes one free,' but Galicia and Radam had fallen and, as he wrote to Brigitte, whom he told to go on ahead, on 25 July: 'I am getting everything ready [to depart]. Including the fur coat.'

With his new-found zeal to promote Polish-German co-operation he 'received' the Polish Count Adam Potocki, a patriot and landowner. He tried to convince Potocki that the Polish race had a valuable contribution to make to future European undertakings. He telegrammed Hitler (5 October 1944) proposing a co-administration of the Government General with the Poles. Now he believed, or so he said, that the theory of total annihilation, of complete enslavement, of thorough disenfranchisement 'is a terrible violation against the interests of our Fatherland'. He might have said all this, and more along these lines to Count Potocki, but the Count got up and left.

To keep a grip on the administration's loyalty he raised the salary of officials and government employees and industrial leaders – the classic political ruse of a dying regime. He raged impotently when his armoured car was confiscated for service at the front. When news of the horrors of the Maideneck concentration camp broke in the world press, he conferred with colleagues. Then he sat down to compose an essay on 'Justice', which he followed with another on 'Dilettantism', then finally one on 'Administration and Administrative Justice'. His son claimed he was preparing for an easy transition to a comfortable university post after the war. At the same time he tried to cover his tracks *vis à vis* the Reich regime, informing the Minister of Justice Lammers that he rejected 'all responsibility for the failure of the Wehrmacht to prevail in this territory'.

He kept his mistress Lilli beside him as long as he could before sending her westwards to relative safety, back to her home in Bad Aibling and her husband, who was complaisant in their affair.

In his diary, just weeks before he fled from Krakow, he recorded an extraordinary exchange between himself and two Nazi Party workers, Karl Schön and Mitglied Masur, in which his loyalty to the Führer – and more importantly, the Führer's loyalty and support for him – is earnestly debated. As Frank questions them it begins to become clear that other Nazi officials have been talking about him behind his back, casting aspersions and suggesting he is going to be pushed out. He wants to know what they were saying and what was going on. It concerns him greatly that he is called *ein Popanz*, a 'puppet', laughing stock or stooge, and he edgily seeks reassurance, blustering and bullying as he does so, from these two faithful Nazis, that he has not lost Hitler's trust and is not about to be dropped. He tells them, ending abruptly, and referring to himself in the third person, 'Frank will investigate this business further!'

That same evening, 9 December, Frank went to the opera for the last time in his life. The Krakow State Theatre was giving a performance of Gluck's *Orpheus and Euridice*, in which the hero Orpheus, the inventor of music, descends to the Underworld to find his love and bring her back to the upper world of light. But he commits the forbidden act of looking behind him as he leaves. Hans Frank had generated and ruled over, gluttonously enjoyed, life in the Underworld (*Nebensland*, as he constantly called Poland). From now on he would, after a very brief respite, be forced to look over his shoulder and confront that dark underworld where once he had been king.

Brave to the last, or so he said and liked to believe, he sat like a 'paladin in my castle [to] calm down the others with my composure and self-control'. The Russians then penetrated the outer perimeter of the city and Frank was, inevitably according to his own account, the last to leave (but did not, as the Führer might have insisted, heroically fall on his sword).

The day before he took a final walk 'through the rooms of the castle I had so carefully maintained and so tastefully furnished. In that great coronation and parliament hall, with its magnificent view far out over the wonderful old city, I stood alone and considered the path that had led us here.'

Sunday afternoon, 17 January 1945: 'I had the flag of our Reich lowered. I took it with me and returned to the Fatherland. The Government General had now become history.'

PART FOUR

25

Walpürgisnacht

Possibly on the very day in May 1945 US tanks arrived at the future Cardinal Joseph Ratzinger's front door, Hans Frank, stripped of position but ever the optimist, was arrested not very far away, at Neuhaus am Schliersee.

He had attempted to preserve if not the dignity then the trappings and perks of his office up to the moment of arrest. Since he left Krakow on 17 January he had, in a royal tour kind of way, been on the run, but not as single-mindedly as other Nazi leaders, like Himmler, who had disguised themselves to slip through military checkpoints, or worked escape routes via the Vatican, through Switzerland or Sweden, or had devised other means of flight.

In April 1945, with characteristic, cold-blooded calculation, Himmler had tried to dissociate himself from Hitler and make peace offers to the Allies through the Swedish diplomat Count Bernadotte: it was claimed that he had taken so long to do this only out of his personal oath of loyalty to Hitler. The overtures were rejected and Hitler found out, removing him from office, although he clung to the appearance and trappings of power, driving about in his Mercedes with his SS escort like a mediaeval condottiere. He rejected suggestions to hand himself over, to fly to Bavaria to be with his wife and family and then was arrested by the British south-west of Lüneburg with forged papers and an eye-patch. Upon revealing who he was, he committed suicide with a cyanide capsule during a body search.

There was a Bishop Hudal in Rome (see page 209), it was reported, who, like some other highly placed members of the church, offered to arrange Frank's escape. It points to Frank's sense of entitlement and superiority, and assumption that he would get away with it, that he did not, like other Nazi leaders, avail himself of the opportunity.

Before returning to await the arrival of the US Army in May, Frank indulged in his own twilight of the gods debauchery, in what one might consider his private *Walpürgisnacht*, the famous scene of Goethe's *Faust Part II*. First he visited Breslau to make sure Brigitte and his children were evacuated to the Schoberhof. Brigitte, before she could find a way out of Poland, had been briefly detained with her five children by armed Poles who broke into the Breslau retreat and ordered her and the children up against the wall while they interrogated them about where Frank was hiding. They escaped while the Poles were tearing the house apart to look for him.

In Breslau, on 20 January, Frank heard the Soviet armies were near, so he, the *Landgerichtsrat* Schüler, and his aides Mohr and Fenzke burnt all the official documents of his rule of the Government General. He kept his diaries.

Driving on from Breslau he stayed with Count Manfred von Richthofen in his castle at Seichau. Here he brought with him between twenty and twenty-five of his staff, and his Polish loot including the exquisite Da Vinci 'Lady with an Ermine' and the Rembrandt self-portrait. With amorous breaks to visit Lilli in Bad Aibling, and as the Reich crumbled, Frank found it hard to give up his old ways. In mid-February word of his constant wild partying (in which his friends the architect von Palesieux and the playwright Gerhart Hauptmann joined him) reached Reich headquarters.

A major from the local 4 Panzer headquarters reported back to Bormann in Berlin on the 'cowardly flight' and 'unbelievable behaviour and extravagant excess' indulged in by the Frank *'regierung'* administration. They crashed an eight-cylinder Mercedes laden with large amounts of drink, food and cigarettes into a local 'art treasure building', shedding secret documents. They beat a hasty retreat in advance of the invaders even though the risk of capture was small, abandoning the castle in a filthy state with empty bottles everywhere and leaving behind:

> 14 typewriters
> 5 telexed personal action files
> 3 parcels of art folders
> 4 cigar box books
> 1 room full of art objects
> 18 cylinder Mercedes
> 20 car rugs

Yet Frank was often in merry mood in early spring 1945, as he visited and bedded his lady friends; he took to composing execrable lyrics:

> Ring out spring song
> And sing
> We in sweet lust
> Wow!
> And bring
> Luck and light
> In every breast.

During the next months, as his staff, resources and hope of reversals in the campaigns vanished, we still find Frank in semi-opulent retreat. He was guarded or at least domiciled either at the Schoberhof family home, or nearby where he had taken over the local café, known as the Haus Bergfrieden, as his new 'Governor General Headquarters' and installed his secretary Helene Kraffezyk. He had now 'settled into a relationship' with Kraffezyk, whatever this may mean. He convinced himself, as did those of his retainers who had not already fled, that he could continue running the Government General in exile, and he informed Hans Lammers in Berlin that he had saved everything essential from the Russians. He still spent nights with Lilli, who was only 30km away (the first on 24 January), while 'Ilse T', a fourth admirer or mistress makes a brief appearance as the sender of a love letter which survives. One wonders how and why all these women apparently stood by him, especially his wife Brigitte, but they did. Helene attested later how kind he was to underlings and friends. 'He had a soft heart. In order not to show it he often hid it behind an aloof or gruff exterior ... He gave orders to his men without listening to their arguments, which naturally made cooperation difficult.'

On 1 May at the Schoberhof Hans told his children he must be the only minister who was looking forward to his arrest because he was handing over his diaries, and, as every day was accounted for, had 'nothing to fear'.

Lieutenant Walter Stein, of the US 7th Army, arrested him on 4 May 1945 and escorted him into custody. Stein took charge also of Frank's well stocked wine cellar and larder (according to the Soviet prosecutor General Rudenko at Nuremberg) and '38 volumes of taped documents covering Frank's life from 1939-1945, 33 of them bound in linen, five in file covers, together with minutes of government conferences, NSDAP meetings; and personal diaries'.

Despite his insistence, like most captured Nazi leaders, on his very special status, his US captors gave him short shrift, transferring him from prison in Miesbach, where he was known as the 'Jewish Butcher of Krakow' and beaten and verbally abused, having to run a gauntlet of jeering guards on arrival, to a military camp near Hitler's retreat at Berchtesgaden. In particular, two GIs savaged him before they dumped him in a truck and covered him with tarpaulin.

After better treatment in the new camp the US Command moved him to the Palace Hotel in Mandorf-les-Bains, Luxembourg, where he joined high-rankers of his own kind, selected for an exemplary trial of Nazi war leaders. Here, at first described by Colonel B.C. Andrus as a 'pitiful wreck', in the company of Von Ribbentrop, Julius Streicher and Göring, he recovered not only his self-esteem, but his usual loquacity.

He began to define himself in the new role he would play among the fifty-two prisoners, that of penitent. On being shown a film of Buchenwald concentration camp, he reported in his confessional book *Facing the Gallows*, he held a handkerchief to his mouth and 'gagged' for fifteen minutes. Like most Nazi leaders, he had never set foot in a death camp.

Hearing of his beloved leader's recent suicide, Frank attempted suicide, possibly twice, although by now he was starting to voice anti-Hitler statements and claim to have been betrayed by him. He cut his left wrist, his arm and his throat, but, like much of what he did, it stopped short of a categorical act and remained frozen as a theatrical gesture. He severed some nerves, and was left with moderately severe paralysis of the left hand. Throughout the subsequent trials he wore a glove. And sunglasses, that prop of petty tyrants and gangsters.

'Since my arrest,' he wrote, now taking up the pen in his defence, 'I have lost all will to go on living, and see the future as black and threatening.'

There remained only one way out, one way to work his ticket, which would become as controversial (as regards its sincerity) as much, if not all, of his life up to this point:

'Oh Lord/ Now we are alone together,/ Only you and I!/ Thus it was when I was born,/ So it is now that I depart!/ Admit me now to Your Heavenly home,/ Oh, I beseech you, hear my prayer!/ I bring but woe and shame,/ And return now to Your heights!/ My soul trembles within./ It yearns for You./ It knows I am in torment,/ And broken through and through.../ My play is done,/ I'm bound for home.../ I relinquish now my role/ Of happy earthly toil./ The one you choose me to play,/ To speak and learn and say,/ My strength has reached its borders,/ I have carried out my orders.../ Bestowed with all honour once craved,/ I yearn now alone for my grave./ O Lord!/ Your earth is a single wound./ But to blessed health I'm now bound./ Heavy toil, heavy tasks fore-gone,/ And all mercy and grace foresworn.../ Our myriad gain/ Is but torment and pain –/ Only torment and pain.'

The God of his youth was about to make a comeback.

26

To Nuremberg

We want to learn the why of the Third Reich.

Nuremberg psychologist Dr Kelley

The devastation of its beautiful cities apart, the ancient kingdom of Bavaria had prospered during the war and continued to do so even in defeat. Peasants were now selling food by the cartload to the occupation forces at black market prices. How many of the farmers would, if they were being honest, declare how good everything had been under Hitler?

The conquering armies, often less well fed than the local Germans (with the exception of US personnel), laid down a marker for the future celebration of criminals as celebrities when Hermann Göring appeared on television. The actor Peter Ustinov, serving in the British Army in Paris, reports having seen it:

There had been no mention whatsoever of his capture, no hint even. He was, to our astonishment, surrounded by American officers who were posing with him for pictures, smiling, patting his back in friendly fashion, demanding autographs on behalf of small relatives, who would live close to history from that day on, and offering to initiate him in the mysterious rites of chewing-gum. Göring looked sallow and thinner than I had imagined, quite apart from being distinctly nervous. Having been informed about the Allied war aims, he certainly had every right to his nervousness.

This began to wear off, however under the relentless impact of these big puppies, leaping all over him and licking his face. By the time the lights went up in the auditorium, he was as relaxed and playful as any of his captors, and we spectators could only look at each other in petrified amazement.

Nazi war leaders, those who had not died, been killed, and were not in hiding, were soon to be placed in the glare of the world spotlight. Göring, together with twenty others, including Frank, was moved to Nuremberg by military convoy, then plane, from Mandorf on 12 August 1945 to stand trial in Nuremberg. Frank, now recovered in confidence and spirit, felt well prepared, with his diaries and with his legal expertise, to show himself before history and the court as being ultimately as innocent as the whole German people, and by this escape the death penalty.

In 'Peace-in-our-time' Munich, where Joseph Ratzinger had in the latter years of the war manned an anti-aircraft battery, and Hans Frank at a similar age marched with the murderous *Freikorps*, Hitler's Braunes Haus, with its marble statue of his mentor, Dietrich Eckart, philosopher and playwright, had been reduced to rubble. Other Munich shrines to the soul of Nazism were heaps of wreckage. The *Haus der Deutschen Künst*, high temple of Hitler kitsch, with its monstrous white colonnades, hid its ruin under a flapping, dark green net. Another shell was the great Deutsches Museum.

Nuremberg was no less a burnt-out shell, that city of half a million where the Nazi flags had annually flapped over two or three million hoarse, screaming Reich enthusiasts. The year 1938 had seen the ultimate *Parteitag* – Party Day, flags in the streets and bands of men marching with banners and standards – just like the leaves of Canetti's German forest. Hitler himself had devised the Wagnerian dedication of the flags which called the roll of the Nazi martyrs who were now residing in Valhalla with the spirits of their valiant ancestors. In the home of the *Meistersingers* and Albrecht Dürer, the victors found only a few shivering women and children 'hollow-cheeked and hollow-eyed', crawling into the caves they had dug for themselves in the rubble of their former homes. The film-maker Roberto Rossellini caught the mood in his 1948 *Germany Year Zero*, shot amid Berlin's rubble, showing 'the corruption of an ideology which strays from morality and Christian charity, sweeping children from one horrendous crime to another in which, with the ingenuousness of innocence, they think to find release from guilt'.

The primitive Gothic prison of Nuremberg housing the twenty-one accused was built of brick, three storeys high with a wide inner corridor, and cells on either side. Each inmate was in a solitary 9ft x 13ft cell, with toilets at each end of the corridor without seats or covers, where prisoners' feet could be kept in view. Outside, the guards from the Big Four nations shared surveillance. Inside, American personnel kept twenty-four hour watch and maintained security. Communication between the accused was kept to a strict minimum. Meals were communal, but because Göring dominated the other prisoners he was put in a room to eat by himself. Psychiatrists divided the rest into five carefully chosen groups. Defence lawyers were allowed daily access to their charges, though guards were ever-present.

On 18 October 1945, the International Military Tribunal began its proceedings nearby in the spacious refurbished upper chamber of the rambling Palace of Justice. The proceedings continued until verdicts were delivered on 1 October 1946. Mountains of documentary evidence were taken from the meticulous Nazi records. The court heard the testimonies of 200 witnesses taken down by stenographers in four languages, a total of more than 5 million words. There were eight judges, two from each nation. The Russians wore military uniforms, the others judicial robes with their national flags draped behind

them. The judicial system was republican and American, the
Chief Prosecutor and President of the Court, Robert Jackson
of the US Supreme Court. The judges were led by the English-
man Lord Geoffrey Lawrence.

The twenty-one defendants attended every day of the trial
(Martin Bormann, the twenty-second, who was almost certainly
dead, but whose body could not be found, was tried *in absen-
tia*). Robert Ley, head of the German Labour Front, who had
believed the Nazis could finally overcome their enemies by the
use of death rays, and had comforted Hitler in his bunker with
the crackpot notion that so many Germans would flee westwards that they would flood the West and overrun it, committed
suicide in custody before being put on trial.

Guards brought the prisoners in two-by-two, dressed drably
now without their insignia and glittering decorations. They
passed through a covered viaduct from the prison into the Palace
and up in an elevator, each watched over in a steel cabinet, to
the courtroom where they took their place in two rows facing
the judges. All were provided with earphones to follow the proceedings in German.

Ranked Number One in the front row, reduced in weight by
30kg, Göring mocked, pulled faces and tried to steal the show,
denying whenever possible the right of the court to sit in judgement over him and his peers. Frank was also placed in the front
row; he sat sullenly between the Nazi philosopher and art plun-
derer, Alfred Rosenberg, stripped of his Ariosophic and Hindu
mysticism, and the Jew-baiter, Julius Streicher, who, like Frank,
took part in the failed putsch of 1923.

Frank wore his glove on his left hand, and the dark glasses. He
spent all of the autumn and winter of 1945–46 listening to and
watching his Nazi colleagues pleading not guilty and defending their record. He finally took the stand on 10 January 1946,
after evidence of his war crimes was given by US trial counsel,
Lt Colonel H. Baldwin. His life out of the courtroom and in the
cells as he suffered depression and suicidal urges, expanded to

the grandiose Faustian proportions of earlier times. He was now playing himself, and had no distractions. He found a 'fit audience though few'.

⁓

Frank had kept relationships going with four women at the same time. That he was back with his wife and cared for his family put a strain on Lilli. He wrote to his mother Magdalena on 21 February:

> I journeyed yesterday evening to spend a whole day again with old Lilli. I am on much better terms with her husband than with her. Life is so strange! Lilli is a lovely adorable person and has brought to me everything that's good and sympathetic. Inside she is closely and warmly tied to me. But as you surely know she also finds something about me that's very heavy to bear. It must be revenge, and had she not been married for twenty five years all would have been well, also for her.

It is not known what Hans told Lilli about his involvement with, or knowledge of, the death camps, and the mass murder of Poles. It is likely he said little or nothing that could implicate him in her eyes. Therefore, when his indictment was published in August 1945, she finally saw that Hans had lied to her by omission, or had blamed all the murder and extermination on Himmler and Krüger. Both of these were out of the way. Krüger committed suicide by swallowing cyanide (Oberösterreich, 10 May 1945), Himmler the same at Lüneburg on 23 May, after his spell of avoiding capture disguised as 'Heinrich Hitzinger'. Both of these enemies were gone, and so with neither able to answer for himself, Frank could hold them responsible for all the atrocities. The rest would be silence.

When Field Marshal Keitel signed Germany's unconditional surrender on 9 May 1945, and the United States Army settled in, the Catholic Church in Bavaria had seemed unsure as to what its role should be. According to Niklas Frank, the locals at Neuhaus went on calling his mother 'Frau Minister' until mid-May. It was difficult to drop the habit of subservience, while an occupying force, however benign and friendly, always remains the enemy. Moreover, the almost universal suffering to some degree or other, either from civil destruction and hunger, mass flight from Russian rape and revenge in the East, or the many other causes of bereavement and deprivation, now quickly assuaged bad consciences.

The vast majority of Germans had no qualms about their reversal from conquerors into victims. As Gunter Grass notes, 'the crimes coming to light with peace, the flip side of war, were making victims out of perpetrators'.

Most began to orientate themselves towards their new leaders, covering up as best they could what they did or failed to do. The chief hierarchical structure that remained was Cardinal Faulhaber's diocese of Munich, and those of his fellow bishops, some of whom had shown themselves far from resistant to Nazism. Catholic bishops bickered with their Lutheran counterparts as to who was more responsible for or more supportive of Nazism, caught between faith and patriotism.

While the Frank family hit penny-pinching and hungry hard times, Frank continued to appeal to Faulhaber from prison to obtain papal clemency. Niklas Frank believed that their fortunes began to change when, even though they had moved out of the Schoberhof into less grand dwellings, Faulhaber sent his twelve-cylinder ecclesiastical buggy to Neuhaus with vittles that dwarfed the American basic care packages.

They were invited to the Archbishop's Palace in Munich, and people started, recorded Niklas, to treat them once more as part of the league of big shots. Faulhaber, who had welcomed the German invasion of Russia in 1941, 'with great satisfaction' – only Berlin's Bishop Konrad von Preysing had refused to support it – played an equivocal and somewhat defiant role. He protested, on 20 June 1945, on behalf of imprisoned NSDAP members and German military prisoners, claiming in a joint letter to the US command with the Lutheran Bishop of Bavaria, Hans Meiser, that imprisonment and atrocities and unclarified sudden deaths in POW camps would make it difficult to rehabilitate the German people.

It would seem that once Frank's trial began in November, Faulhaber's patronage and support for Brigitte rapidly ground to a halt – so much so, that Frank threatened to reveal secret agreements made between the Vatican and the Nazis, which he soon realised would not exactly fit in with the general drift of his whitewash and his image as penitent. Niklas Frank reports in *Meine deutsche Mutter*, his account of Brigitte's life, that Faulhaber approved of some proposal his father made as Justice Minister in 1933 or 1934 in the negotiations between the Nazis and the Church, calling it in German '*genial*': brilliant. At first, Faulhaber had supported Frank's plea for mercy, but when the Polish delegation in Nuremberg became aware of this he immediately stopped his intervention with Pope Pius XII in Rome.

Meantime, with the competition cut down to nil, and with Lilli now grown deaf to Frank's repeated appeals to write to him, attend the trial or visit him in the cells, Brigitte once more had him all to herself. She did all she could to create sympathy for Frank, defend her children, excuse and whitewash his record.

The question remains, were there secret documents? Joseph Ratzinger's refusal to authorise scrutiny of Vatican documents relating to Pacelli's pre-war diplomacy in Germany and the Second World War until 2014, which has been criticised by some Jewish leaders, suggests there was something to cover up, even if there wasn't.

The number of Nazis who received help from the Vatican to disguise themselves, to filter through military checkpoints, or work escape routes through the Vatican itself, through Switzerland or Sweden, or devise other means of flight, has been estimated at over 30,000. To this day there are whole communities

in Argentina and Brazil whose founder members are alleged
to have arrived after the war from Nazi territories. The main
organiser of this exodus, known as the Vatican Ratline, was
the notorious anti-Semite Austrian cleric, Bishop Alois Hudal,
Rector of the Pontificate Santa Maria dell'Anima, where he
looked after the interests of German-speaking Catholics in Italy.
A close friend of Hudal was Monsignor Giovanni Montini, later
Pope Paul VI.

Through his office Hudal arranged papers, passports, exit
visas and work permits for escaping Nazis, among them many
well known criminals such as Klaus Barbie, Adolf Eichmann,
Heinrich Müller, Gustav Wagner and Franz Stangl. Hudal convinced Montini that leniency was needed, and as the war ended
he made the transition from pro-fascist to anti-communist, and
was then appointed by Pius XII as the official Spiritual Director
of the German People in post-war Germany.

Not surprisingly, there was considerable scientific as well as
worldwide public curiosity about this clutch of 'the greatest
group of criminals the human race has ever known'. Even so,
sartorially speaking, the Americans treated them with consideration. At first they were stripped of their suits and made to
don cotton gabardine fatigues dyed black; then the Americans
allowed them to choose items for cleaning from their own
clothes. 'Every detail,' said Speer, 'was discussed with the commandant down to the matter of sleeve buttons.' Every night
their suits were pressed for the next day's session. Psychologists made them constant objects of observation, and gave them
Rorschach and IQ tests to evaluate their mental processes and
personality traits. Most of the defendants, who saw themselves
as members of the *Herrenrasse* or master race, were only too
keen to show their vanquishers their intellectual prowess, and
all scored highly.

Both Dr Kelley and Dr Gilbert gave Frank the inkblot tests. The cigar-puffing Kelley declared, 'In my life I've run across some strange birds, but I've never met twenty-one people who considered themselves so pure and lily white.'

The inkblot tests established that most of the Nazis were essentially normal, suggesting to Kelley that the potential to act like Nazis may exist in many of us. He added, importantly, 'the almost utter destruction of the whole world will have gone for nought if we do not devise some conclusion concerning the forces that produce such chaos'. He extrapolated from his observation that the leaders were not spectacular types, and that there was 'little in America today [1947] which could prevent the establishment of a Nazi-like state'. His observations flew in the face of the general prevailing demonisation of the Nazi leaders as one-off monsters (a convenient theory to which the future Cardinal Ratzinger later subscribed). However, Kelley did believe that Hitler was the exception – 'abnormal and mentally ill'. He had never met Himmler, Goebbels or Bormann.

As a guide to Frank's exotic and even florid associations with the inkblots he was given, and without the key to what they could or did mean, Frank's Rorschach record delves into and reveals his bizarre personality. It exhibits considerably more, perhaps, than his gift for words and showmanship. In contrast to Speer's frankly dull, uncooperative, prosaic responses (Speer was undoubtedly not only the most gifted of the captured men, but also the cleverest, too) Frank sees in these fairly simple blots cosmic symbols of belief, the Eiffel Tower, women's breasts, an advertisement against venereal disease. His startling range and high suggestibility covers beautiful prima ballerinas, legion eagles, negro women with white wings, bats, masqueraders and clowns making faces, crabs and flying fish. At one point, in his second test, he sees a blot as 'one eye in a criminal head and a beard', the nose is illuminated, like a mast. He cries out '*Scheusslich! Wider lich!* Awful! Disgusting! Like Stalin. Did you know that I knew Lenin as a kid in Munich?'

During the tests he was, by turns, excited, full of wonder and surprised, and would gasp with enthusiasm at what he read into the inkblots: sometimes perhaps it was a regurgitation or revisiting of all the varied artistic symbolism and richness of the Polish works of art he pillaged in previous years ('wreaths hanging from cross over grave; two weeks after burial, therefore Christ's figure not finished on cross; blue silk banners of 18th century hanging across trophy room'). Finally, he has this comment to make:

> It's uncanny … they're just inkblots, but it shows that beauty and a deeper meaning can be concealed in the most unassuming forms … You know it is terrifying … a man wants to make an inkblot … and the ink itself makes a symbol of life! It just shows that the spiritual world is greater than any man's will. You psychologists are ingenious in using such methods.

I reconstruct the following scenario from the reported results of the IQ test as described by Speer and the psychologists (using contemporary witnesses):

> In this pre-trial communal gathering Speer, Hans Frank, Schacht, Seyss-Inquart, Admiral Dönitz, are holding and studying a count of marks for IQ tests. Göring is here too, but he is scornful and fulminates apart from the others. US Guards watch.
> 'Twenty-one of us!' said Speer aloud to himself. He was not interested in the score. Speer sees himself not as one of the others but definitely superior. He was writing to his wife: 'I must regard my life as concluded …' was his usual theme. The guards read and censored mail, so they knew what went in his letters. Schacht says suddenly, 'I got the highest score!'

Speer put down his pen and asked, 'Have you read the indict-ment?'

Schacht ignores this. 'No, no, no! I mean, look at the list of the marks. I got the highest actual score!'

'You didn't!'

Overhearing this, Göring has come over, and in a sulky and prima-donna fashion says, 'I am among the top scorers.' The leader has spoken. This is true; Göring had a phenomenal intelligence and memory. But Schacht had the highest score: over 150.

'Yes, you came top – but only because of your age!' Seyss-Inquart complains to Schacht. 'They gave you a senility bonus.'

'It's a good job Himmler's not here,' answered Schacht. 'He would have got the highest mark.'

Seyss-Inquart was not to be outdone. 'I don't agree. If it had been a test on the *Bhagavad-Gita, Thus Spake Zarathustra* – then that might be so.'

Speer has grown impatient.

'What in God's name are you talking about? Guilt? – Are you discussing the score of marks for debt? Where is your guilt? We have the same word.'

'Shut up, Speer! We all know you would betray us, and the Führer, given the chance. They had you quoted in the British press criticising Hitler.'

'That was lies,' answered Speer.

'Like Frank here, you were ready to desert the ship. A fair-weather Nazi, Frank had his face on a postage stamp. He thought he was greater than Hitler. What a joke.'

Frank protested. 'Perfidious Albion. They sent a card to Himmler with my face on a stamp next to the Führer's.'

'Stop arguing.' Schacht had grown tired of the bickering. 'We are going to be here for months. Stop arguing! This is an intelligence test.'

'Look at us!' Again Speer spoke with contempt, but saw himself as different. 'Who would have thought that you, Reichsmarshalls, Grand Admirals, Reichsleiters, would be squabbling over the marks of an IQ test set by a Yank military psychologist. No doubt he is a Jew. Many brilliant people are. We slipped up here, didn't we? Listen – ' he read from the charge sheet:

'"Indictments: one: Crimes Against Peace – planning, preparation, initiation, and waging of a war of aggression, or a war in violation of international treaties, agreements, and assurances ..." Well? –' he looked at Schacht, who snatched the sheet from him, and continues reading:

'"Second: War Crimes: violations of the laws or customs of war. To include, but not be limited to murder, extermination, enslavement, deportation to slave labour ... killing of hostages, plunder of private property, murder or ill-treatment of prisoners of war, slave labour, use of outlawed weapons, wanton destruction of cities or devastation not justified by military necessity. Three: Crimes Against Humanity. including inhuman acts committed against any civilian population, before or during the war, or persecutions on political, racial, or religious grounds ... whether or not in violation of the domestic law of the country where perpetrated" ... Further, "the official position of defendants, whether as Heads of State or responsible officials in Government departments, shall not be considered as freeing them from responsibility or mitigating punishment."'

'What is your response, Herr Reichsmarshall?' Speer mildly inquires of Göring.

Göring tapped his fingers on the table and irritably asked Frank, 'What do you say, Hans? You're the eminent lawyer?'

Before Frank could answer, Schacht interrupts:

'What about what they did to us? Saturation bombing of Dresden ... systematic murder of civilians, the old, women and children ...'

Frank speaks: 'They have gone into that. The tribunal has decided that it will not allow us to defend ourselves by claiming that the powers against us have also committed crimes, such as the carpet bombing of German cities. In a murder trial it is no defence for the accused to say that your accusers, too, have killed.'

The lawyer has spoken. Silence.

'Well now, the learned counsel has given his advice,' sneers Göring. 'Let us not take it seriously, gentlemen. It is all a charade. It is, purely and simply, revenge. The victims are getting their own back on the conquered.'

Schacht agrees. 'And, moreover, talking of murder, none of us ever killed anyone, did we? I certainly never did. What about you, Speer, did you ever shoot or strangle a soul?'

'Never. But I know for a fact Himmler did. Göring, you must have killed plenty of people in your time?'

'Not after 1934, when we got rid of Röhm and his crowd. They're not indicting us for that. I led the German Air Force in World War One. I shot down fourteen or fifteen English planes. Once, during a dogfight, I had an English ace in my sights and was about to blow him to kingdom come. But I could see he had run out of ammunition. It wasn't a fair fight. I let him live … But, of course we all know Goebbels was a killer. A serial murderer.'

'We were only transmitting orders that came from above. Who can blame us? We carried out orders. We were true, loyal servants of Germany,' says the banker Funk.

'And what about King Stanislaus here?' Göring bates Frank. 'Hitler called you Stanislaus, and said you were too soft on the Poles. I bet you never dirtied your hands with Polish blood. Too squeamish, eh? Why don't you answer? What about you, Frank? Come on, answer. You never shot anyone, or put anyone to death, did you?'

'Did I? Did I? You know, when it comes down to it, I cannot remember. One thing for sure, I never gave orders, never gave an order, never gave a direct order to anyone to resort to terror or execution.' He talks in a slightly nervous staccato. 'I issued policy directives to protect the Reich and German sovereignty. I only ever wanted good management. Good efficient management of the Reich's resources. Good clear execution of the means by which our dreams and ambitions could be achieved … It was Himmler, wasn't it, Himmler was the one who believed the solution to all our problems was to eliminate any obstacle with death squads and industrialised extermination. Himmler was mad to obey the Führer's orders and kill every last Jew in the world. He even took the best SS units from the Russian front to achieve his aim.'

'We all hated Himmler. We hated him more than the Jews.'

'I quarrelled with Himmler. I shall bring that out at the trial in my defence. I believed in the execution of the law. In a fair trial! Himmler acted behind my back. Himmler subverted my authority both in Bavaria where I was Minister of Justice and in Poland … I believe in justice. We will be given a fair trial.'

27

The Butcher's Conversion

Hans Frank's return journey to faith was rapid, sudden and very public. I doubt he ever read Marlowe's *Doctor Faustus*. But if he had, he surely would have identified with the tortured Faustus:

> I see an angel hover o'er thy head,
> And, with a vial full of precious grace,
> Offers to pour the same into thy soul.

The Church preached that it was never too late to gain redemption, and Hans, in his own mind a great tragic figure, saw his redemption and salvation as belonging to history. He would make sure that nothing about it would be uncommunicated. Again without knowing it, it seemed he emulated Marlowe's Faustus, when Mephistopheles had fixed to come and collect his soul an hour before midnight:

> ... or let this hour be but
> A year, a month, a week, a natural day,
> That Faustus may repent and save his soul!
> *O lente, lente currite noctis equi!*

The dramatic side of Frank wasted no time. 'Show and tell,' it said. As soon as Father Sixtus O'Connor, a US Army chaplain,

entered his cell (according to the Franciscan priest), he found
Frank prostrated on the floor, kneeling before him. He said,
'When I was a little boy, every morning before I went to school
my mother would make the sign of the cross on my forehead.
Please, Father, do that for me now.' He felt more like following
the Goethe version than Marlowe's, and was ready to negotiate
himself a place in heaven.

The Benedictine's instruction of Frank proceeded apace,
with the advantage he had been baptised as a child and taken
communion. He was re-baptised or 'converted' in his cell
on October 25 1945. Now, according to his psychiatrist, he
became aloof and withdrawn. He made a very full secular
confession as well (private confession was never going to be
enough, because he was, as we know, on the world stage) to
Dr Gustave Gilbert:

> 'Yes, many things have become clear to me in the loneliness
> of this cell. The trial is neither here nor there, but what a
> spectacle of the irony of fate and heavenly injustice! You
> know, there is a divine punishment which is far more devas-
> tating in its irony than any punishment man has yet devised!
> Hitler represented the spirit of evil on earth and recognized
> no power greater than his own. God watched this band of
> heathens puffed up with their puny power and then simply
> brushed them aside in scorn and amusement.' Frank brushed
> them aside with his gloved hand. 'I tell you, the scorn-
> ful laughter of God is more terrible than any vengeful lust
> of man! When I see Göring, stripped of his uniform and
> decorations, meekly taking his 10-minute walk under the
> curious, amused eyes of the American guards, I think of how
> he revelled in his glory as President of the Reichstag. It is
> grotesque! Here are the would-be rulers of Germany – each
> in a cell like this, with four walls and a toilet, awaiting trial
> as ordinary criminals. Is that not a proof of God's amuse-
> ment with men's sacrilegious quest for power?' His smile

gradually froze and his eyes narrowed to slits. 'But are these people thankful for these last few weeks in which to atone for their sins of egotism and indifference, and to recognize that they have been in league with the *devil incarnate*? Do they get on their knees and pray to God for forgiveness? – No, they worry about their own little necks and cast about for all kinds of little excuses to absolve themselves of blame! Can't they see that this is a horrible tragedy in the history of mankind, and that we are the symbols of an evil that God is brushing aside?

He raised his anger at Hitler to such a pitch that he apologised to the guard outside, who had grown restive: 'He played art-and-music-lover, but he had no conception of art. He liked Wagner, naturally, because he could see himself playing god with dramatic splendour.' Hitler was incapable of appreciating the nude that for him 'represented merely a protest against convention'. As for those fascinating, formerly hypnotic eyes, they now gave out the stare of the hard, insensitive psychopath. Intriguingly, he confirmed Thomas Mann's reading of the Nazi soul as wilful primitive egotism or hubris, and that the hatred of form and convention was the key to his personality: 'He took Bavaria, his *Secretär* Wien [after Schiller's character in *Kabale und Liebe*] and Himmler into his confidence, because they were reflections of his hatred of form and convention.' Frank raised a warning forefinger and wagged it at Dr Gilbert: 'Beware of the legend-builders, *Herr Doktor*! Himmler would not have dared to carry out this program of mass murder if Hitler had not directly approved it or ordered it!'

And now, commented the much younger but level-headed Gilbert (he is called fresh-faced, pleasant in the accounts), Frank really felt spiritually liberated as never before. His dreams 'take him beyond the confines of his cell', noted Gilbert, who was transfixed by Frank, and had not made up his mind as to whether he was sincere or not:

Recently he dreamed of Hitler, and that made him doubly resolved to take an upright stand and admit common guilt. It is all so realistic. Sometimes he has nocturnal emissions. In one recent dream he was standing at the seashore and watching the waves, and then a girl appeared – he thinks his daughter – then the mountains and the yodelling and the vast spaces. – He awoke with an incredible feeling of emotional relief. Went on talking about how independent one could be of the restrictions of the environment if one had inner fortitude.

How long would this last? And had the lawyer and politician, still intent on controlling the salvation of his body and soul, finally and for ever renounced evil?

Unfortunately for him, this Faust had not just an hour but nearly six months to wait in a suspended state of guilt and contrition before judgement in the dock. Would he last the course? Would he be able to prove the depth and integrity of his penitence, and steal a march upon his criminal confederates?

There's no art to see the mind's construction in the face.

Macbeth, act 1, scene 4, 1

Dr Gilbert and Dr Kelley continued their appraisal of Nazi evil. Kelley, who spoke no German, became fixated on Göring, sucked into a love-hate relationship with this complex, charismatic figure, and inclined anyway, from projection of his own mood and personality, to see the Nazis in darker and more occult forms. Kelley had little of Gilbert's range, speed and sensitivity.

In the Court Room on 29 November, Commander Donovan told the prisoners that they were to be shown a documentary of the atrocities US troops found on arrival at the concentration camps. Dr Gilbert omits to say that Frank, Göring and the others had already been shown a similar film about Buchenwald at the Palace Hotel in May that year. Drs Gilbert and Kelley were sat at each end of the prisoners' dock, and Gilbert jotted notes on their responses every few minutes:

Frank swallows hard, blinks eyes, trying to stifle tears ... Fritzsche watches intensely with knitted brow, cramped at the end of his seat, evidently in agony ... Göring keeps leaning on balustrade, not watching most of the time, looking droopy ... Funk mumbles something under his breath ... Streicher keeps watching, immobile except for an occasional squint ... Funk now in tears, blows nose, wipes eyes, looks down ... Frick shakes head at illustration of 'violent death' – Frank mutters 'Horrible!' ... Rosenberg fidgets, peeks at screen, bows head, looks to see how others are reacting ... Seyss-Inquart stoic throughout ... Speer looks very sad, swallows hard ... Defence attorneys are now muttering, 'for God's sake – terrible.' Raeder watches without budging ... von Papen sits with hand over brow, looking down, has not looked at screen yet ... Hess keeps looking bewildered ... piles of dead are shown in a slave labor camp ... von Schirach watching intently, gasps, whispers to Sauckel ... Funk crying now ... Göring looks sad, leaning on elbow ... Dönitz has head bowed, no longer watching ... Sauckel shudders at picture of Buchenwald crematorium oven ... as human skin lampshade is shown, Streicher says, 'I don't believe that' ... Göring coughing ... Attorneys gasping ... Now Dachau ... Schacht still not looking ... Frank nods his head bitterly and says, 'Horrible!' ... Rosenberg still fidgeting, leans forward, looks around, leans back, hangs head ... Fritzsche, pale, biting lips, really seems in agony ... Dönitz has head buried in his hands ... Keitel now hanging head ... Ribbentrop looks up at screen as British officer starts to speak, saying he has already buried 17,000 corpses

... Frank biting his nails ... Frick shakes his head incredulously at speech of female doctor describing treatment and experiments on female prisoners at Belsen ... As Kramer is shown, Funk says with choking voice, 'The dirty swine!' ... Ribbentrop sitting with pursed lips and blinking eyes, not looking at screen ... Funk crying bitterly, claps hand over mouth as women's naked corpses are thrown into pit ... Keitel and Ribbentrop look up at mention of tractor clearing corpses, see it, then hang their heads ... Streicher shows signs of disturbance for first time ...

In the cell afterwards, Gilbert found Frank depressed and agitated, full of abject shame and rage:

'To think that we lived like kings and believed in that beast! – Don't let anybody tell you that they had no idea! Everybody sensed that there was something horribly wrong with this system, even if we didn't know all the details. They didn't *want* to know! It was too comfortable to live on the system, to support our families in royal style, and to believe that it was all right. You treat us too well,' he said, pointing to the food on the table, which he hadn't touched. 'Your prisoners and our own people starved to death in our camps. – May God have mercy on our souls! – Yes, *Herr Doktor*, what I told you was absolutely right. – This trial has been willed by God.'

He had, he said, a vision of Hitler in the courtroom, repeating it in mystical ecstasy: 'You have sworn faithfulness to me unto death – come!'

Other defendants pestered Gilbert, asking if he had felt the terrific power of Hitler emanating from the screen. Gilbert replied he hadn't. Ribbentrop told him that had Hitler come to his cell he would do it all over again: 'Can't you really feel the terrific magnetism of his personality?'

But then we see Frank observing Frank, the cunning operator (and 'normal' as Gilbert noted): 'I wrote it down as I thought it might interest you psychologically.'

Frank then railed against his fellow prisoners, distancing himself from them: 'They still don't know what is taking place.' On his walk with Göring in the prison yard, he said, Göring 'stopped and looked at me, waiting for me to take my proper place at his left because he is the senior officer'. The Lutheran Chaplain Gerrecke told Gilbert after the film that Göring said he would attend chapel services – to do the chaplain a favour, 'Because as ranking man of the group, if I attend the others will follow suit.'

Frank also made some interesting and arguably prophetic statements to Gilbert about 'old Europe', and how barbarism was a strong German racial characteristic. He was terrified, he said, at 'the thought that Hitler is only the first stage of a new type of human being in evolution, which will end in destroying itself. Europe is finished.'

In a new Europe that, it can be argued, is becoming more and more innured to unnatural genetic selection such as was advocated in Nazi Germany, to euthanasia and mercy suicide, as well as mass abortion, perhaps Frank's warning should be taken just a little seriously. Parts of Hitler's Darwinian *Mein Kampf* are being implemented, albeit in gentler, outwardly more humane form. Has the IT revolution created a new type of human being contemptuous of individuality, ready to worship images or idols, intent on submerging him or herself in mass identity, and discarding responsibility for greed or gratification? The Polish Pope John Paul II, a survivor of over five years spent in Frank's Krakow, repeatedly pointed to the present-day danger of Nazi totalitarianism, a 'culture of death' existing in another form. Joseph Ratzinger, while cardinal, and after the crumbling of the Soviet bloc, echoed Frank in his prophetic scenarios: at that time he did not read 'any secondary literature', for it was 'important to be in conversation only with the greats

... Perhaps the possibilities of our Western culture have been exhausted, as in the ancient world.' He saw 'a violent change, with great losses ...'

Frank often reiterated his defiance of Göring and the diehard Nazis until the beginning of 1946, but away from the prison cells, and in advance of his appearance in the courtroom, his naively honest and uncensored diary had already built the case against him. Major Walsh, for the prosecution, read such statements to the hushed court as, 'That we sentence 1,200,000 Jews to die of hunger should only be noted marginally.' Walsh also presented a 75-page SS report by General Stoop, boasting of setting every block of the Warsaw ghetto on fire, where the residents 'finally jumped from windows, a great number of Jews who could not be counted were exterminated by blowing up sewers and dugouts'.

After General Jodl shouted against this 'SS swine' boasting at such a length while major campaigns against well-armed enemies hardly merited mention, Major Walsh also quoted Frank on Polish Jews in December 1941. Frank stated they had '2,500,000 malignant gluttons in the Government General'; but then later, in January 1944, this had come down sharply: 'at the present time, we still have in the GG perhaps 100,000 Jews.'

When Gilbert later asked Frank about these statements in his cell, Frank said such cold-blooded stuff belonged to the time of his blind fanaticism, and that he had turned over his diaries so the truth could be told. He said, 'Let the axe fall where it may.'

At lunch breaks Frank now openly harangued the others, his face red with mounting rage, in particular his old boss Göring, who also had come round to saying that he thought Hitler had gone too far. A general consensus among the prisoners emerged that Hitler had possibly gone crazy by 1942, certainly by 1943. When Frank appealed to the others on the necessity of telling the whole truth for the German people and the world to know, 'Rosenberg tried to hark back to the old tactic of Allied aggressions and how America was going to be faced with the same racial problem. He looked to Speer for moral support, but Speer laughed in his face with a sarcastic wave of the hand.'

Speer was playing a cool game for tactical exoneration. As the minister for armaments who had miraculously maintained massive production to the end, and as the architect of Hitler's megalomaniac plans for new cities, he had somehow managed to distance himself from the way this was achieved.

28

Governor Faust takes the Stand

Most of the defendants, inspired or cowed by Göring's cynicism and scepticism, slipped back from their *mea culpa* mood after the film into entrenched myopia. Nazi youth leader von Schirach: 'I doubt very much whether a German woman could have deliberately had lampshades made out of human skin,' he told Gilbert. 'Then it was done by a German man and she accepted it as a matter of course,' he retorted. 'What difference does it make?' Schirach sat back with a despondent look.

Frank's fellow-accused were, by the year's end, turning on him more and more. He wallowed in self-pity and shame, but still asserted the need for the world to be shown the truth. His hero worship transferred to his captors:

> Oh, *ja* – the shame is devastating. – Such fine men, those judges and the prosecuting attorneys – such noble figures – the Englishmen – the Americans, – especially that tall fine Englishman [Judge Lawrence]. – And they sit on the opposite side and I sit here among such repulsive characters as Streicher – Göring – Ribbentrop.

He was beginning, under the influence of Father Sixtus, to enjoy the additional restrictions of solitary confinement imposed on them – the authorities didn't like the clubhouse twittering of the defendants that had grown among them and had stopped the communal lunches and exercise. Frank endorsed Hitler's *bête noire*, Pastor Martin Niemöller, who had survived his Nazi ordeal and who now told the German people that they talked too much about the hardship and not enough about their guilt. Well-fed prisoners apparently soon forget their crimes, it seemed to Frank.

In January 1946 it seemed something in Frank snapped. He became once again the Brechtian Bavarian of divided soul, like Mr Puntila who one day will abuse his servant Matti when drunk, then become the soul of love the next day.

It happened like this.

Suddenly, as the court's lens zoomed in on Frank's face, and the evidence against him was laid before the judges, those present were startled to hear Frank's young counsel from Munich, Dr Seidl, halt the proceedings with an accusation clearly approved by Frank. Seidl had qualified as an attorney in 1937, and joined the Nazi Party the same year. Described by Himmler's grand-niece as a 'master of specious argument', he defended numerous Nazis, but also later made a name for himself as Bavarian Minister of the Interior, one of his duties being the surveillance of extreme right-wing groups.

Dr Alfred Seidl was a good bet as far as Frank was concerned, as he simultaneously defended Rudolf Hess, Hitler's former deputy, who actually escaped with his life. Like Hitler and Himmler, Hess had an abiding belief in astrology and, as he told Dr Douglas Kelley, one of his astrologers told him he was destined to bring about peace between 'the two great Nordic powers'. Owing to his mental condition and Seidl's defence, he ultimately escaped hanging.

Frank's general line of defence would be to say that he had little defence. Göring contemptuously described Seidl as just like Mickey Mouse.

But now Dr Seidl was to stun the hushed court, which had been listening to Frank's own testimony of his crimes, by asking the judges whether the Vatican was helping the prosecution. If the answer to this was in the affirmative, Frank had told Seidl to say, on his behalf, that 'his Client would have to leave the Church'.

Suddenly the whole of Frank's public conversion, the whole of his contrition and confession, came down to a threat, repeating that which he had made to Sapieha once before. What Frank meant was that he resented the Church, which had been reinforced by his wife's animus, who now felt ditched by Faulhaber, for not coming to his aid. Since the trial began, the Bavarian Church had distanced itself from the accused.

In briefing Seidl to take this course he had again plunged into one of those judicial muddles from which he at once wriggled to free himself. Before the court opened the next day, 10 January, he told Gilbert that Seidl had 'misunderstood him' – arguing that he had merely 'wanted to know' whether the Catholic Church, which should be above such matters, was helping the prosecution.

He denied saying that he would leave the Church, although neither Dr Gilbert nor anyone else, it seemed, believed his denial. He had merely said, he asserted, in a rather eerie echo of Pius XII's explanation of why he did not denounce Hitler, that 'it would put all the German Catholics in a difficult position'. Again, here is an echo which goes back to the Concordat of 1933 and the really 'difficult position', not to say stranglehold, in which Pius, then as Pacelli, and the Vatican, had all German Catholics. Why should Faulhaber be deserting the Nazi cause now, when in a sermon in Munich in 1937, he declared:

> At a time when the heads of the major nations of the world faced the new Germany with reserve and considerable suspicion, the Catholic Church, the greatest moral power on earth, through the Concordat, expressed its confidence in the new

German government. This was a deed of immeasurable significance for the reputation of the new government abroad.

Frank then gave the game away, and was to become much-
quoted:

> It was just another one of those times when I suddenly
> get startled [gasps] and jump right in ... It is interesting to
> observe one's own reactions. It is as though I am two people.
> – Me, myself, Frank here – and the other Frank, the Nazi
> leader. And sometimes I wonder how that man Frank could
> have done those things. This Frank looks at the other Frank
> and says, 'Hmm, what a louse you are, Frank! – How could
> you do such things? – You certainly let your emotions run
> away with you, didn't you?' Isn't that interesting? I am sure
> as a psychologist you must find that very interesting. – Just
> as if I were two different people. I am here, myself – and that
> other Frank of the big Nazi speeches over there on trial. –
> Fascinating, isn't it?

To this Dr Gilbert added in his account, 'Very fascinating, in a
schizoid sort of way.'

Over the next months until 18 April, Frank wavered. He did
not much like L.N. Smirnov, the Soviet prosecutor, who called
him 'the unnecessary evil gnome of jurisprudence [whom]
Hitler needed to clothe in legal form the inhumane theories of
fascism'. Confident words from a Stalinist lackey!

Gilbert found him back-tracking in his violent renun-
ciations. Should he have made his last stand with the Nazi
leaders, Frank wondered. He even expressed admiration for
Göring – 'so charming at times'. These unstable, situational
developments came and went, still with doubts – 'The Russians have no business in this court' (they had been shown a
Soviet atrocity film of acres of executed Soviet soldiers). But
when Kaltenbrunner took the stand and the main executioner

denied he knew anything about the death camps, Frank again changed his mind. Kaltenbrunner's out-and-out perjury outraged Frank.

On 15 April 1946, Colonel Rudolf Höss calmly testified in a matter-of-fact, apathetic way, that he had carried out Himmler's orders, murdering the 2.5 million Jews under his direction at Auschwitz.

Frank's outrage and recantations came and went in fits and starts. Sometimes it was vanity that swung him back, and his sense of innocence was wounded by the evidence in court. Gilbert overheard him talking after the court heard how women's hair was packed into bales for commercial use at Auschwitz:

> Frank, in spite of the revival of remorse which he professed to me yesterday, was overheard using some of the stock Nazi defensive rationalizations in a conversation with Rosenberg, within hearing of Kaltenbrunner, during the morning recess. 'They are trying to pin the murder of 2,000 Jews a day in Auschwitz on Kaltenbrunner – but what about the 30,000 people who were killed in the bombing attacks on Hamburg in a few hours? – They were also mostly women and children. – And how about the 80,000 deaths from the atomic bombing in Japan? – Is that justice too?' Rosenberg laughed, 'Yes, of course – because we lost the war.'

Maundy Thursday, 18 April 1946, the first Holy Day of the first peacetime Easter celebration for six years. A nervous, self-conscious Frank, still in his sunglasses pleading conjunctivitis, left hand in glove, waited to take the stand.

Seidl rose to his feet; at first he proposed the tribunal hear the witnesses he brought to the court before he called Governor Frank. Frank's first line of defence were the witnesses who would attest to his good relations with the Church in Poland, how he patronised and protected the arts, proposed more rations for Polish workers, founded an orchestra ...

Judge Lawrence wouldn't have it. He instructed that they should hear the accused first and then, if doubt remained over his guilt, they would hear witnesses.

Frank began by giving the jury his CV: the usual stuff. Legal advisor to Hitler and the Nazi Party; Reichstag member in 1930; President of the German Academy of Law in 1933; Governor General of Poland in 1939.

Dr Seidl asked: 'What part did you play in the events in Poland beginning in 1939?'

The answer surprised the packed and hushed courtroom: 'I bear the responsibility. Ever since April 30, 1945, when Hitler ended his life, I have been determined to reveal my responsibility to the world as clearly as possible.' He then mentioned handing over the volumes of his diary.

Seidl's next question was: 'Witness, are you conscious of any guilt in having countless crimes against the rights of nations or against human rights?'

Frank did not know how to answer and hesitated. But Judge Lawrence interceded and said: 'That is a question the court has to decide.'

So Seidl rephrased his question: 'Witness, what do you say regarding the accusations that have been brought against you in the indictment?'

Frank responded by saying that he would ask the Tribunal to decide on the degree of his guilt at the end of the trial. But then, he took a deep breath, adding:

'I myself, speaking from the very depths of my feelings, and after the experience of the five months of this trial, want to say that now, after I have gained a full insight into all the horrible atrocities that have been committed. I am possessed by a deep sense of guilt.'

The court stirred again with surprise. Frank's co-accused, who sat in two ranks, miserably cowed and broken men arranged according to age and seniority, turned to one another in shock and anger. Once they had had more power than any comparable ministers, generals or heads of civil service in any world power. Like an empty sack that has lost its stuffing, in seat Number One, pulling an outraged face, sat an almost naked Göring. Naked not in flesh, but stripped of all insignia and medals and 7kg lighter. Gone was the braiding of the 'golden pheasant'. His overalls were a sackcloth grey. Usually he was the centre of all attention, the celebrity playing to the gallery, the judges or the cameras. He would have made a successful chat-show host. Now he just glared, looking ready to shout in fury, but too proud to be silenced by the court officials. Frank had a snipe at him, lying that while running Poland he had never had the time to collect art treasures.

Next to Göring was the amnesiac Hess, hairless, wan, with tiny shrunken eyes. Whether Hess had lost his mind – or just intermittently for the sake of convenience – is one of those questions which would engage theorists and engender speculation forever. Von Ribbentrop next to him, once a grafter who had paid for his title, now carried the look of a greasy slumdog. He had wriggled so much under questioning, changing his story from day to day. And *Nummer Vier*, Kaltenbrunner, mild-mannered murderer; then edgy, chip-on-shoulder Alfred Rosenberg, the superior philosopher with no blood on his hands, just a twisted mind that fed the blood lust of the others.

Frank's place was usually between him and the unrepentant soap-box viper Streicher. There was fawning Funk, and Dr Schacht, nose turned up, a Brooklynite by birth, disdainful that he was slotted in with the Third Reich hard-core. Then behind, Franz von Papen, former German Chancellor and aristocrat, 'Satan in a Top Hat' who in the first instance let Hitler in and crowned him Chancellor, then cashed in a stack of honours and positions Hitler conferred upon him, a shape-shifter supreme. He sat alongside the rigid and upright generals and admirals. So Frank was breaking ranks – or was he?

'What were your aims when you took over the Government General?'

'I was not informed about anything ... My aim was to safeguard justice without doing harm to our war effort ... You must look at all the heavy responsibilities and workload I had. I was utterly and totally powerless, I was in this area of administering the General Government. The ones really responsible for everything were Himmler and Krüger, Koppe and the SS. None of them had checked their annihilation orders with me in advance.'

Here he was denying all those speeches he made, all those orders he issued when he ran the Government General. They were collected in a remarkable volume published in London in 1941–42, named *The Black Book*, detailing the many thousands of atrocities committed in Poland, along with the Government General laws drawn up by Frank, and scores of horrific documentary photographs. Both the endless list of decrees and the more euphemistically described exterminations were confirmed as truth in his diaries:

'Will you tell us the size of the Government General [asked Seidl]?'

'One hundred seventy to one hundred eighty thousand square kilometres. Please, your honour, please – I request you do not try to pin me down to the exact number of square kilometres!'

'What can you be thinking of, Mr Frank? You will answer precisely. Your frivolous tone is not appropriate to the proceedings.'

Seidl then put to Frank the crucial question: 'Did you ever in any way participate in the annihilation of the Jews?' They were in for another oration:

I say yes: and the reason I say yes is because, having been so affected by the five months of this trial, and particularly after having heard the testimony of the witness Höss, Commandant

of Auschwitz, my conscience does not allow me to cast off
the responsibility solely onto small people. I myself never set
up an extermination camp for Jews, nor did I ever support the
existence of such camps; but it is Adolf Hitler personally who
has inflicted that dreadful responsibility on his people, then it
is mine, too, for we have led the battle against the Jewry for
years; and we have indulged in the most horrible utterances –
my own diary bears witness against me. And, therefore, it is
no more than my duty to answer your question, in this sense
and in this connection, with 'yes'. A thousand years will pass
and this guilt of Germany will still not be erased.

Frank prepared himself well for this moment. This last utterance
became widely quoted. It produced uproar in the courtroom,
and many thought it an honest answer, perhaps the first ever
uttered by a dyed-in-the-wool Nazi. Seidl was shoved by members of the gallery who came down. As order was restored by the
judges, Seidl went over to talk to Frank, speaking to him quietly
so no one could hear:

'Did you really mean to say that?'
  'Was it wrong of me?'
  Seidl spoke quickly to Frank. The noise subsided suddenly.
Silence. Seidl could be heard.
  'Dr Frank, were you, witness …?'
  'I beg your pardon?'
  'I will ask again. Can you tell me what was in your capacity
as General Governor, your policy regarding the conscription
of labourers for the Reich?'
  'My policy was laid down in my decrees. No doubt they
will be put forward as evidence against me by the prosecu-
tion. I consider that it will save time if I answer that question
later, with the permission of the Tribunal.'
  'The accused is quite correct in his reply,' agreed
Lord Lawrence.

'Can you tell us now when was the first time you heard the name Maidanek?'

'This was in connection with the foreign news dispatches. I had heard rumours, and the stench of these rumours seemed to be penetrating my very walls.'

'And therefore you didn't know of the conditions in Treblinka, Auschwitz and the others? Did Treblinka belong to Maidanek, or is that a separate camp?'

'I don't know. It seems to have been a separate camp. Auschwitz was not within the territory of the Government General. I was never in Maidanek, nor in Treblinka, nor in Auschwitz.'

'Yet those names do occur with some frequency in the diaries.'

'One has to take the diary as a whole. You can't go through forty-two volumes and pick out single sentences and separate them from their context.'

'What I ask myself is, how can we possibly reinterpret his statement about turning the Poles and Jews into mincemeat to mean that all Poles, including the Black Madonna of Czestochowa, were invited to visit his Chopin Museum? What as? Mincemeat. I've tried it, and believe me, it doesn't work.'

'As for the rest, however, I would like to say here that I do not want to argue or quibble about individual phrases. It was a wild and stormy period, filled with terrible passions.'

'Passions' excused everything. Anti-Semitism, the court was asked to understand, and the extermination of whole races of people, now turned out to be 'passions in a stormy period'.

'And when a whole country is on fire in such storm and stress, and a life-or-death struggle is going on, such words can easily be used …'

Hans Frank veered into one of his rambling and ineffectual explanations. He sensed this himself but continued. Dr Seidl tried to interrupt:

'Some of the words are terrible; I must admit myself that I was shocked at many of the words I had used.'

'The prosecution has given er ... From a conference in 1939 with the Administrative chief of Uber-Ost. It says here, "During the first conversation which the Chief of the Central Department had with Reichsminister Dr Frank on October 3, 1939, in Posen, the latter explained the task that had been given him by the Führer and the economic-political principles on which he intended to base his administration in Poland. According to that, it could be done only by ruthless exploitation, by the gutting of the country. Therefore, it would be necessary to conscript manpower to be used in the Reich ..." and so on. That's a close approximation. I have summarized it, Mr President.'

'Those utterances were surely not made in the way that they are put down here,' said Frank.

'But you do not wish to say that you never spoke with that man?' asked his counsel.

'I cannot remember it at all. It has escaped my powers of recollection.'

During the morning recess, Frank joined his fellow-accused, anxious, noted Gilbert, gaining words of encouragement from Von Papen and Seyss-Inquart. Seidl questioned him, 'Should I ask you what part of the intellectual responsibility – ', 'No, let it go as it is,' interrupted Frank.

Fritzsche did not at all like Frank identifying his guilt with that of the German people, while Schacht said Frank was right. Sachel whispered to Göring, 'Did you hear him say that Germany is disgraced for a thousand years?' Göring: 'Yes, I heard it ... I suppose Speer will say the same thing. The weak-kneed cowards!'

Frank was in the dock again after the recess. This time he was under heavy fire from Chief Justice Smirnov, the Soviet prosecutor, who wore a military uniform. Frank was becoming the worse for wear and now seemed more hesitant, as if that former display of courage and honesty was under threat. Dr Gilbert asked himself, 'Would he be able to stand firm in his desire to tell the truth?'

Smirnov put the question: 'Will the defendant tell us who was the actual leader of the National Socialist Party in the Government General?'

'I can't hear anything. I can't hear anything at all,' answered Frank.

'I am asking you ...' Smirnov spoke in Russian. Something must be wrong with the interpreting, which was relayed by four linguists encased in glass booths wearing telephone handsets, and with mics set in front of them.

'I hear nothing ...' Dr Gilbert suspected he may be trying to toy with the court. Frank seemed able to switch easily between chess master, crafty Bavarian peasant, and crooked lawyer.

'You didn't hear of the existence of Maidanek until the year 1944. Is that correct?' persisted Smirnov.

'In the year 1944 the name Maidanek was brought to my attention *officially* for the first time by Press Secretary Gassner.'

'I place before you your report to Hitler of May 1943. I shall read you an excerpt from your report, and I should like to remind you that the report is dated May 1943. Excuse me, it is from June 19, 1943. I quote ...'

He proceeded to quote the wrong passage, but finally got to the point with the right one:

'"A large part of the Polish intelligentsia, however, would not let itself be influenced by the news from Katyn and held against Germany alleged similar crimes, especially Auschwitz." I shall now omit the next sentence and continue quoting from your report: "Among that portion of the working class which is not communistically inclined, this is scarcely denied; but at the same time it is pointed out that the attitude of Germany toward the Poles is not any better." Please make note of the next sentence: "I have reports that there are concentration camps in Auschwitz and Maidanek where likewise the mass murder of Poles is taking place systematically as in a production line." How can one reconcile this passage from your report which mentions Auschwitz and Maidanek where systematic mass murder was taking place, with your statement that you heard of Maidanek for the first time at the end of 1944? Well, your report was dated June 1943, and there you mention not only Maidanek, but Auschwitz as well.'

'With reference to Maidanek, we were speaking about the extermination of Jews. The extermination in Maidanek became known to me during the summer of 1944.'

Frank's answers, it seemed, were lapsing into that 'cowardly crap' which made his son Niklas so contemptuous of his father: 'Along with your courage, your control of the German language [was] always so strikingly perceptive.'

'Up to now the question of Maidanek had been mentioned always only in connection with extermination of Jews.'

'Pathetic', thought Niklas – the one-time brilliant lawyer so adroit at fighting on behalf of Hitler stumbles! Even the Soviet was grinning ... He continued scornfully:

'Consequently I must understand you to be saying the following – I refer to the text submitted to you: In May 1943, you learned of the mass murder of Jews?'

'I beg your pardon? ... 1944, about the extermination of the Jews in Maidanek, yes the official documents have been delivered to me in the foreign press, yes.'

'Your "Ordinance for Combating Attacks Against German Economic Buildup in the Government General." Paragraph One. It says, "Non-Germans who – with the intention of preventing or disrupting German construction activities in the Government General – violate laws, other ordinances, or official decrees or directives are to be sentenced to death." Let us look at Paragraph Six. "The verdicts of the Drumhead Court Martial of the Security Police are to be carried out immediately."'

Just a little while before, in his exchange with Seidl, Frank had been boasting about his authority to grant amnesty to the condemned:

'I ask you to tell us who the members of this Court Martial, this *Standgericht*, were?'

'The Security Police, yes.'

'But you were telling us of your hostile attitude toward the SD, the Security Police. Why ever would you have given the SD the right to deal oppressively with the Polish population?'

'Because that was the only way I could exert any influence over the verdicts. If I had not promulgated this ordinance, then there would have been no possibility of control, and the police could have simply acted blindly.'

So, it seemed, Smirnov had him in a corner, exposing his previous fear and moral cowardice. Here was a repeat of his behaviour on the telephone with Hess and Hitler over the execution of Röhm, and his pusillanimous climb-down over Lasch with Lammers and Hitler.

His son Niklas commented on the proceedings: 'You're squeaking like a rat in mortal terror!'

'You spoke of the right of amnesty that was entrusted to you. Perhaps you might direct your attention to Paragraph Six of this ordinance. I would like to remind you of this paragraph: "The verdicts of the Drumhead Court Martial of the Security Police are to be carried out immediately." I should like to remind you again that there was only one possible verdict: death. How could you change it if the condemned person was to be shot or hanged immediately after the verdict?'

'Nevertheless the verdicts had to be submitted to me for my approval.'

'Yes, but the verdicts were to be carried out immediately, were they not?'

So he was behaving just like he had over the Röhm putsch. And then came Frank's telling and self-condemning answer, the answer of the German Everyman Faust. 'Nevertheless, the verdict had to be submitted to me for my approval.'

He was saying, in effect, if he put his signature to an order he could or would never change, because it was for him ultimately to obey and keep his position even if he disagreed: this was better than if it went through without his signature. He had confirmed he was guilty, and condemned himself.

And here one surely has to ask, following the words of Smirnov, had not the Concordat done exactly this, too? The Church, in order to keep its authority on paper, had signed over to the Führer the right to deal oppressively with the Catholics in Germany because, like Frank, this was the only way the Church could exert an influence, which was illusory, and keep its sense of being in authority. As Frank said, this was the 'only way I could exert any influence over the verdicts'.

So, like the Vatican's control over the German Church, Frank's power was illusory, in the eye of the beholder.

Gilbert called Frank's confession his 'confession' (the inverted commas signifying his scepticism). Frank felt it was a victory, a triumph that raised him up in the eyes of God:

Well, today is Good Friday, and I am at peace because I kept my oath. Yesterday I stood before the black gates, and now I have passed through to the other side. – I stood before the black gates in bare feet and sackcloth with a candle in my hand like a penitent sinner – or a Vestal Virgin – and spoke once more before God and the world. – Now I have paid my bill and passed through the black gates and do not belong to this

> world any more … God is a most generous Host. He allows
> you to run up as big a bill as you please. – He lets you order
> anything you want – but He demands payment in full at the
> end! He doesn't allow any default of payment! Haha! – He is a
> most generous Host, but he demands payment in full!

Here again the eerie echo of the Faust story. Frank paused for
a minute, having exhausted the possibilities of his metaphors,
then went on with a review of his defence. He ended with
his habitual condemnation of Göring, and then expressed the
fulsome sentiment: 'But I had to confess my sin, so that I may
be at peace with God, and perhaps raise my eyes to Him a
little bit.'

And this is about as far as it would go, until the court retired
to consider its judgements. Frank's fellow-prisoners had
doubts about the genuineness of his confession. The mutual
mudslinging went on. Rosenberg thought Frank's stand
showed how 'musical and sensitive' he was, and those 'musical people are all whacky. You could never predict what Frank
was going to say.' He thought the 'thousand years disgrace'
comment was going pretty far, and laid down a mind-set for
the accused to follow, which became more prevalent as they
got ever more nervous about the verdicts. Gilbert dubbed it
resorting to 'historical defensive rationalization'; it went like
this in Rosenberg's words:

> How about the murder of 3,000 Chinese in the Opium War
> and the degradation of perhaps 3 million Chinese by the British,
> through their opium traffic? And how about the 300,000 exter-
> minated by an atomic bomb in Japan? And how about all the air
> attacks on our cities? That is all mass murder too, isn't it?

This provoked Gilbert, who demanded that there should be
greater admission of guilt from the prisoners, more calling a
spade a spade. So he retaliated:

'The whole war was unnecessary mass murder, and you can thank your Führer for deliberately starting it when the people of no country in the world wanted it – not even your own. Even Göring admits that. You might take a share of the blame yourself for your *Führerprinzip* and your own propaganda that constantly stirred up hatred instead of seeking some conciliation.'

Rosenberg squirmed and protested, rationalized and counter-attacked. It was certainly not his fault, he said, that the war started and that things have gone to such extremes. It was the Versailles Treaty and the vicious, vengeful French and the imperialistic British and the threat of Communist world revolution, etc., etc.

In their bickering and recrimination, the old North-South German antipathy surfaced again: with Seyss-Inquart, Dr Gilbert questioned why Dönitz and Göring said Höss was a southern German, and that a Prussian could never do what he had done. Gilbert mentioned the popular notion that Austrians and Bavarians were very similar people. Seyss-Inquart launched into an interesting distinction:

Yes, as I told you, the southern German has the imagination and emotionality to subscribe to a fanatic ideology, but he is ordinarily inhibited from excesses by his natural humaneness. The Prussian, on the other hand, does not have the imagination to conceive in terms of the abstract racial and political theories, but if he is told to do something, he does it. When he has an order, he doesn't have to think. – That is the categorical imperative; orders are orders. In Höss you have an example of how Nazism combined the two. Hitler would never have gotten anywhere if he had remained in Bavaria, because while the people would have followed him fanatically they never would have gone to such excesses. But the system took over the Prussian tradition as well and amalgamated the southern emotional anti-Semitism with the Prussian

thoughtless obedience. – Besides, the Catholic authoritarianism achieves the same effect as Prussian militarism – you need
only look to the Jesuits for an example of that. When fanatic
ideology is combined with authoritarianism, there is no limit
to the excesses it can go to – just as in the Inquisition.

It would be hard to find anywhere else such a succinct and
trenchant summary.

Baldur von Schirach, who was spared execution for a twenty-
year German prison sentence, strongly denied the post-war
German argument that Hitler forced and brainwashed young
Germans against their will. In 1931, when Hitler made von Schirach Hitler Youth leader and Poet Laureate, Nazism was twice
as strong in numbers among university students as among the
population as a whole. A former student at Munich University,
von Schirach married Henriette Hoffmann, daughter of Heinrich Hoffmann, Hitler's court photographer. Hitler appointed
von Schirach Gauleiter of Vienna, a role he played with *folie des
grandeurs*, becoming known as 'Pompadour of Vienna'. He denied
any pressure was used to get Hitler Youth members into the Nazi
Party when they were 18. He told George Clare, 'Good God,
they all rushed to get into the party. A proper stampede it was.'

29

Punishment

Frank finally – what? – reverted to type? Told the truth? Throughout the trial he had been writing pious letters of self-endorsement to Gertrude and his children, in which the negative shadows were consumed in soothing phrases that demonstrated to his family and himself that he had wooed and won God over to his side.

In his summation addressed to the Nuremberg judges in mitigation, for the most part he took back his earlier confession and admission of guilt:

> I must still rectify one of the statements that I made here earlier. In the witness stand I spoke about the one thousand years that could not erase the guilt from our nation on account of Hitler's behaviour. However, not only the fact that the behaviour of our enemies toward our people and our soldiers has been so carefully excluded from the proceedings of this Tribunal, but also the gigantic mass atrocities of the most horrible kind … which, as I have now learned, were committed against Germans, above all in East Prussia, Silesia, Pomerania and in the Sudetenland by Russians, Poles, and Czechs, and are still being committed – all this has completely cancelled out, even today, any possible guilt on the part of our people and nation!

The defence of the accused finished on 25 July 1946. The next day Robert Jackson, the chief prosecutor, wound up:

> Mr President and members of the tribunal. It is impossible in summation to do more than outline with full strokes the vitals of this trial's mad and melancholy record, which will live as a historical text of the twentieth century's shame and depravity. It is against such a background that these defendants now ask this tribunal to say that they are not guilty of planning, executing or conspiring to commit this long list of crimes and wrongs. They stand before the record of this tribunal as bloodstained Gloucester stood by the body of his slain king. He begged of the widow, as they beg of you: 'Say I slew them not!' And the queen replied: 'Then say they were not slain, but dead they are.' If you were to say of these men that they are not guilty it would be as true to say that there has been no war, that there are no slain, that there has been no crime.

On 2 September the judges retired to consider their verdicts. They spent four weeks doing this. On 30 September the defendants assembled in court for the last time to hear Lord Lawrence read out the judgements. Eleven were sentenced to be hanged, including Göring, whose wife had believed all through the trial he would be exiled to an island like Napoleon! Three were acquitted, and seven, including Hess, Speer, and Von Papen, given long prison sentences.

Ribbentrop's reaction to the death sentence, reports Dr Gilbert, was 'Death! – Death! Now I won't be able to write my beautiful memoirs!' Kaltenbrunner 'clasped hands that did not show in his insensitive face'. 'Death!' he whispered. Göring demanded a firing squad, which was refused. Streicher gave a crooked smile: 'Just what I expected,' he told Gilbert:

Frank smiled politely, but could not look at me. 'Death by hanging,' he said softly, nodding his head in acquiescence. 'I deserved it and I expected it, as I've always told you. I'm glad that I have had the chance to defend myself and to think things over in the last few months.'

A few days after the verdict, Göring asked Dr Gilbert what the inkblot test told him about his personality. Gilbert answered:

'Frankly, they showed that while you have an active, aggressive mind, you lack the guts to really face responsibility. You betrayed yourself with a little gesture on the inkblot test.' Goering glared apprehensively. 'Do you remember the card with the red spot? Well, morbid neurotics often hesitate over that card and then say there's blood on it. You hesitated, but you didn't call it blood. *You tried to flick it off with your finger*, as though you thought you could wipe away the blood with a little gesture. You've been doing the same thing all through the trial – taking off your earphones in the courtroom, whenever the evidence of your guilt became too unbearable. And you did the same thing during the war too, drugging the atrocities out of your mind. You didn't have the courage to face it. That is your guilt. I agree with Speer, you are a moral coward.'

The Lutheran pastor refused Göring the rites of the Last Supper, i.e. Holy Communion, and the blessing of the Church. Chaplain Gereide said he had not shown any sign of repentance. Two hours before he was due to be hanged, at 10.45 p.m. he took a capsule of potassium cyanide.

Dr Kelley later commented that, 'shrouded in mystery' and showing 'the impotency of the American guard', this was 'a skillful, even brilliant finishing touch, completing the edifice for the Germans to admire in time to come'.

Kelley was suspected of slipping the capsule to Göring. Later Professor of Criminology at Berkeley, an expert at conjuring and on the psychology of 'misdirection', Kelley committed suicide on New Year's Eve, 1957, with a cyanide capsule he had allegedly taken from Nuremberg Prison and kept as a souvenir.

Should Father O'Connor have given Frank extreme unction and blessed him on the scaffold as he did? To the last, Hans Frank had done nothing but try to gain the approval of all those near to him and from the world. His atonement, his penitence, had all the marks of superficiality. It was above all his vanity, the blindness to that particular sin, some claimed, that showed how little he had really repented.

One psychiatrist pointed out that his beatific tranquility merely hid his own tensions. But what did such carefully acted-out piety really signify? Did not his hastily cultivated yet forceful and theatrical piousness have something about it that was too patently flimsy?

Frank was not only criminal in his acts and attitudes, which he acknowledged. In the way Frank called attention to himself in every possible way and on every possible occasion, he represented a destructive vanity which today remains a significant part of everyday culture.

Unlike Ribbentrop, who lamented that he would never be able to write his 'beautiful memoirs', Frank wasted no time during the trial and had gone ahead. He had composed his memoir, *Facing the Gallows*, with a dedication from Goethe's *Werther*, subtly changing the wording to bolster his self-serving account of 'former and partial guilt' – to make it sound as if God endorsed it, which was not the sense of the original.

Facing the Gallows, introduced and promoted by Gertrude, became a best-seller. Winifred Wagner, as we have said, found his account of Hitler 'the best character study of Hitler that I have ever read'. It was to win Hans Frank thousands of posthumous admirers. As one 1952 letter put it, 'He was a great European in the finest sense of the word.' It was perhaps the beginning of a revisionism which some claim is still a discernible part of German culture.

On 16 October the US hangman, John C. Woods from San Antonio, placed the noose round the neck of Hans Frank, fifth in the queue, after Ribbentrop, Kaltenbrunner, Rosenberg and Keitel, in the prison gymnasium where the gallows had been set up. Kinsbury Smith, an American journalist who was present, described the event:

> There was a brief lull in the proceedings until Kaltenbrunner was pronounced dead at 1.52 a.m.
> Hans Frank was next in the parade of death. He was the only one of the condemned to enter the chamber with a smile on his countenance.
> Although nervous and smiling frequently, this man, who was converted to Roman Catholicism after his arrest, gave the appearance of being relieved at the prospect of atoning for his evil deeds.
> He answered to his name quietly and when asked for any last statement, he replied in a low voice that was almost a whisper, 'I am thankful for the kind treatment during my captivity and I ask God to accept me with mercy.'
> Frank closed his eyes and swallowed as the black hood went over his head.

When Niklas questioned him about his father's death, Father Sixtus O'Connor told him, 'These words were on his lips when the trapdoor opened under him. I heard it clearly: "Jesus, have mercy." Before the snapping sound. That, you see, was the terrible thing about your father's death, that sound of his neck cracking.'

Niklas imagines he opens his mouth and bites into his father's heart, feels him screaming and screaming ... 'until I swallow you and your last flood of lies [and] ... until your heart stops beating and goes limp'. To this day he carries in his wallet a photo of his father dead, which he calls his form of revenge.

Other thoughts and quotations might be cited or serve by way of bitter farewell. It does seem Frank died without consistent or significant insight into himself, without self-knowledge, and protected from his own feelings by Father O'Connor. Yet, on record, and questionable though the smile may have been, he was the only one of these Nazi criminals who died smiling.

Christopher Marlowe's Second Scholar says of Faustus:

> ... he was a scholar once admired
> For wondrous knowledge in our German schools.

Invoking the Faust myth finally may be going too far. Transcendence, the appeal to a higher good, is what gives the myth its value. The argument against applying it to this story is that fascism is an impersonal mechanism, an amplified yet banal evil, which therefore could or should not be explained, even less enobled, by bringing in a mythical devil. From the example of Hans Frank's life we perhaps need to ask, can there ultimately be drawn any other meaning or wider value, and how is it linked – if not inexplicably – with all our experience of the mystery of good and evil?

Appendix

Definition of the Term 'Jew' in the Government General

Decree Concerning the Definition of the Term 'Jew' in the Government General.

Dated July 24, 1940
By virtue of Par. 1, Section 5 of the Decree of the Führer and Reich Chancellor relating to the administration of the occupied Polish territories, dated October 12, 1939 (*Reichsgesetzblatt* I, p. 2077), I decree:

Section 1
Where the term 'Jew' is employed in the legislative and administrative regulations of the Government General, it shall be interpreted to mean:

(1)   Anyone who is or is regarded as a Jew under the legislative regulations of the Reich.
(2)   Anyone who, being a former Polish citizen or Stateless, is or is regarded as a Jew according to Section 2 of the present Decree.

Section 2
(1)   Anyone who is descended from at least three racially entirely Jewish grandparents, is a Jew.

(2) Anyone who is descended from two racially entirely
     Jewish grandparents is regarded as a Jew,
     (a) if belonging to the Jewish religious community
          on September 1, 1939, or accepted thereinto after
          that date;
     (b) if married to a Jewish spouse when the present
          Decree comes into force, or has married one since;
     (c) if born from extra-marital intercourse with a Jew in
          the sense of Par. 1, and born after May 31, 1941.
(3) A grandparent is regarded as entirely Jewish if he or she
     belonged to the Jewish religious community.

Section 3
(1) Where the term 'Jewish extraction' is employed in the
     legislative and administrative regulations of the 'Govern-
     ment Central', it shall be interpreted to mean:
     (a) anyone who is of Jewish extraction according to the
          legislative regulations of the Reich;
     (b) anyone who, being a former Polish citizen or State-
          less, is descended from one or two racially entirely
          Jewish grandparents, unless regarded as a Jew
          according to Par. 2, Section 2.
(2) The provision of Par. 3, Section 2 applies accordingly.

Section 4
(1) A concern shall be regarded as Jewish if the proprietor is a
     Jew in the sense of Section 1.
(2) The concern of a private company shall be regarded as Jewish
     if one or more of the personally liable partners are Jews.
(3) The concern of a legal entity shall be regarded as Jewish:
     (a) if one or more of the persons entitled to its legal
          representation, or if one or more of the members of
          the board are Jews;
     (b) if Jews participate decisively with capital or voting
          rights. Decisive participation with capital is present

> if more than one quarter of the capital is held by Jews; decisive participation with voting rights is present if the votes of the Jews reach one half of the total votes.

(4) A concern shall also be regarded as Jewish if it is in fact under dominant Jewish influence.

(5) The provisions of Pars. 1 to 4 apply correspondingly to societies, foundations, institutions and other undertakings.

Section 5

Legislative and administrative regulations relating to Jews extend to persons of Jewish extraction only if this is specially mentioned.

Notes

p.19 'The Russians ...' Thomas Mann, *Doctor Faustus* (Penguin, 1976), 123

p.20 'Etienne Mantoux ...' Paul Johnson, *A History of the Western World* (Weidenfeld & Nicolson, 1983), 30

p.20 'the economic is simply ...' Mann, 119

p.21 'Ernst Hanfstaengl ...' Claus Hant, *Young Hitler* (Quartet, 2010), 318–19

p.22 'the front Hitler ...' Hant, 359–62

p.23 'eliminates any complexity ...' Ibid., 372

p.23 'a secret known by ...' Ibid., 365

p.23 'with the certainty ...' Munich Speech, 14 March 1936

p.24 'The prohibition on universal ...' Elias Canetti, *Crowds and Power* (Gollancz, 1952), 181

p.26 'The mark of the man ...' Niklas Frank, *In the Shadow of the Reich* (New York, 1991), 40

p.27 'He played an important role ...' Dieter Schenk, *Hans Frank: Hitlers Kronjurist und Generalgouverneur* (Frankfurt am Main, 2006), 24, 25

p.27 'a Jewish lawyer ...' Gustave Gilbert, *Nuremberg Diary* (Da Capo Press, 1995), 280

p.27 'Anyone who got involved ...' NF, 46

p.28 'My dear Frau ...' Ibid., 65

p.29 'Today I mustered ...' Ibid., 34

p.29   'People of Germany ...' Ibid., 4 December & 15 December 1918

p.31   'were suitably prepared ...' Katrin Himmler, *The Himmler Brothers* (Pan, 2008), 43

p.31   'The ties between Heinrich ...' KH, 114

p.32   'A woman is loved ...' Ibid., 106

p.35   'of a piteous martyrdom ...' Upton Sinclair, *Between Two Worlds* (T. Werner Laurie, 1941) 159

p.36   'And opposed to that ...' Schenk, 26

p.38   'Munich, from which ...' KH, 43, 64

p.38   'Turks were slaughtering ...' *Between Two Worlds*, 44

p.39   'Oh what energy is locked ...' NF, 39

p.41   'France, Tibet and India ...' Hant, 349; V. and V. Trimondi, *Hitler, Buddha, Krishna* (2002)

p.42   'hungered after marriage ...' 36

p.43   'The more I tried to achieve clarity ...' *Mein Kampf*, 205–6

p.43   'The conglomeration ...' Ibid., 123–24

p.44   'While in ranks of their supporters ...' Ibid., 43–44

p.48   'That I was poor ...' Ibid., 224

p.48   'One trait of Hitler ...' Hant, 352; *Hitler's Table Talk, 1941–1944*

p.49   'Hitler sent ... Dr Block ...' Hant, 352

p.49   'He must be a bachelor ...' Shirer, 84–85

p.51   'The revival of ritual ...' Mann, 359

p.51   'For myself, I have ...' *Hitler Speaks*, 1940

p.52   'I had never seen ...' Streicher, Testimony at the Nuremberg Trials, 26/4/46, 194–95 on Von Schirach whom Hitler made 'Poet Laureate', George Clare, *Berlin Days 1946–47* (Pan, 1989)

p.55   'the upper part of his nose ...' Shirer, 640

p.57   'There were an estimated ...' Oosterhuis & Kennerley, *Homosexuality and Male Bonding in Pre-Nazi Germany*, etc. (Harrington Park Press, 1991), 183

p.58   'There was a very masculine ...' Alfred Rouse, *Homosexuals in History: Ambivalence in Society, Literature and Art* (2002), 214

p.59   'Walther Langer suggests ...' Walther Langer, *The Mind of Adolf Hitler* (New York, 1972), 192. See also CH, 349–51 p.60 'The answer is simple ...' Irwin J. Haeberle, *Swastika, Pink Triangle and Yellow Star* (Meridian, 1989), 369

p.60 'What, are you really still studying ...' Schenk, 102–12

p.60 'I quoted from Goethe's ...' Gilbert, 144

p.66 He had been wounded ...' Shirer, 113

p.66 'Then suddenly all was quiet ...' Hans Frank, *Im Angesicht des Galgens* (Munich, 1953), 580

p.67 'In the middle was our ...' KH, 98

p.68 'looked like a delicatessen ...' Johnson, 78, 135

p.69 'His first lover ...' HF *Im Angesicht*, 47

p.71 'Your fate was sealed ...' NF, 50–51

p.76 'a girl of eighteen ...' CH, 341

p.79 'The future lies ...' Shirer, 196

p.82 as Joseph Ratzinger recalls in *Milestones: Memoirs 1927–1979* (Ignatius Press, 1980), 78

p.85 'On a trip from Budweis ...' Albert Speer, *Inside the Third Reich* (Weidenfeld & Nicolson, 1970), 152

p.85 'brutal, unjust ...' Walter Langer, and CH, 344

p.86 'Gilbert told Toland ...' John Toland, *Explaining Hitler* (Doubleday, 1976), 26

p.86 'Frank's lack of integrity ...' Gilbert, 84

p.87 'Did I tell you a gypsy ...' Oswold Spengler, Martyn Housden, *Hans Frank, Lebensraum and the Final Solution* (Palgrave Macmillan, 2003) 236, Note 108

p.91 'In general, self-control ...' Speer, 152

p.91 'He permitted each individual ...' Fest, 183

p.91 'Just imagine! ...' NF to author, 2010

p.92 'The Minister of Justice ...' NF, 76

p.93 'According to some sources ...' Shirer, 370; Konrad Heiden, *Der Führer*, 746–47

p.94 'There was a brief pause ...' Note 24, Proconsuls, Trial of Germans; NF 85–86

p.94 'The two SA officers ...' Shirer, 307–12

p.95 'Christianity has infused ...' Telford Taylor, 20

p.96 'There is no independence of law ...' Shirer, 370

p.97   'I'll have my reckoning ...' Speer, 184–85

p.98   'Nietzsche prophesised ...' Shirer, 146–47

p.99   'Distinguished Arabs told him ...' Speer, 150–51

p.100   'Friction produces warmth ...' Steven Evans, 25

p.101   'Wherever you drove you saw ...' Upton Sinclair, *Dragon's Teeth*, 395

p.102   'But they were civilized cats ...' Ibid., 413

p.102   'Never get boring ...' HM, 145

p.102   'Cardinal Faulhaber had ...' Gunter Lewy, *The Catholic Church and Nazi Germany*, 41

p.102   'We bishops are being asked ...' Saul Friedlaender, *Nazi Germany and the Jews*, Ch 2, Vol. 1

p.104   'Music turns the equivocal into a system ...' Mann, 129

p.107   'It is my conviction ...' Cardinal Faulhaber, Burns Oates, 1934

p.107   'The Führer commands ...' John Cornwell, *The Hitler Pope* (Viking Press, 1999), 181

p.108   'army and forest transfused ...' Canetti, 173

p.108   'My life is and remains ...' Housden, 41, Note 35

p.109   'He had another such fit ...' Speer, 184–85

p.110   'We live in an age of the final ...' *Third Reich in Power*, 25, Note 106

p.112   'You shall love peace as ...' Nietzsche, *Thus Spake Zarathustra*, Part One

p.114   'And in order to demonstrate ...' HF, Diary

p.115   'Firmly erect, swaying ...' Schmidt, 71

p.118   'He even considered sending ...' Schenk, 135

p.119   'I will give a propagandistic cause ...' Gilbert, 44

p.119   'We get a good picture ...' Schenk, 124, 112

p.120   'Afterward Hitler sat alone ...' Speer, 156–57

p.122   'Though their minds were deliberately ...' Shirer, 353

p.124   'The activities they were denied ...' Canetti, 181

p.124   'In round-the-clock raids bombers knocked out ...' Davis, 80

p.125   'I received instructions to ...' Ibid., 214

p.125   'Was it not also love ...' Mann, 151

p.126   'Ah, I am a unique specimen ...' Gilbert, 151

p.126 'Goethe was such a figure ...' CH, 420

p.127 'The advance of the German ...' *The Black Book*, 546

p.129 'On February 14, 1940 ...' Ibid., 54–55, 47–48

p.129 'My relationship with the Poles ...' *HF, Diary*

p.130 'systematic colonization of Poland ...' John Michalczyk, *Confronted* (New York, 2004), 110

p.131 'He let things come ...' quoted in Michael Burleigh, *The Third Reich: A New History* (Macmillan, 2000)

p.132 'It is forbidden (1) ...' NF, 113

p.133 'He dispatched chalices, pyxes ...' BB, 35 ff

p.134 '*So holen wir die ...*' NF, 110–11

p.139 '"The principle," he answered ...' Davis, 366

p.140 'In this country ...' Housden, 28

p.140 'Next they employed the *lapanka* ...' *The Eagle Unbowed*, 114–15

p.142 'I should like to be told ...' André Gide, *Journal* (Penguin, 1984), 7 July 1940, 648–49

p.143 'About the development ...' Eichmann Trial Record, mimeographed, 1961, Document 983

p.143 'With hindsight one of ...' Otto Dietrich, *My Years With Hitler* (Chicago, 1983), 83

p.144 'One thing is certain: the authority ...' Piotrowski (ed.), *Hans Frank Diary*, 214

p.145 'to decimate the Slav population ...' Johnson, 414, Note 1960

p.145 'Before me sat Frank ...' quoted in Housden, 13

p.147 'If I wished to order ...' Shirer, 874–75

p.147 'It happened in Poland ...' Ibid., 872, Note 203

p.150 'the Jews called these deals ...' *Trial of the Germans*, 454, Notes 9 & 10

p.151 'There is no state within ...' Ibid., 216

p.152 'a slight fluttering of the eyes ...' NF, 163

p.154 'I know why Hitler loves me ...' *HF, Diary*

p.155 'Should you ever again hear ...' NF, 181

p.157 'A few weeks ago she told ...' Schenk, 175–81

p.159–61 Reconstructed on the basis of all the various sources quoted above. The precedent for this is Peter Ackroyd's ground-

breaking life of Charles Dickens, which uses such bio-dramatic
interpolations, in this author's view, perfectly legitimately

p.162 'She had no orgasm …' NF, 3

p.164 'In a circular dated November 9 …' *Ich Adolf Eichmann*

p.167 'Evening harmonious …' This exchange and the following
based on *HF, Diaries*, 22 and NF, 215–20

p.168 'In April 1942, he opposed the …' Housden, 55–58

p.171 'he should have shot himself …' Shirer, 1219

p.172 'we are the symbols of an evil …' Gilbert, 20–21

p.174 'Frank is pursuing a policy …' Schenk, 321–28

p. 175 'I can still see my father …' Elizabeth Heisenberg, *Inner Exile*
(Boston, 1984), 49

p.175 'Here in Munich I was in school…'

p.178 'From then on …' Davis, 114, 115

p.179 'Last month one of the crematoriums …' Primo Levi, *If This is
a Man*, 154–55

p.180 'We must not be squeamish …' Housden, 200ff

p.185 'It is outrageous …' NF, 260–61

p.186 'Last June it was 25 years …' *HF, Diary*, 17 February 1944

p.188 'The Church is maintaining …' Ibid., 2 March 1940

p.188 'I observe in increasing measure …' Ibid., 19 December 1940

p.189 'To illustrate the resistance …' Davis, 184

p.189 'The Polish clergy …' *HF, Diary*, 14 April 1944

p.192 'That the enemies we had …' Ibid., 17 February 1944

p.193 'I see, Herr Governor General …' *Universal Father*, 93–99.
Niklas Frank completely dismisses this as untrue

p.198 'Frank will investigate ….' Schenk, 12–15

p.198 'through the rooms of the castle …' HF, *Im Angersicht*

p.200 '… sense of entitlement …' John Loftus, *The Vatican, the
Nazis, and the Swiss Banks*

p.200 '… constant wild partying …' Schenk, 262–63

p.201 'Ring out spring song …' Ibid., 365

p.201 'settled into a relationship …' Ibid., 360–65

p.203 'Oh Lord/ Now we are alone …' NF, 323

p.204 'There had been no mention …' Peter Ustinov, *Dear Me*, 187 p.206 'the corruption of an ...' Roberto Rossellini, *The War Trilogy* (The Viking Press, 1973), 353

p.207 'I journeyed yesterday evening ...' Schenk, 264

p.209 'At first, Faulhaber had supported ...' NF to author, 2010

p.210 'the greatest group of criminals ...' Gilbert, 80

p.210 'the almost utter ...' Preliminary Studies, Kelley, 47

p.210 Ibid., Kelley, 238

p.211 'It's uncanny ...' Eric A. Zillmer (ed.), *The Quest for the Nazi Personality* (Laurence Erlbaum Associates, 1995), 201ff

p.215 'I see an angel ...' *Doctor Faustus*, Act 5, Scene 1

p.217 'Yes, many things have ...' November 1946, Gilbert, 47–49

p.217 'Recently he dreamed ...' Ibid., 21

p.218 'Frank swallows hard ...' Ibid., 68

p.221 'Rosenberg tried to hark ...' Ibid., 21

p.223 'master of specious ...' KH, 294

p.226 'It was just another one ...' Gilbert, 116

p.235 'Yes, as I told you ...' Ibid., 286–87

p.235 'Baldur von Schirach ...' Clare, 198

p.237 'Frank smiled politely ...' Gilbert, 432

p.238 'shrouded in mystery ...' Kelley, 82, Zillmur, 76

Select Bibliogaphy

(1939–41) *The Black Book – Vol 2 – The German New Order in Poland*. Hutchinson

Alexander, Eben (2012) *Proof of Heaven*. Piatkus

Bernstein, Jeremy (2006) *Heisenberg in Poland*. American Association of Physics Teachers

Clare, George (1989) *Berlin Days, 1946–47*. Pan

Cornish, Kimberley (1999) *The Jew of Linz*. Arrow

Cornwell, John (1999) *Hitler's Pope*. Penguin

Crankshaw, Edward (1963) *The Fall of the House of Habsburg*. Papermac

Davidson, Eugene (1966) *The Trials of the Germans*. Macmillan

Dietrich, Otto (1958) *Hitler's Regency*. Chicago

Evans, Richard J. (2005) *the Third Reich in Power*. Allen Lane

Faulhaber, M Von (1936) *Judaism, Christianity and Germany*. Publisher Unknown

Fest, Joachim, C. (1999) *The Face of the Third Reich*. Da Capo Press

Frank, Niklas (1991) *In the Shadow of the Reich*. Alfred A Knopf

Frank, Niklas (2005) *Mein deutsche Mutter*. Goldmann

Gide, André (1984) *Journals, 1889–1949*. Penguin

Goebbels, Joseph (2008) *Diaries*. Pen & Sword

Hant, Claus (2010) *Young Hitler*. Quartet

Heisenberg, Elizabeth (1948) *Inner Exile*. Boston

Himmler, Katrin (2008) *The Himmler Brothers*. Pan
Housden, Martyn (2003) *Hans Frank, Lebensraum and the Final Solution*. Palgrave Macmillan
Keneally, Thomas (1983) *Schindler's Ark*. Hodder & Stoughton
Kershaw, Ian (1998) *Hitler 1889–1936: Hubris*. Penguin
Kochanski, Halik (2012) *The Eagle Unbowed*. Allen Lane
Kubizek, August (1955) The *Young Hitler I Knew*. Open Source
Johnson, Paul (1983) *A History of the Modern World*. Weidenfeld & Nicolson
Lang, Peter (2004) *Hitler's Voice: The Völkischer Beobachter, 1920–1933*. Mühlberger, Detlef
Levi, Primo (2000) *If This is a Man*. Everyman
Mann, Thomas (1976) *Doctor Faustus*. Penguin
Mann, Thomas (1951) *The Holy Sinner*. Penguin
Murphy, Paul I., Arlington, Rene R. (1983) *La Popessa*. Warner Inc.
Orange, A. *The Religious Roots of Alcoholics Anonymous and the Twelve Steps*. Ch 8 www.orange-papers.org
Pietrowski, S. (1961) *Hans Frank's Diary*. Warsaw
Ravenscroft, Trevor (1973) *The Spear of Destiny*. Red Wheel
Reed, T.J. (1996) *The Uses of Tradition*. Oxford University Press
Rosenbaum, Ron (1998) *Explaining Hitler: The Search for the Origins of His Evil*. Macmillan
Schenk, Dieter, (2006) *Hans Frank: Hitlers Kronjurist und Generalgouverneur*. Frankfurt an Main
Schmidt, Paul (1951) *Hiter's Interpreter*. W Heinemann
Shirer, William L. (1959) *The Rise and Fall of the Third Reich*. Simon & Shuster
Sinclair, Upton (1942) *World's End*. T. Werner Laurie
Sinclair, Upton (1945) *Presidential Agent*. T. Werner Laurie
Sinclair, Upton (1950) *Dragon's Teeth*. T. Werner Laurie
Speer, Albert (1970) *Inside the Third Reich*. Weidenfeld & Nicolson
Styron, William (1979) *Sophie's Choice*. Corgi
Taylor, Telford (2013) *The Anatomy of the Nuremberg Trials*. Skyhorse

Trevor-Roper, H.R. (1953) *Hitler's Table Talk, 1941–44*. Weidenfeld & Nicolson

Ustinov, Peter (1977) *Dear Me*. Penguin

Victor, George (1998) *Hitler: The Pathology of Evil*. Brasseys

Williamson, Gordon (2006) *The SS: Hitler's Instrument of Terror*. Amber

Winter, Edward (2009) *Hans Frank and Chess*. www.chesshistory.com/winter

Zillmer, Eric A. (ed.) (1995) *The Quest for the Nazi Personality*. Laurence Erlbaum Associates

Index

No military ranks or official civil positions are given as they changed for individuals throughout the period described.